WITHDRAWN

Margreet de Heer

RELIGION
A DISCOVERY
IN COMICS

NANTIER • BEALL • MINOUSTCHINE
Publishing inc.
new york

Original title: Religie in Beeld
Published originally in Dutch by Uitgeverij Meinema, 2011

Publication in the U.S.: NBM Publishing, 2015
Printed in China
1st printing July 2015

ISBN 978-1-56163-994-6
Library of Congress Control Number 2015943277

Text & drawings: Margreet de Heer
Colors: Yiri T. Kohl

Also available wherever e-books are sold

CONTENTS

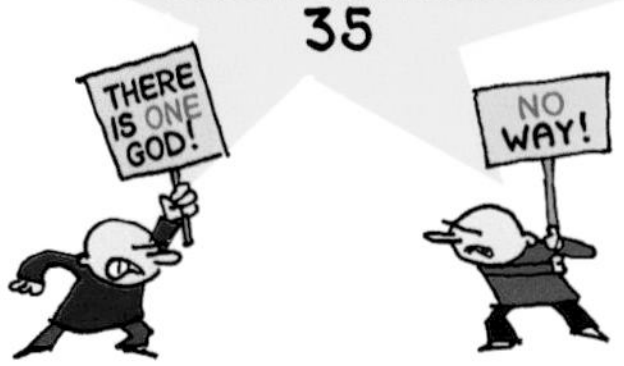

THERE IS ONE GOD!
NO WAY!

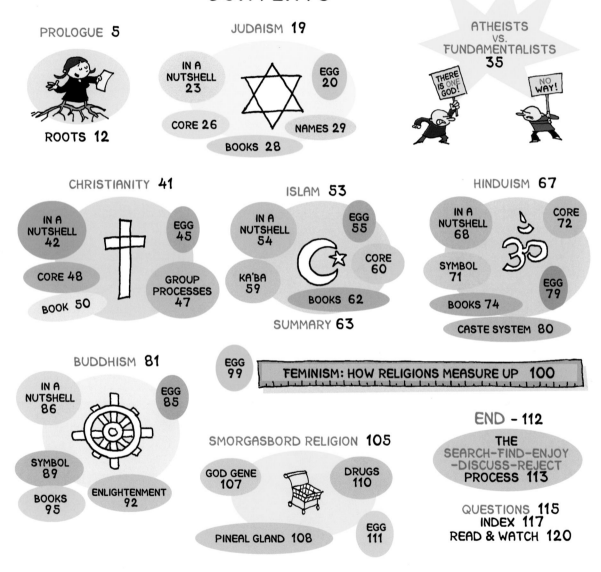

THIS BOOK IS DEDICATED TO:

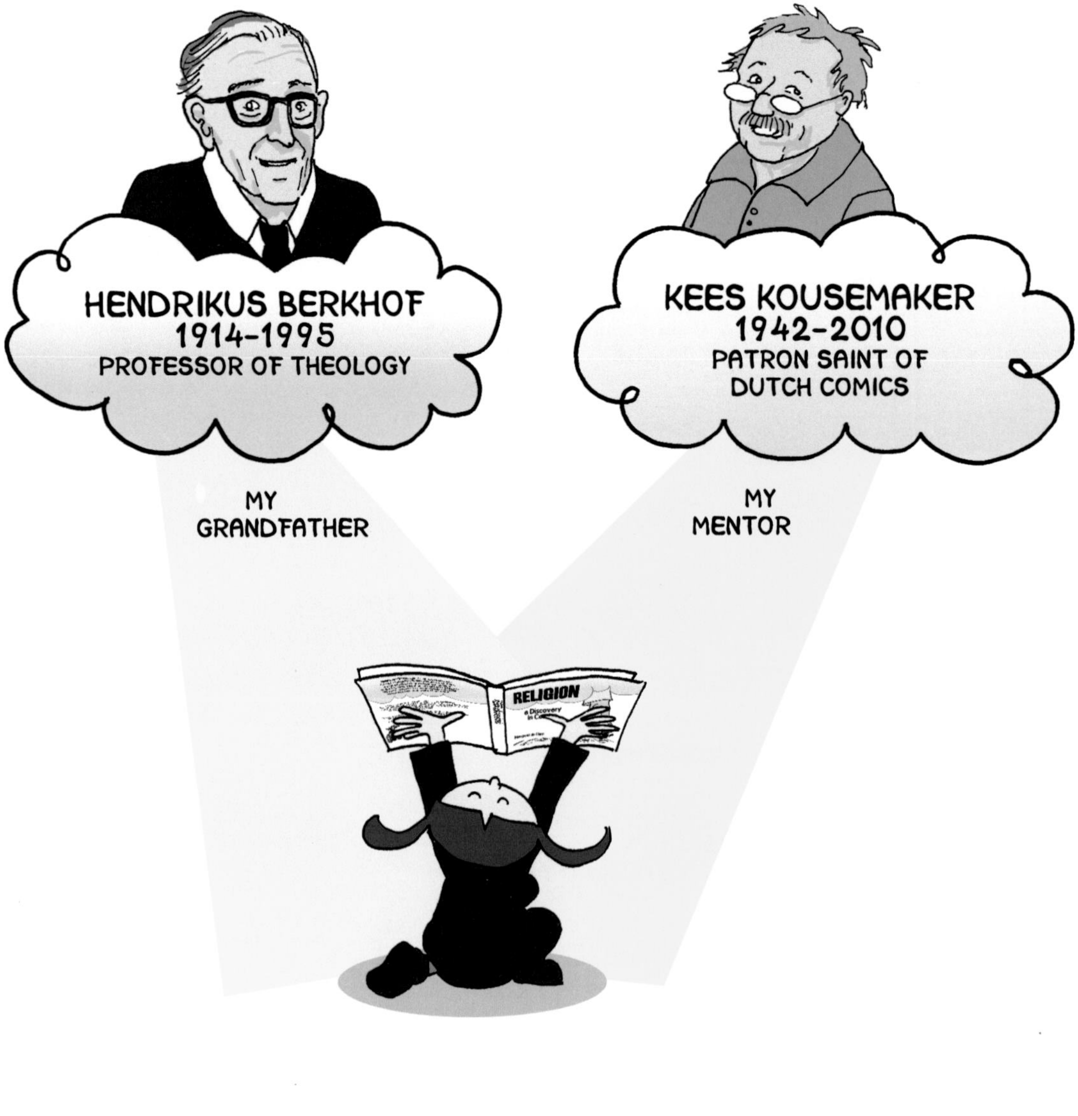
HENDRIKUS BERKHOF
1914-1995
PROFESSOR OF THEOLOGY
KEES KOUSEMAKER
1942-2010
PATRON SAINT OF
DUTCH COMICS
MY
GRANDFATHER
MY
MENTOR
RELIGION
a Discovery

PROLOGUE

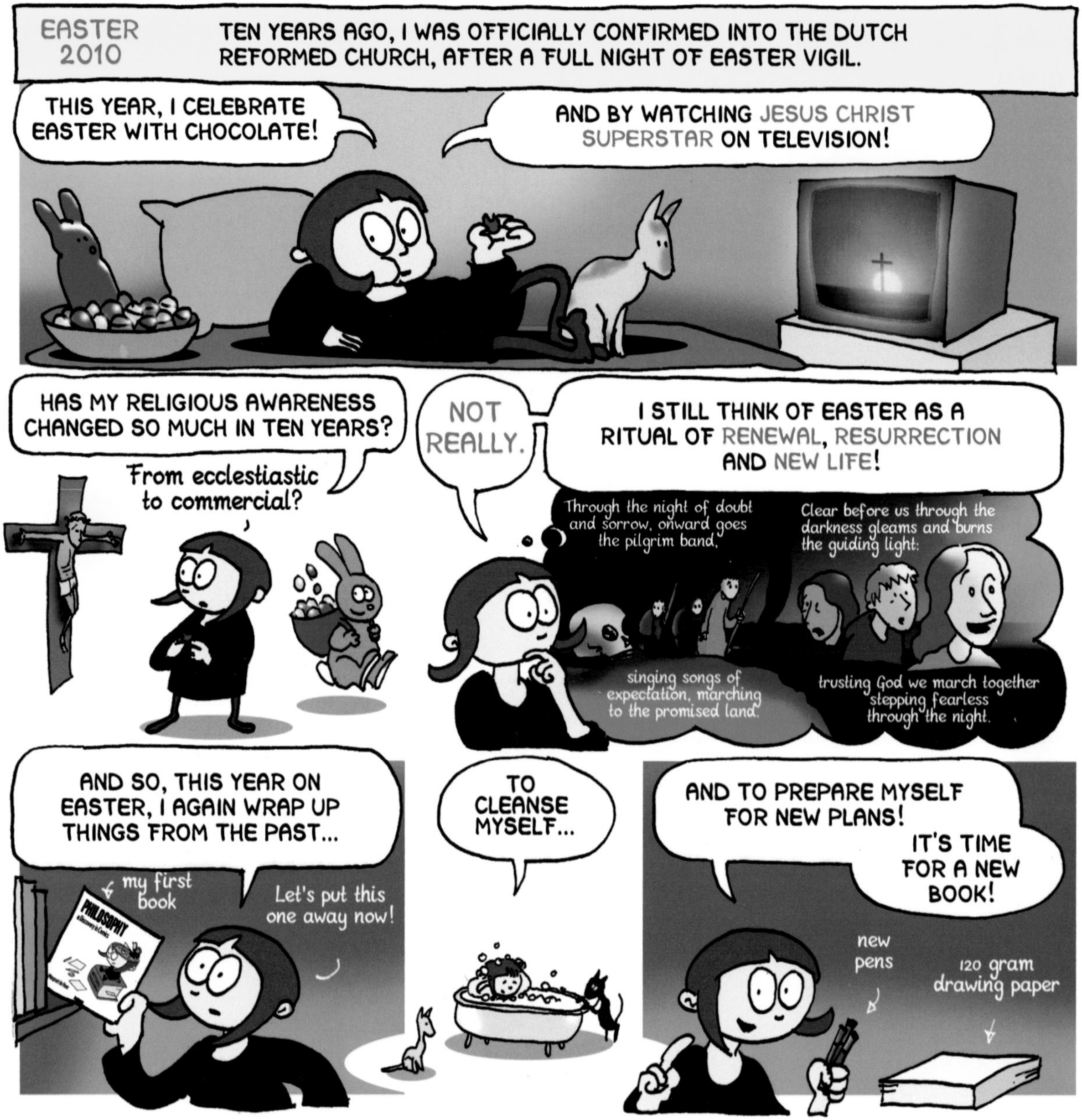
EASTER 2010
TEN YEARS AGO, I WAS OFFICIALLY CONFIRMED INTO THE DUTCH REFORMED CHURCH, AFTER A FULL NIGHT OF EASTER VIGIL.
THIS YEAR, I CELEBRATE EASTER WITH CHOCOLATE!
AND BY WATCHING JESUS CHRIST SUPERSTAR ON TELEVISION!
HAS MY RELIGIOUS AWARENESS CHANGED SO MUCH IN TEN YEARS?
From ecclestiastic to commercial?
NOT REALLY.
I STILL THINK OF EASTER AS A RITUAL OF RENEWAL, RESURRECTION AND NEW LIFE!
Through the night of doubt and sorrow, onward goes the pilgrim band,
singing songs of expectation, marching to the promised land.
Clear before us through the darkness gleams and burns the guiding light:
trusting God we march together stepping fearless through the night.
AND SO, THIS YEAR ON EASTER, I AGAIN WRAP UP THINGS FROM THE PAST...
my first book
PHILOSOPHY
Let's put this one away now!
TO CLEANSE MYSELF...
AND TO PREPARE MYSELF FOR NEW PLANS!
IT'S TIME FOR A NEW BOOK!
new pens
120 gram drawing paper

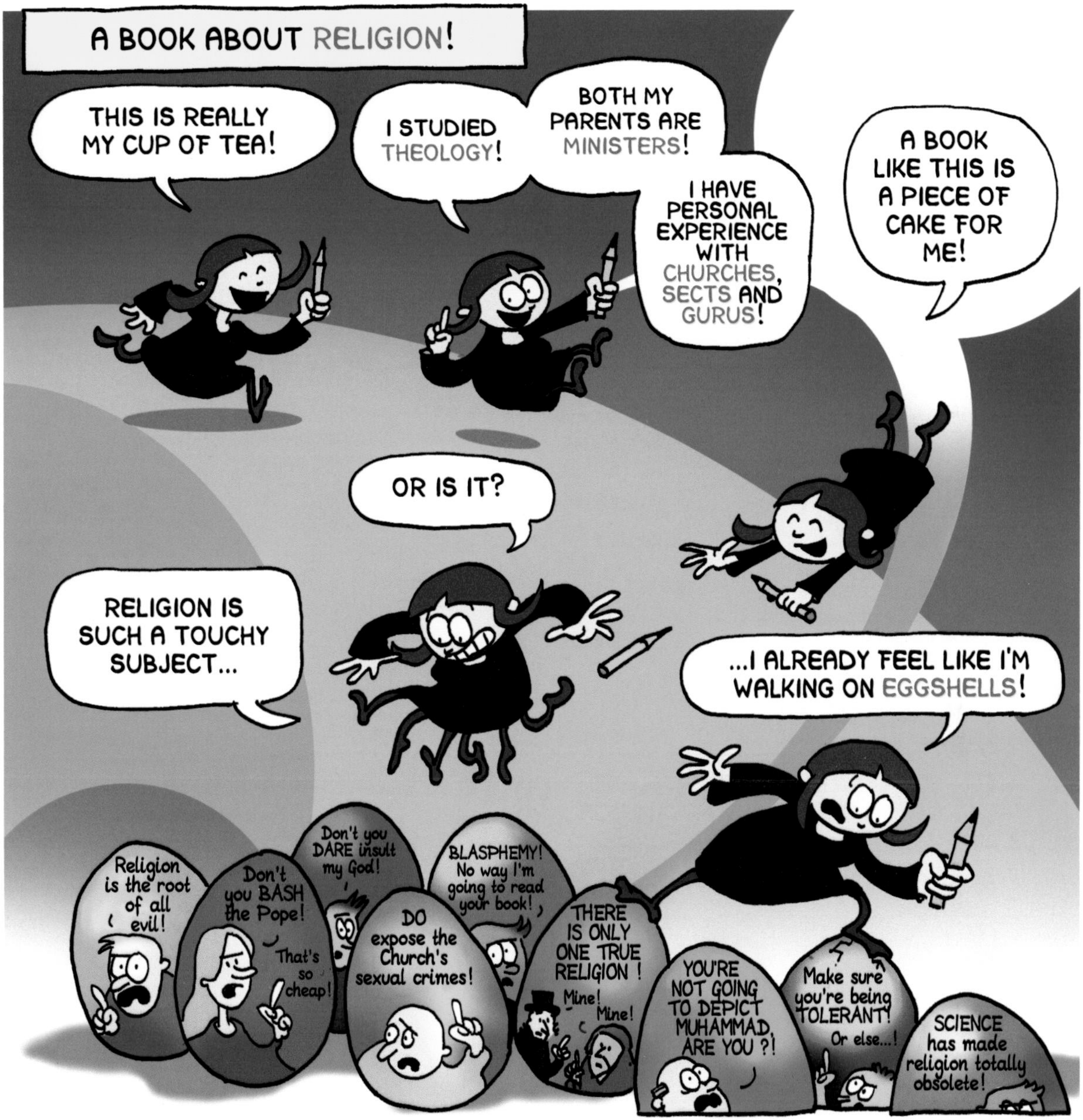
A BOOK ABOUT RELIGION!
THIS IS REALLY MY CUP OF TEA!
I STUDIED THEOLOGY!
BOTH MY PARENTS ARE MINISTERS!
I HAVE PERSONAL EXPERIENCE WITH CHURCHES, SECTS AND GURUS!
A BOOK LIKE THIS IS A PIECE OF CAKE FOR ME!
OR IS IT?
RELIGION IS SUCH A TOUCHY SUBJECT...
...I ALREADY FEEL LIKE I'M WALKING ON EGGSHELLS!
Religion is the root of all evil!
Don't you BASH the Pope!
That's so cheap!
Don't you DARE insult my God!
DO expose the Church's sexual crimes!
BLASPHEMY! No way I'm going to read your book!
THERE IS ONLY ONE TRUE RELIGION!
Mine!
Mine!
YOU'RE NOT GOING TO DEPICT MUHAMMAD, ARE YOU ?!
Make sure you're being TOLERANT!
Or else...!
SCIENCE has made religion totally obsolete!

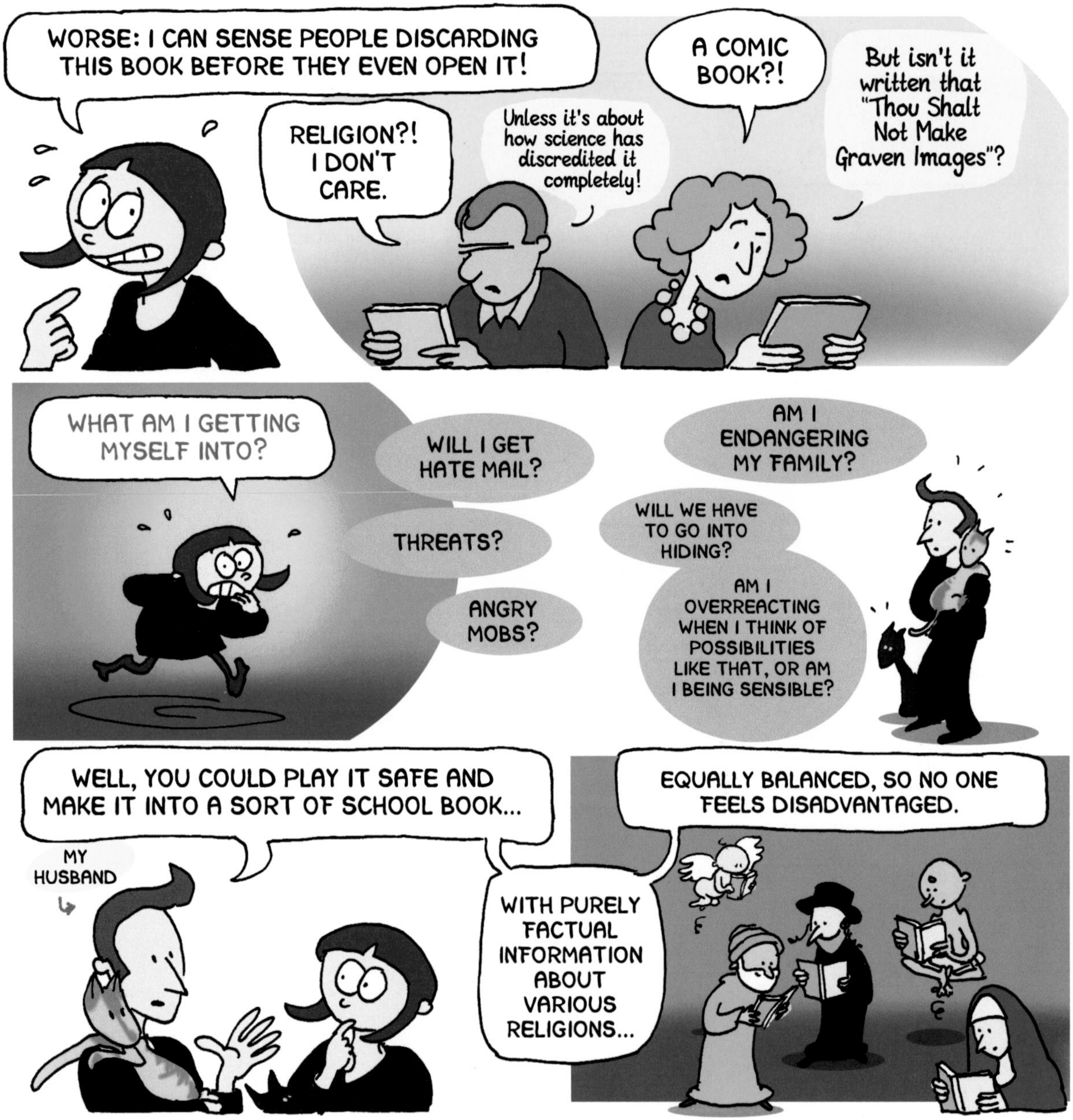
WORSE: I CAN SENSE PEOPLE DISCARDING THIS BOOK BEFORE THEY EVEN OPEN IT!
RELIGION?! I DON'T CARE.
Unless it's about how science has discredited it completely!
A COMIC BOOK?!
But isn't it written that "Thou Shalt Not Make Graven Images"?
WHAT AM I GETTING MYSELF INTO?
WILL I GET HATE MAIL?
THREATS?
ANGRY MOBS?
AM I ENDANGERING MY FAMILY?
WILL WE HAVE TO GO INTO HIDING?
AM I OVERREACTING WHEN I THINK OF POSSIBILITIES LIKE THAT, OR AM I BEING SENSIBLE?
WELL, YOU COULD PLAY IT SAFE AND MAKE IT INTO A SORT OF SCHOOL BOOK...
MY HUSBAND
WITH PURELY FACTUAL INFORMATION ABOUT VARIOUS RELIGIONS...
EQUALLY BALANCED, SO NO ONE FEELS DISADVANTAGED.

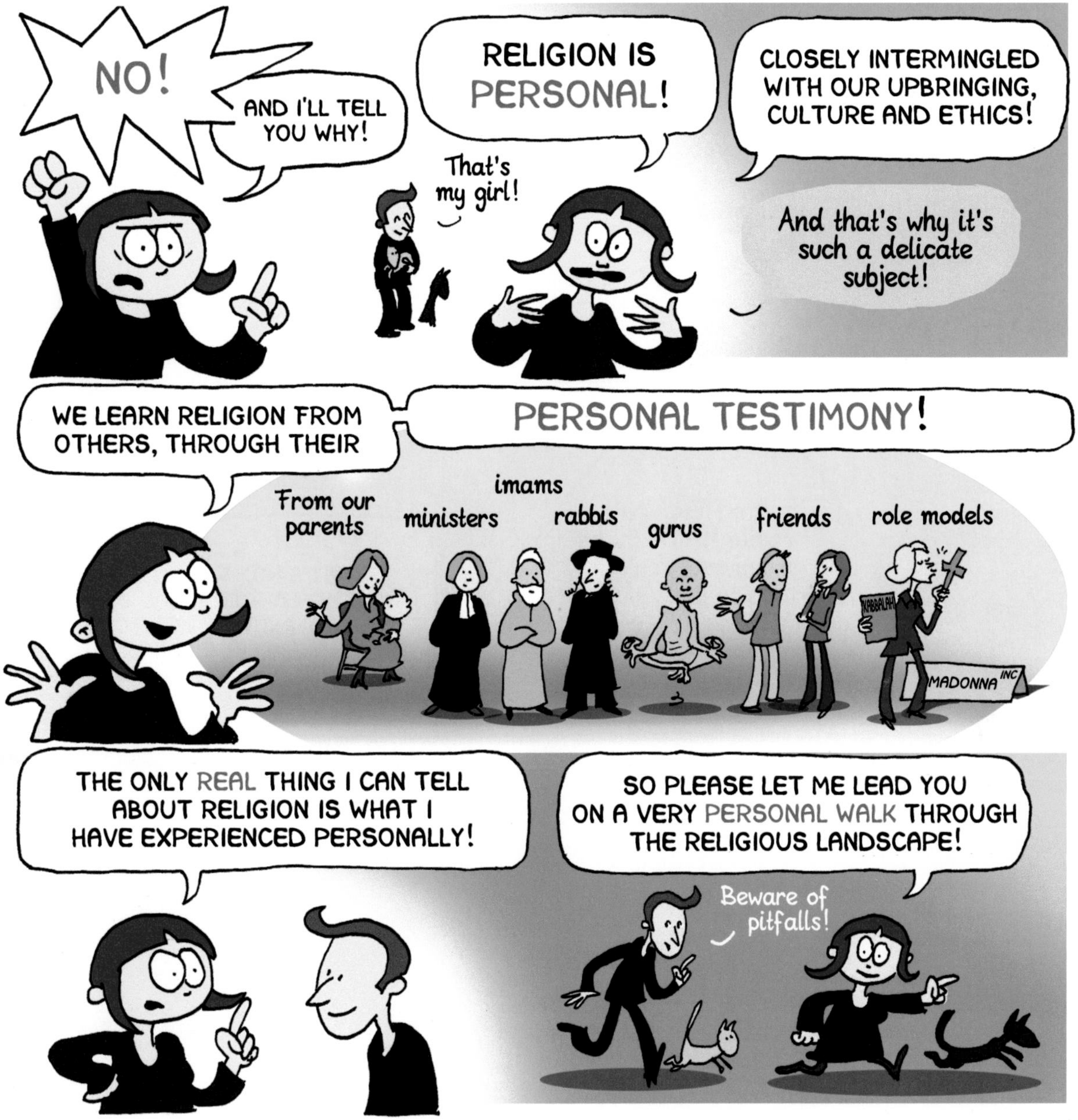

NO!
AND I'LL TELL YOU WHY!
That's my girl!
RELIGION IS PERSONAL!
CLOSELY INTERMINGLED WITH OUR UPBRINGING, CULTURE AND ETHICS!
And that's why it's such a delicate subject!
WE LEARN RELIGION FROM OTHERS, THROUGH THEIR
PERSONAL TESTIMONY!
From our parents
ministers
imams
rabbis
gurus
friends
role models
KABBALAH
MADONNA INC
THE ONLY REAL THING I CAN TELL ABOUT RELIGION IS WHAT I HAVE EXPERIENCED PERSONALLY!
SO PLEASE LET ME LEAD YOU ON A VERY PERSONAL WALK THROUGH THE RELIGIOUS LANDSCAPE!
Beware of pitfalls!

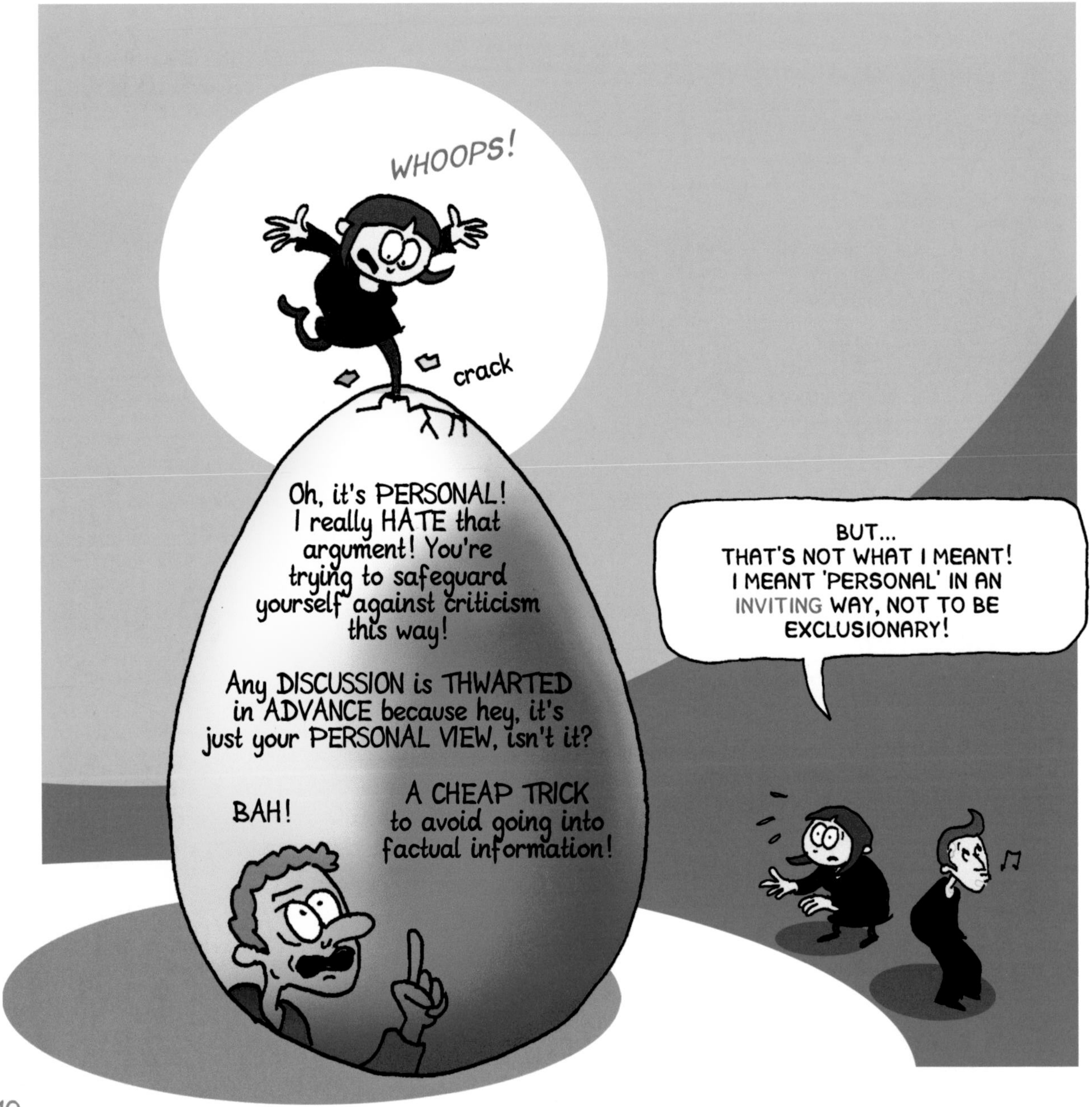
WHOOPS!
crack
Oh, it's PERSONAL! I really HATE that argument! You're trying to safeguard yourself against criticism this way!
Any DISCUSSION is THWARTED in ADVANCE because hey, it's just your PERSONAL VIEW, isn't it?
BAH!
A CHEAP TRICK to avoid going into factual information!
BUT... THAT'S NOT WHAT I MEANT! I MEANT 'PERSONAL' IN AN INVITING WAY, NOT TO BE EXCLUSIONARY!

MY HUSBAND AND I COME FROM DIFFERENT RELIGIOUS BACKGROUNDS:

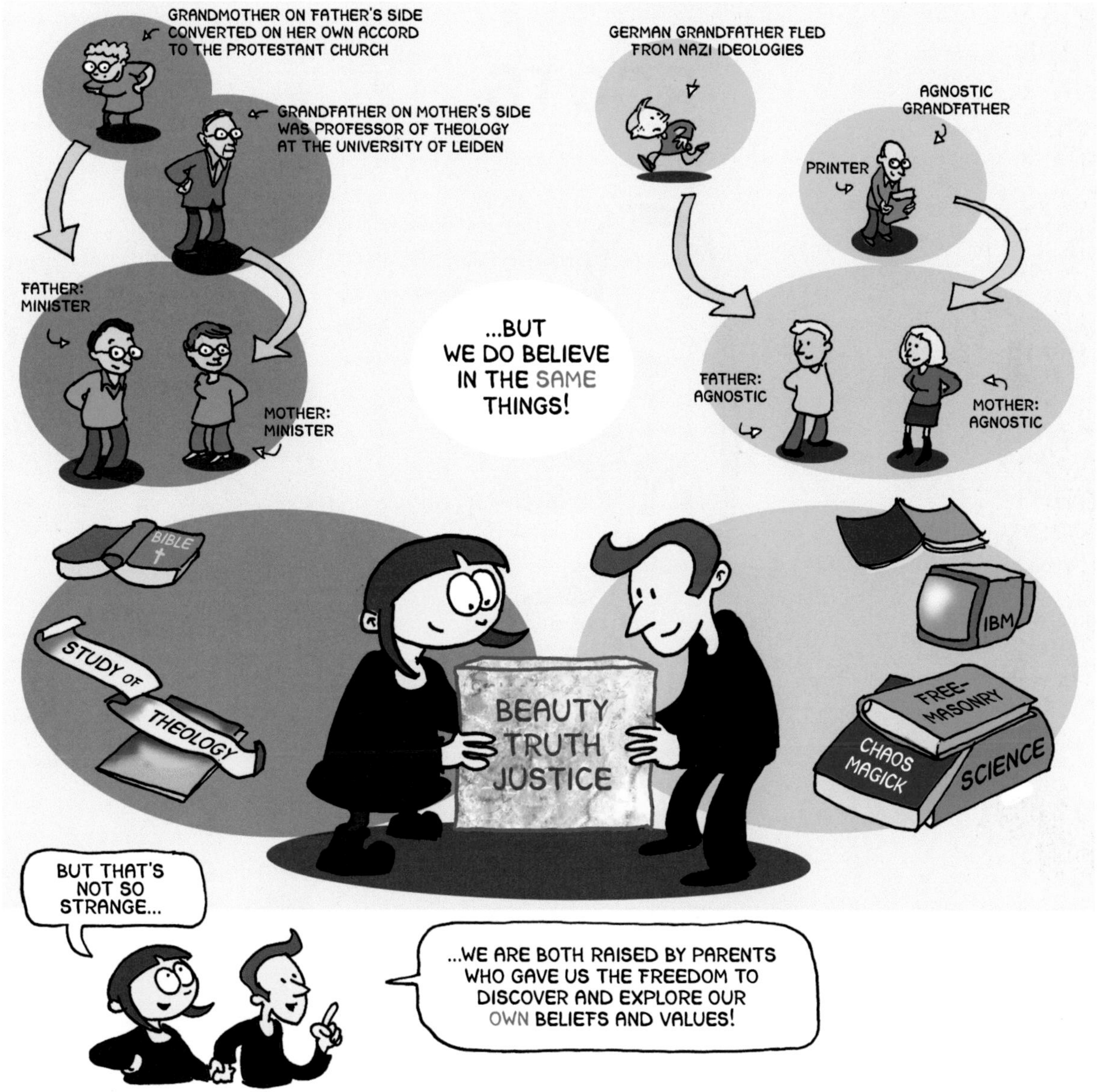
GRANDMOTHER ON FATHER'S SIDE CONVERTED ON HER OWN ACCORD TO THE PROTESTANT CHURCH
GRANDFATHER ON MOTHER'S SIDE WAS PROFESSOR OF THEOLOGY AT THE UNIVERSITY OF LEIDEN
FATHER: MINISTER
MOTHER: MINISTER
GERMAN GRANDFATHER FLED FROM NAZI IDEOLOGIES
AGNOSTIC GRANDFATHER
PRINTER
FATHER: AGNOSTIC
MOTHER: AGNOSTIC
...BUT WE DO BELIEVE IN THE SAME THINGS!
BIBLE
STUDY OF THEOLOGY
BEAUTY TRUTH JUSTICE
IBM
FREE-MASONRY
CHAOS MAGICK
SCIENCE
BUT THAT'S NOT SO STRANGE...
...WE ARE BOTH RAISED BY PARENTS WHO GAVE US THE FREEDOM TO DISCOVER AND EXPLORE OUR OWN BELIEFS AND VALUES!

ROOTS

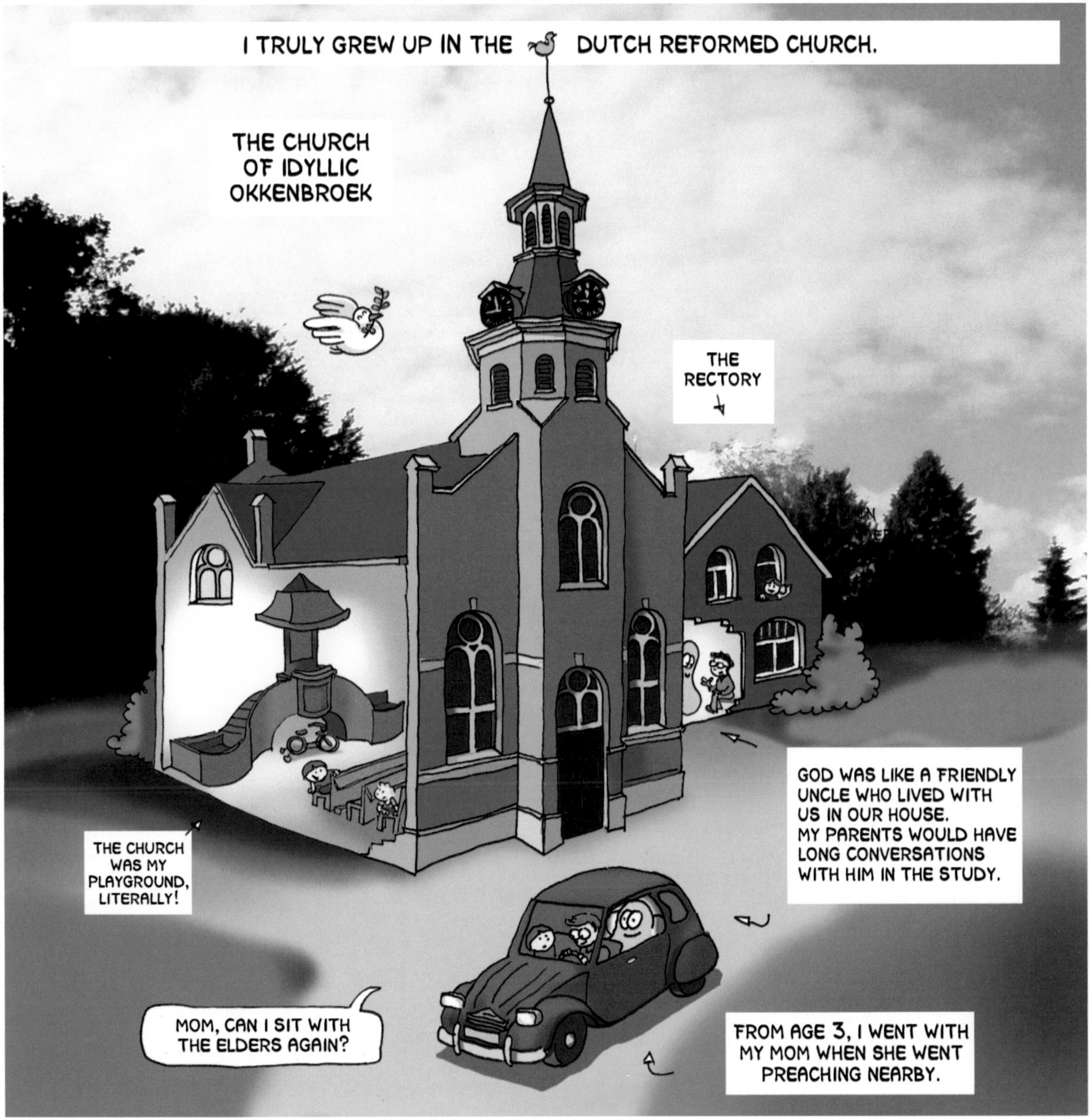

I TRULY GREW UP IN THE DUTCH REFORMED CHURCH.
THE CHURCH OF IDYLLIC OKKENBROEK
THE RECTORY
GOD WAS LIKE A FRIENDLY UNCLE WHO LIVED WITH US IN OUR HOUSE. MY PARENTS WOULD HAVE LONG CONVERSATIONS WITH HIM IN THE STUDY.
THE CHURCH WAS MY PLAYGROUND, LITERALLY!
MOM, CAN I SIT WITH THE ELDERS AGAIN?
FROM AGE 3, I WENT WITH MY MOM WHEN SHE WENT PREACHING NEARBY.

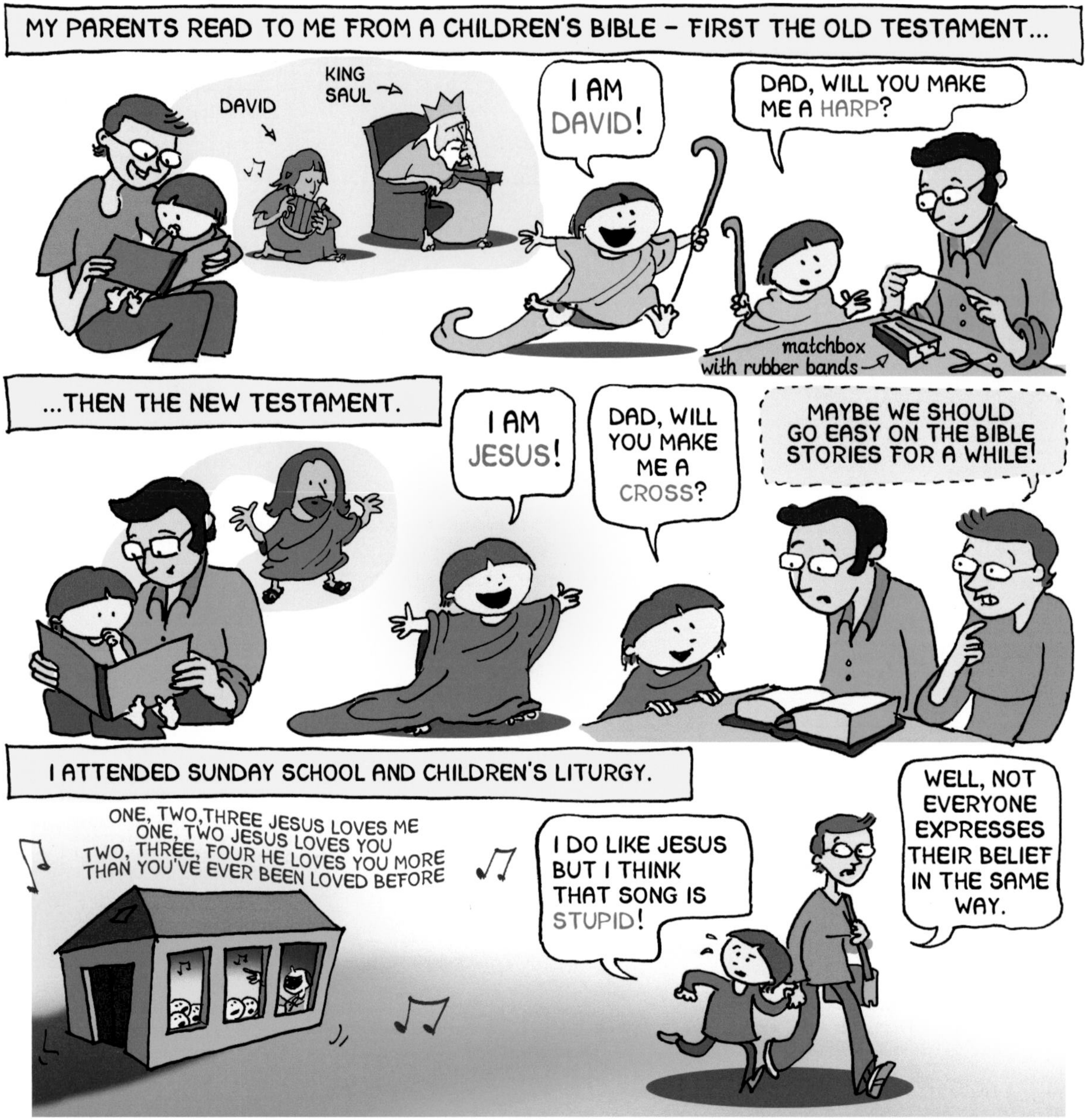
MY PARENTS READ TO ME FROM A CHILDREN'S BIBLE – FIRST THE OLD TESTAMENT...
DAVID
KING SAUL
I AM DAVID!
DAD, WILL YOU MAKE ME A HARP?
matchbox with rubber bands
...THEN THE NEW TESTAMENT.
I AM JESUS!
DAD, WILL YOU MAKE ME A CROSS?
MAYBE WE SHOULD GO EASY ON THE BIBLE STORIES FOR A WHILE!
I ATTENDED SUNDAY SCHOOL AND CHILDREN'S LITURGY.
ONE, TWO,THREE JESUS LOVES ME
ONE, TWO JESUS LOVES YOU
TWO, THREE, FOUR HE LOVES YOU MORE
THAN YOU'VE EVER BEEN LOVED BEFORE
I DO LIKE JESUS BUT I THINK THAT SONG IS STUPID!
WELL, NOT EVERYONE EXPRESSES THEIR BELIEF IN THE SAME WAY.

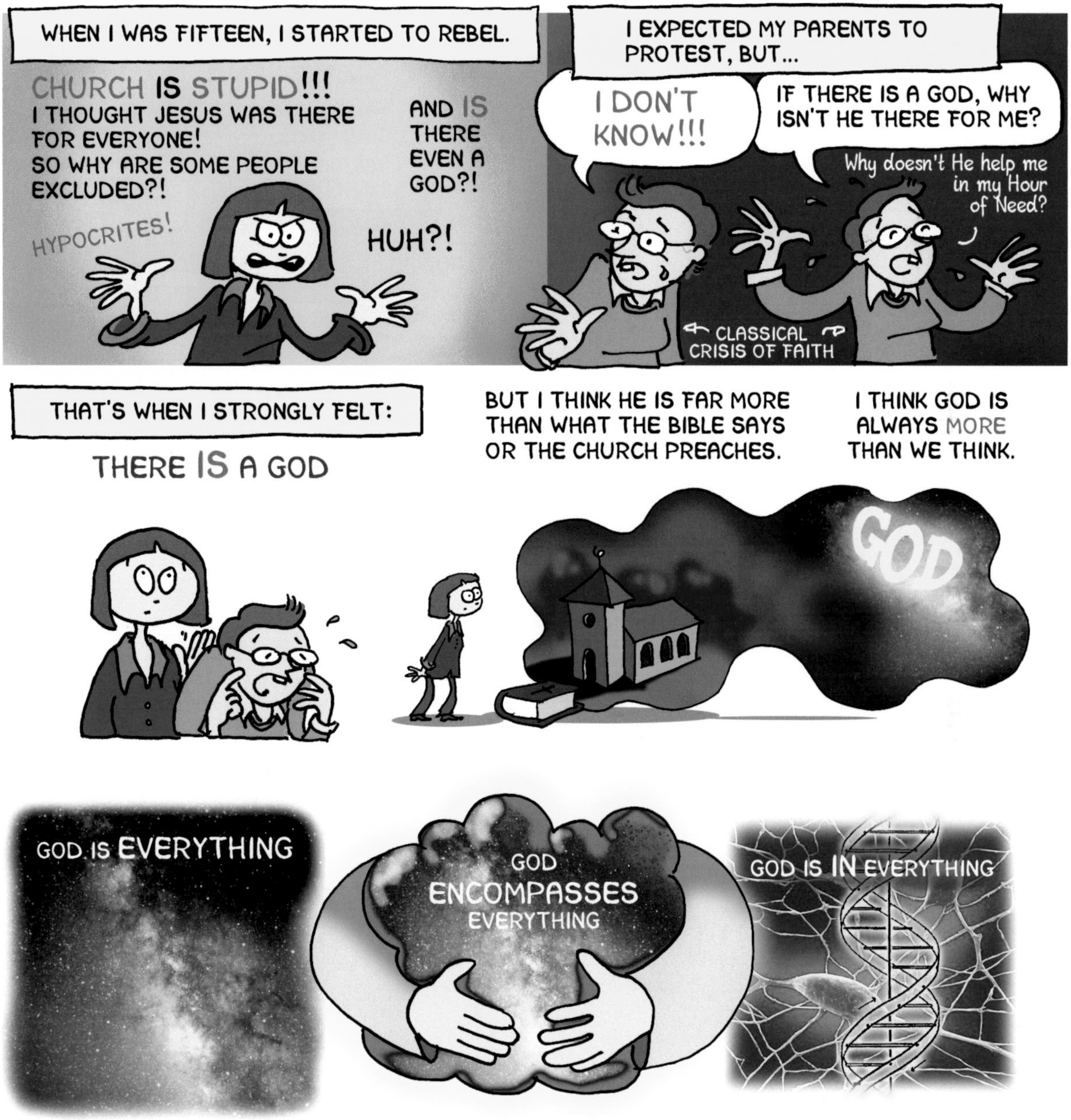
WHEN I WAS FIFTEEN, I STARTED TO REBEL.
CHURCH IS STUPID!!!
I THOUGHT JESUS WAS THERE FOR EVERYONE!
SO WHY ARE SOME PEOPLE EXCLUDED?!
AND IS THERE EVEN A GOD?!
HYPOCRITES!
HUH?!
I EXPECTED MY PARENTS TO PROTEST, BUT...
I DON'T KNOW!!!
IF THERE IS A GOD, WHY ISN'T HE THERE FOR ME?
Why doesn't He help me in my Hour of Need?
CLASSICAL CRISIS OF FAITH
THAT'S WHEN I STRONGLY FELT:
THERE IS A GOD
BUT I THINK HE IS FAR MORE THAN WHAT THE BIBLE SAYS OR THE CHURCH PREACHES.
I THINK GOD IS ALWAYS MORE THAN WE THINK.
GOD
GOD IS EVERYTHING
GOD ENCOMPASSES EVERYTHING
GOD IS IN EVERYTHING

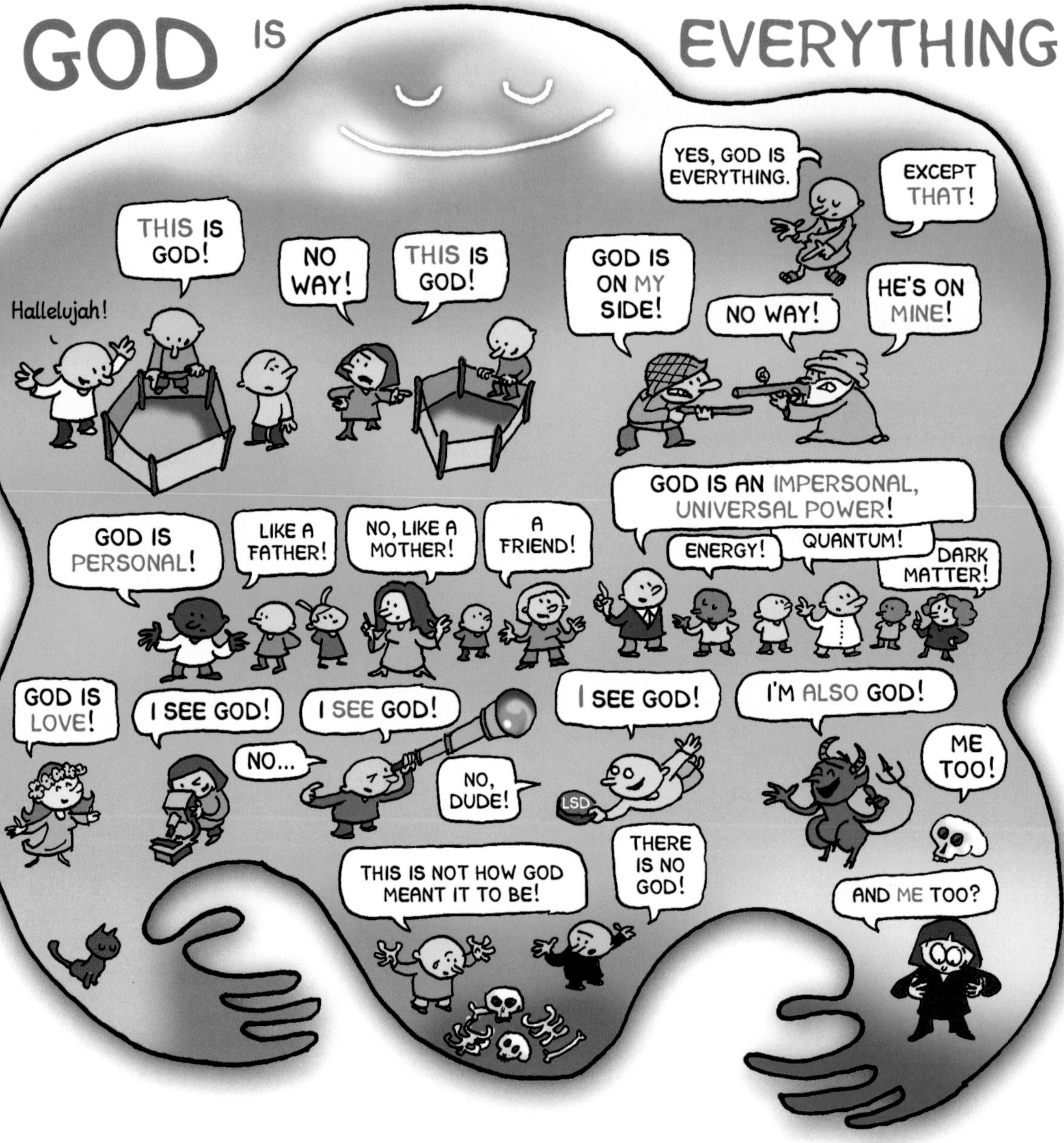
GOD IS EVERYTHING
YES, GOD IS EVERYTHING.
EXCEPT THAT!
THIS IS GOD!
Hallelujah!
NO WAY!
THIS IS GOD!
GOD IS ON MY SIDE!
NO WAY!
HE'S ON MINE!
GOD IS AN IMPERSONAL, UNIVERSAL POWER!
GOD IS PERSONAL!
LIKE A FATHER!
NO, LIKE A MOTHER!
A FRIEND!
ENERGY!
QUANTUM!
DARK MATTER!
GOD IS LOVE!
I SEE GOD!
I SEE GOD!
NO...
NO, DUDE!
I SEE GOD!
LSD
I'M ALSO GOD!
ME TOO!
THIS IS NOT HOW GOD MEANT IT TO BE!
THERE IS NO GOD!
AND ME TOO?

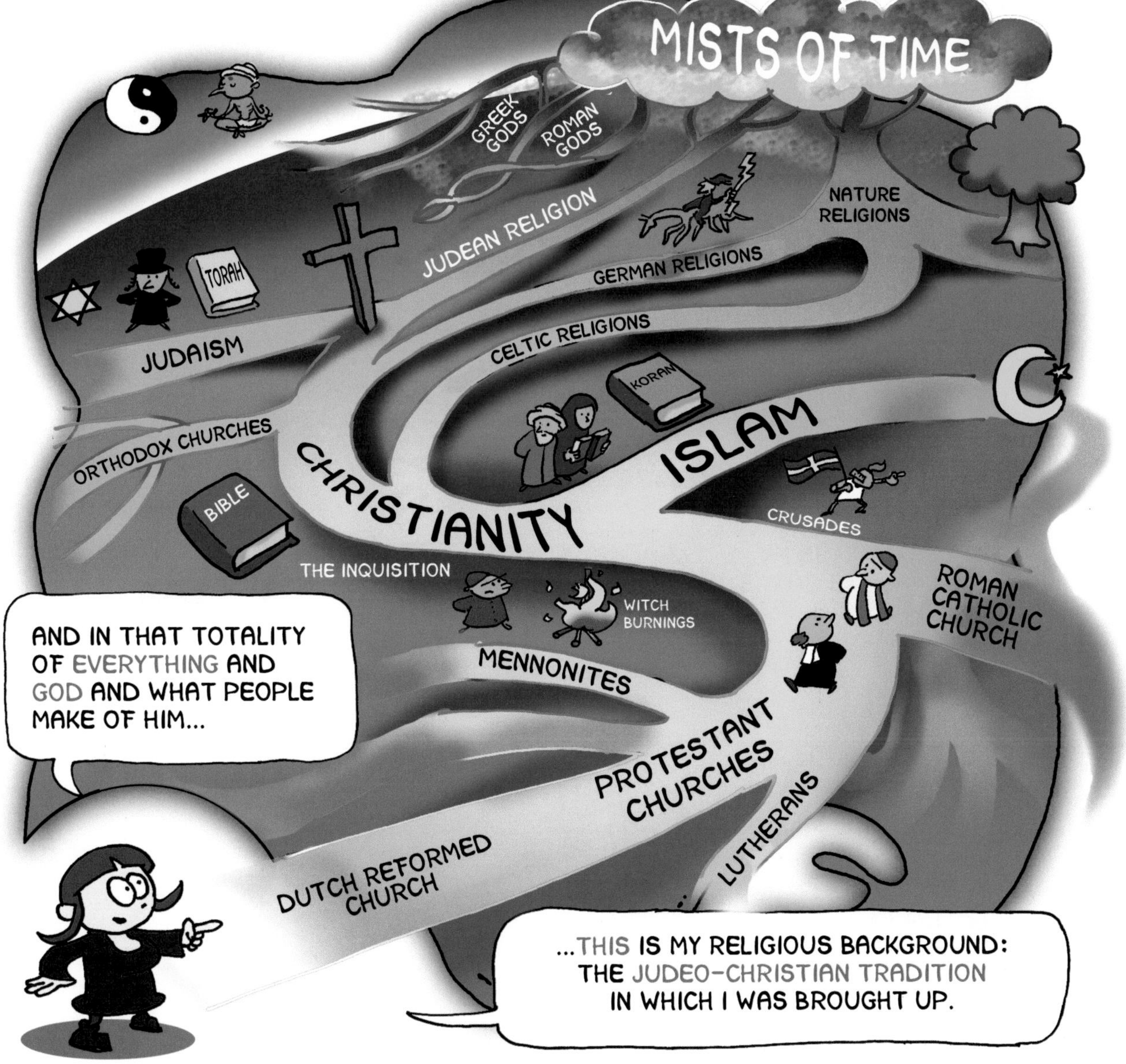
MISTS OF TIME
GREEK GODS
ROMAN GODS
JUDEAN RELIGION
NATURE RELIGIONS
GERMAN RELIGIONS
TORAH
JUDAISM
CELTIC RELIGIONS
KORAN
ORTHODOX CHURCHES
CHRISTIANITY
ISLAM
BIBLE
CRUSADES
THE INQUISITION
WITCH BURNINGS
ROMAN CATHOLIC CHURCH
AND IN THAT TOTALITY OF EVERYTHING AND GOD AND WHAT PEOPLE MAKE OF HIM...
MENNONITES
PROTESTANT CHURCHES
LUTHERANS
DUTCH REFORMED CHURCH
...THIS IS MY RELIGIOUS BACKGROUND: THE JUDEO-CHRISTIAN TRADITION IN WHICH I WAS BROUGHT UP.

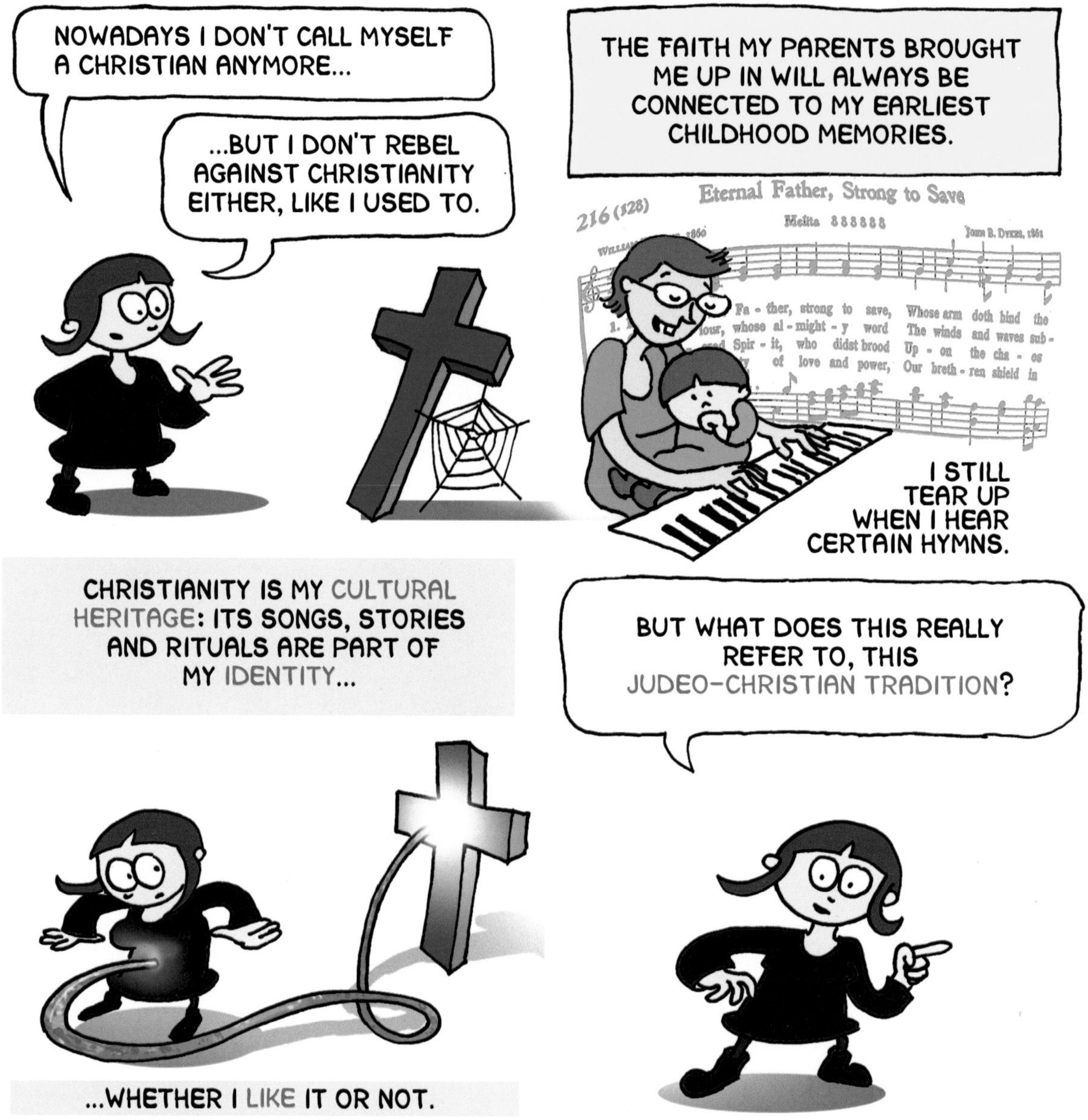
NOWADAYS I DON'T CALL MYSELF A CHRISTIAN ANYMORE...
...BUT I DON'T REBEL AGAINST CHRISTIANITY EITHER, LIKE I USED TO.
THE FAITH MY PARENTS BROUGHT ME UP IN WILL ALWAYS BE CONNECTED TO MY EARLIEST CHILDHOOD MEMORIES.
Eternal Father, Strong to Save
I STILL TEAR UP WHEN I HEAR CERTAIN HYMNS.
CHRISTIANITY IS MY CULTURAL HERITAGE: ITS SONGS, STORIES AND RITUALS ARE PART OF MY IDENTITY...
...WHETHER I LIKE IT OR NOT.
BUT WHAT DOES THIS REALLY REFER TO, THIS JUDEO-CHRISTIAN TRADITION?

CHRISTIANITY

ISLAM

JUDAISM

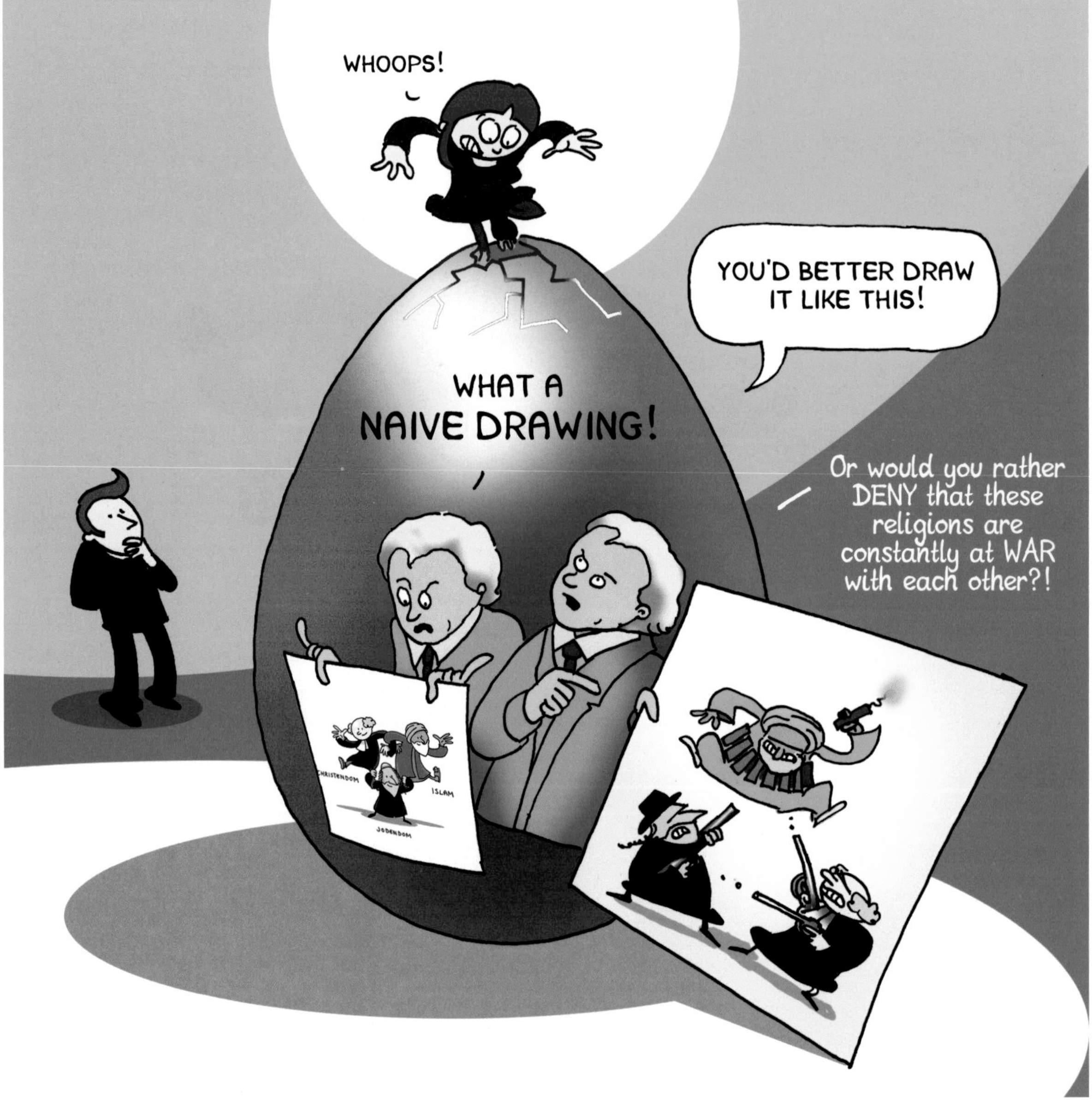
WHOOPS!
WHAT A NAIVE DRAWING!
CHRISTENDOM
ISLAM
JODENDOM
YOU'D BETTER DRAW IT LIKE THIS!
Or would you rather DENY that these religions are constantly at WAR with each other?!

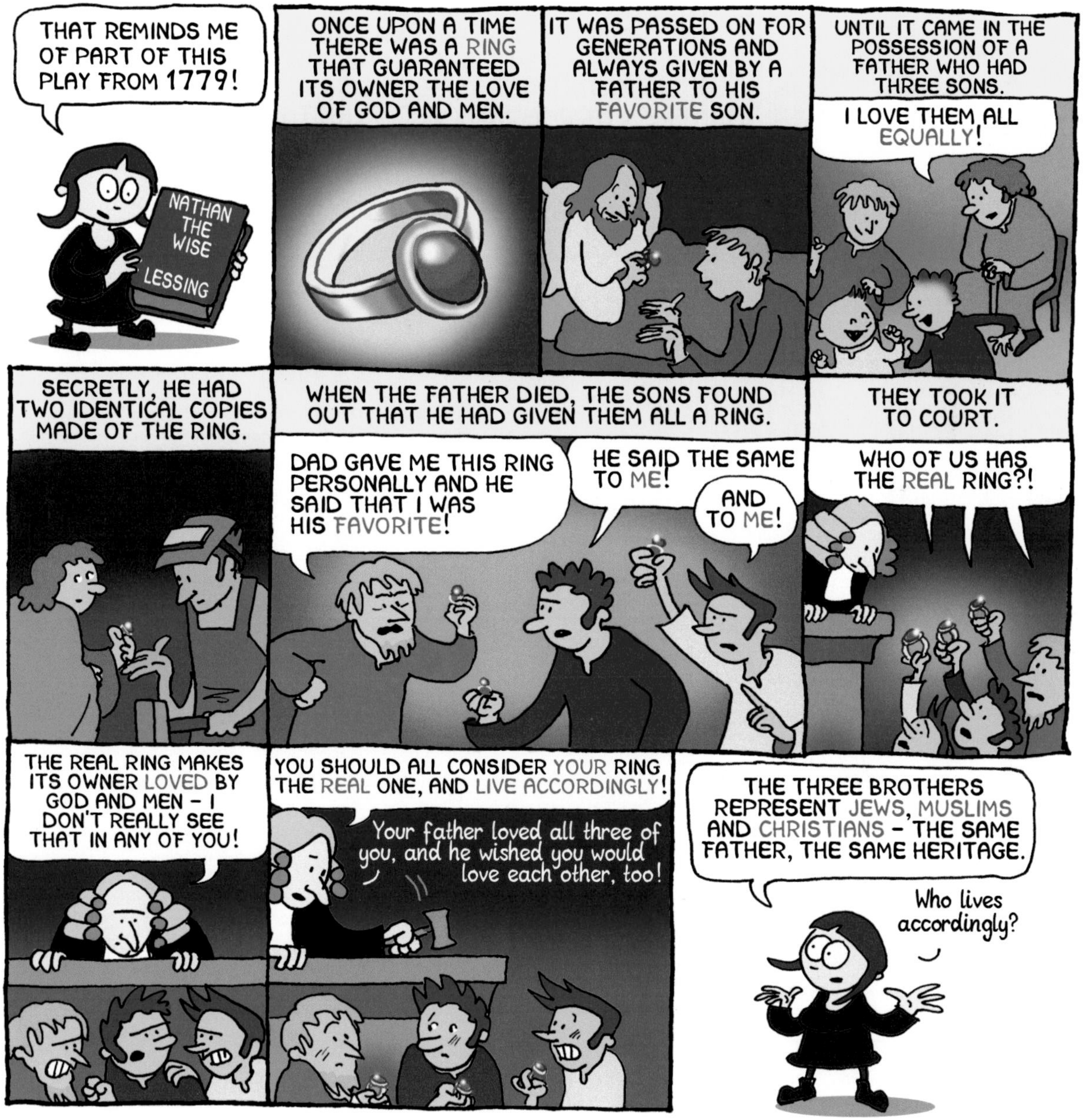
THAT REMINDS ME OF PART OF THIS PLAY FROM 1779!
NATHAN THE WISE
LESSING
ONCE UPON A TIME THERE WAS A RING THAT GUARANTEED ITS OWNER THE LOVE OF GOD AND MEN.
IT WAS PASSED ON FOR GENERATIONS AND ALWAYS GIVEN BY A FATHER TO HIS FAVORITE SON.
UNTIL IT CAME IN THE POSSESSION OF A FATHER WHO HAD THREE SONS.
I LOVE THEM ALL EQUALLY!
SECRETLY, HE HAD TWO IDENTICAL COPIES MADE OF THE RING.
WHEN THE FATHER DIED, THE SONS FOUND OUT THAT HE HAD GIVEN THEM ALL A RING.
DAD GAVE ME THIS RING PERSONALLY AND HE SAID THAT I WAS HIS FAVORITE!
HE SAID THE SAME TO ME!
AND TO ME!
THEY TOOK IT TO COURT.
WHO OF US HAS THE REAL RING?!
THE REAL RING MAKES ITS OWNER LOVED BY GOD AND MEN - I DON'T REALLY SEE THAT IN ANY OF YOU!
YOU SHOULD ALL CONSIDER YOUR RING THE REAL ONE, AND LIVE ACCORDINGLY!
Your father loved all three of you, and he wished you would love each other, too!
THE THREE BROTHERS REPRESENT JEWS, MUSLIMS AND CHRISTIANS - THE SAME FATHER, THE SAME HERITAGE.
Who lives accordingly?

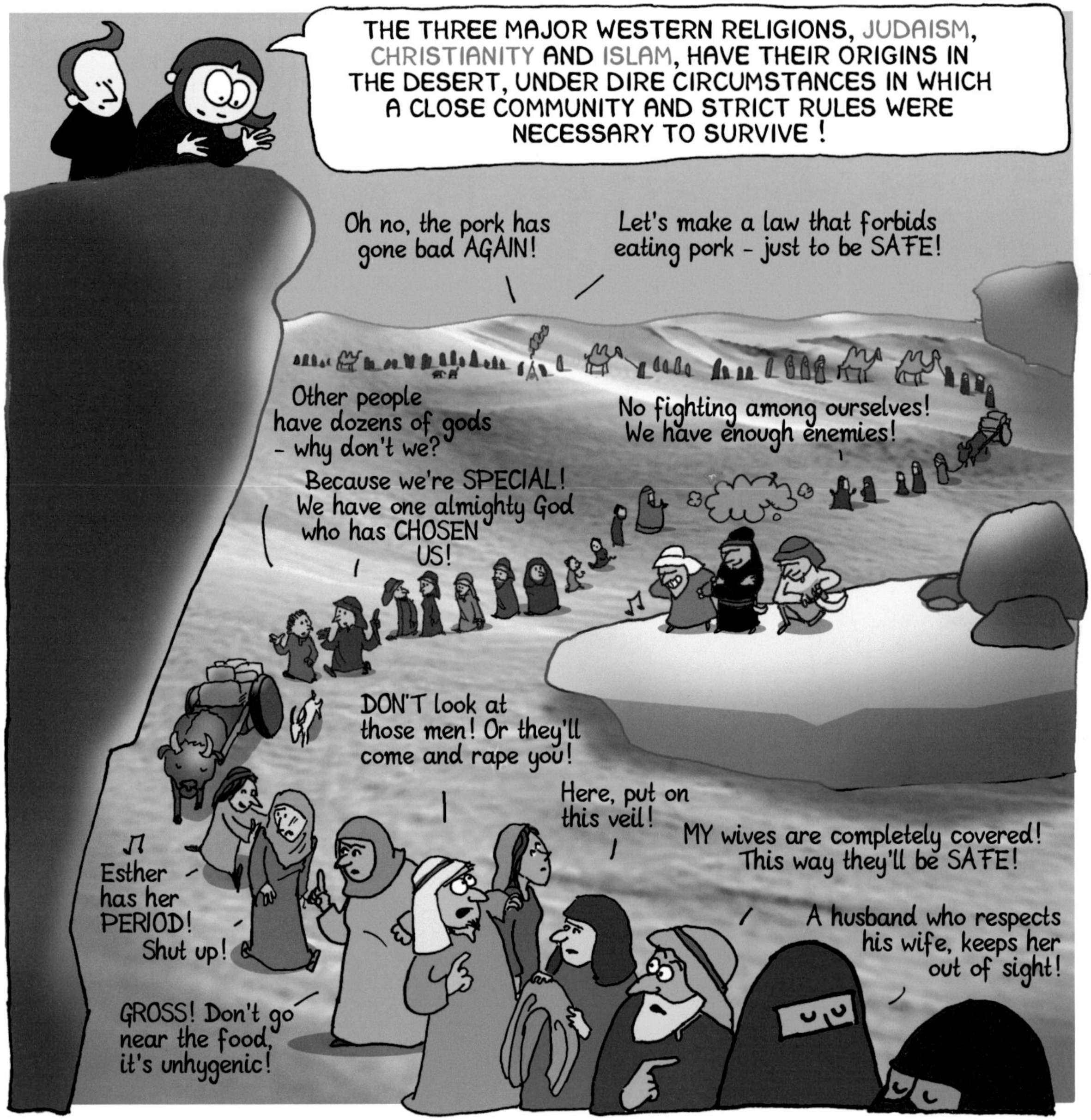
THE THREE MAJOR WESTERN RELIGIONS, JUDAISM, CHRISTIANITY AND ISLAM, HAVE THEIR ORIGINS IN THE DESERT, UNDER DIRE CIRCUMSTANCES IN WHICH A CLOSE COMMUNITY AND STRICT RULES WERE NECESSARY TO SURVIVE !
Oh no, the pork has gone bad AGAIN!
Let's make a law that forbids eating pork - just to be SAFE!
Other people have dozens of gods - why don't we?
No fighting among ourselves! We have enough enemies!
Because we're SPECIAL! We have one almighty God who has CHOSEN US!
DON'T look at those men! Or they'll come and rape you!
Here, put on this veil!
MY wives are completely covered! This way they'll be SAFE!
Esther has her PERIOD!
Shut up!
A husband who respects his wife, keeps her out of sight!
GROSS! Don't go near the food, it's unhygenic!

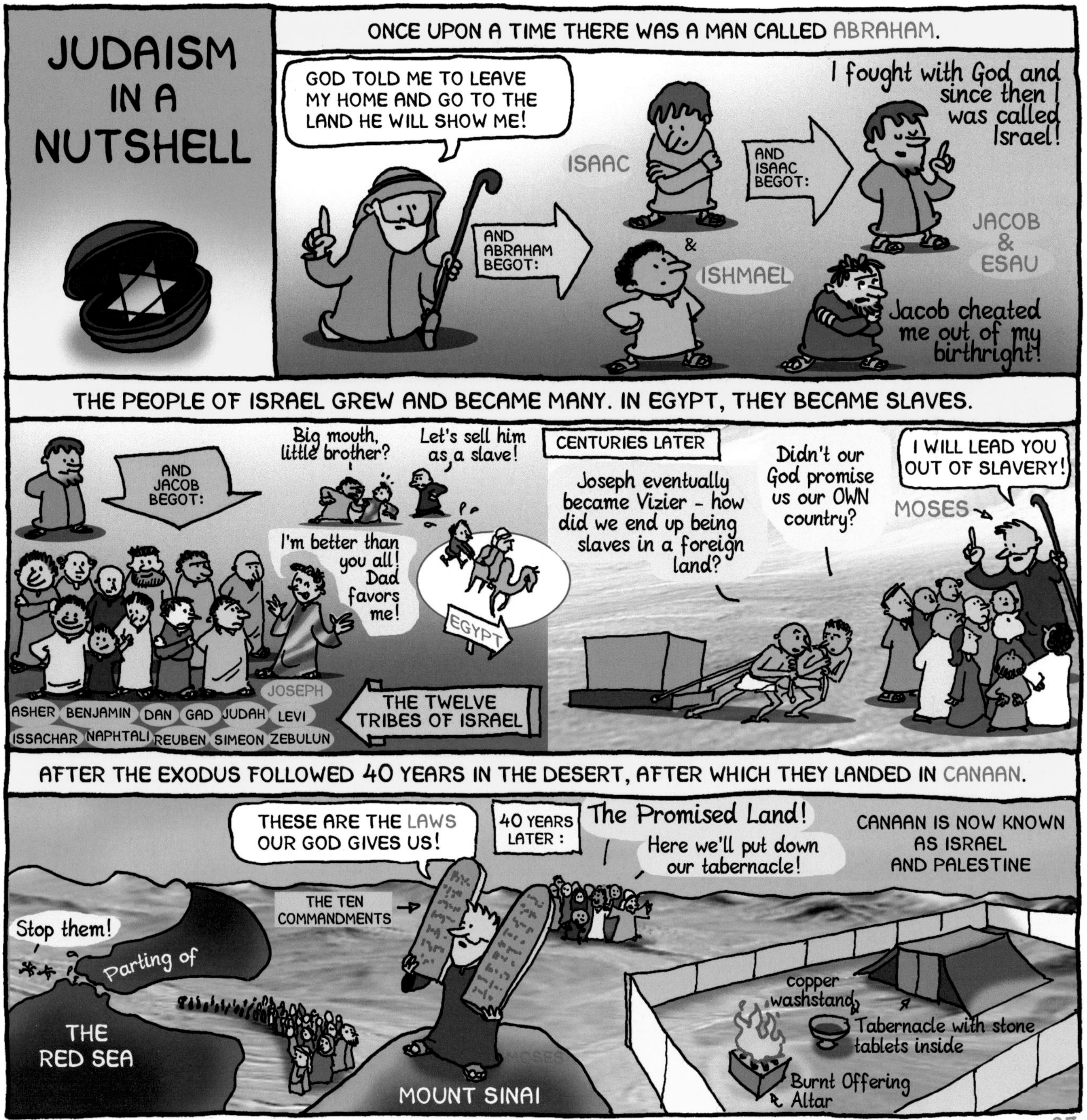

JUDAISM IN A NUTSHELL
ONCE UPON A TIME THERE WAS A MAN CALLED ABRAHAM.
GOD TOLD ME TO LEAVE MY HOME AND GO TO THE LAND HE WILL SHOW ME!
AND ABRAHAM BEGOT:
ISAAC
&
ISHMAEL
AND ISAAC BEGOT:
I fought with God and since then I was called Israel!
JACOB & ESAU
Jacob cheated me out of my birthright!
THE PEOPLE OF ISRAEL GREW AND BECAME MANY. IN EGYPT, THEY BECAME SLAVES.
AND JACOB BEGOT:
Big mouth, little brother?
Let's sell him as a slave!
I'm better than you all! Dad favors me!
EGYPT
JOSEPH
ASHER BENJAMIN DAN GAD JUDAH LEVI
ISSACHAR NAPHTALI REUBEN SIMEON ZEBULUN
THE TWELVE TRIBES OF ISRAEL
CENTURIES LATER
Joseph eventually became Vizier - how did we end up being slaves in a foreign land?
Didn't our God promise us our OWN country?
I WILL LEAD YOU OUT OF SLAVERY!
MOSES
AFTER THE EXODUS FOLLOWED 40 YEARS IN THE DESERT, AFTER WHICH THEY LANDED IN CANAAN.
THESE ARE THE LAWS OUR GOD GIVES US!
40 YEARS LATER :
The Promised Land!
Here we'll put down our tabernacle!
CANAAN IS NOW KNOWN AS ISRAEL AND PALESTINE
Stop them!
Parting of
THE RED SEA
THE TEN COMMANDMENTS
MOSES
MOUNT SINAI
copper washstand
Tabernacle with stone tablets inside
Burnt Offering Altar

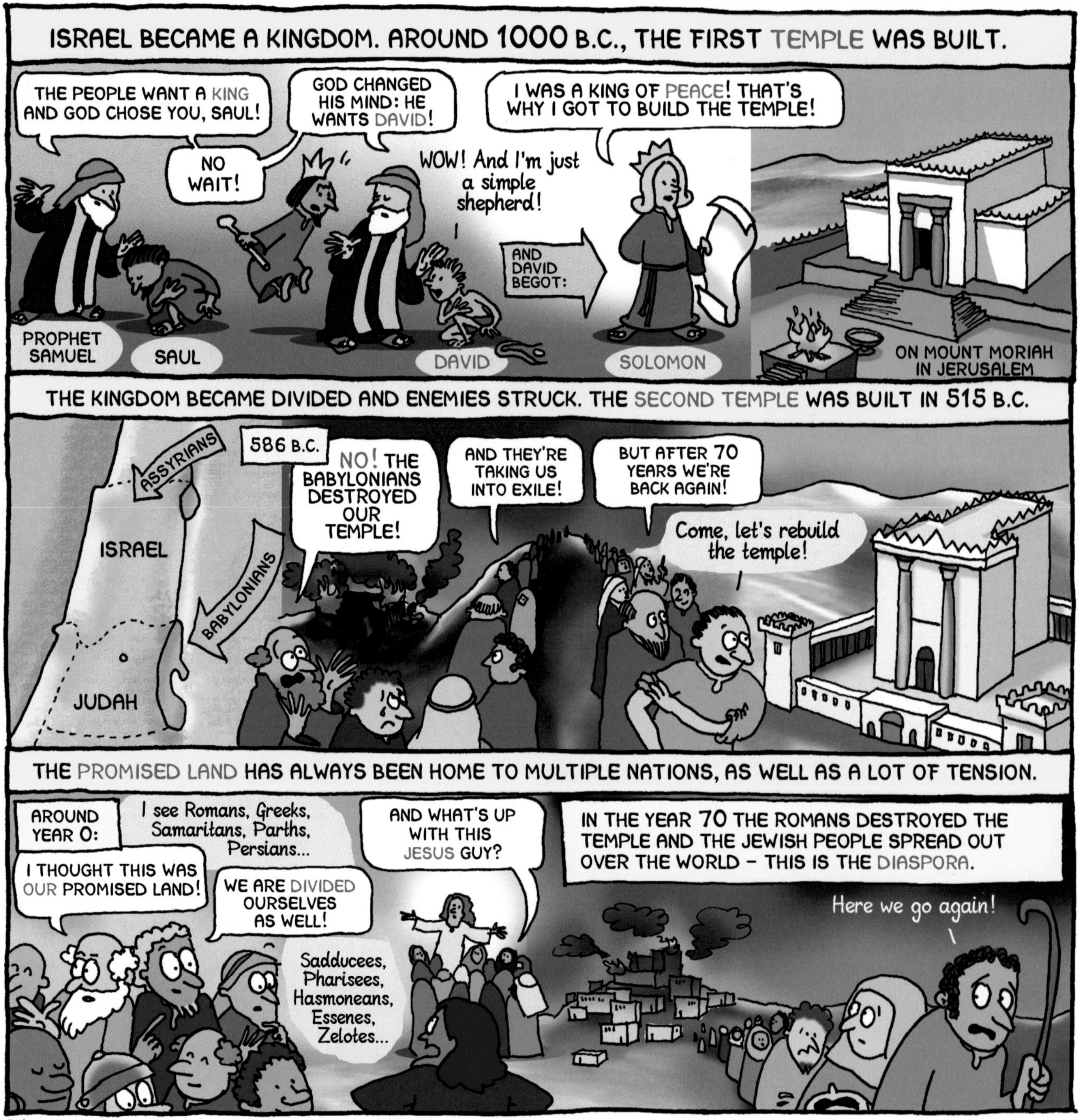
ISRAEL BECAME A KINGDOM. AROUND 1000 B.C., THE FIRST TEMPLE WAS BUILT.
THE PEOPLE WANT A KING AND GOD CHOSE YOU, SAUL!
NO WAIT!
GOD CHANGED HIS MIND: HE WANTS DAVID!
WOW! And I'm just a simple shepherd!
AND DAVID BEGOT:
I WAS A KING OF PEACE! THAT'S WHY I GOT TO BUILD THE TEMPLE!
PROPHET SAMUEL
SAUL
DAVID
SOLOMON
ON MOUNT MORIAH IN JERUSALEM
THE KINGDOM BECAME DIVIDED AND ENEMIES STRUCK. THE SECOND TEMPLE WAS BUILT IN 515 B.C.
ASSYRIANS
ISRAEL
BABYLONIANS
JUDAH
586 B.C.
NO! THE BABYLONIANS DESTROYED OUR TEMPLE!
AND THEY'RE TAKING US INTO EXILE!
BUT AFTER 70 YEARS WE'RE BACK AGAIN!
Come, let's rebuild the temple!
THE PROMISED LAND HAS ALWAYS BEEN HOME TO MULTIPLE NATIONS, AS WELL AS A LOT OF TENSION.
AROUND YEAR 0:
I see Romans, Greeks, Samaritans, Parths, Persians...
I THOUGHT THIS WAS OUR PROMISED LAND!
WE ARE DIVIDED OURSELVES AS WELL!
Sadducees, Pharisees, Hasmoneans, Essenes, Zelotes...
AND WHAT'S UP WITH THIS JESUS GUY?
IN THE YEAR 70 THE ROMANS DESTROYED THE TEMPLE AND THE JEWISH PEOPLE SPREAD OUT OVER THE WORLD – THIS IS THE DIASPORA.
Here we go again!

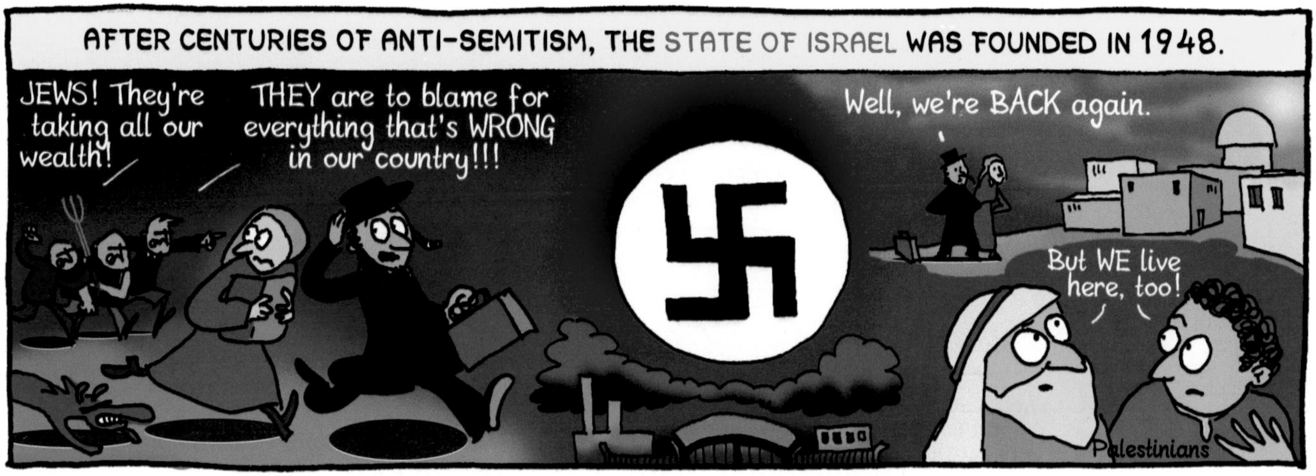
AFTER CENTURIES OF ANTI-SEMITISM, THE STATE OF ISRAEL WAS FOUNDED IN 1948.
JEWS! They're taking all our wealth!
THEY are to blame for everything that's WRONG in our country!!!
Well, we're BACK again.
But WE live here, too!
Palestinians

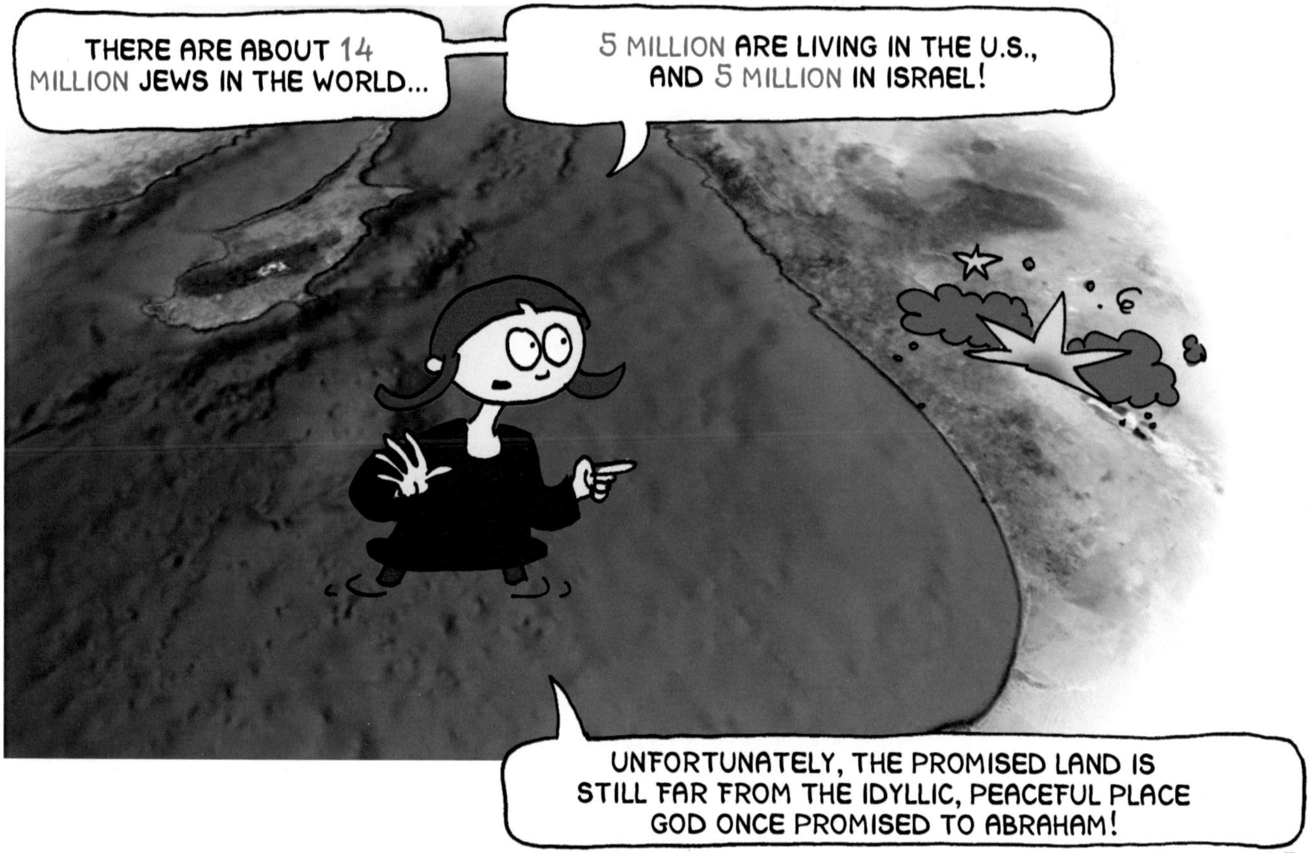
THERE ARE ABOUT 14 MILLION JEWS IN THE WORLD...
5 MILLION ARE LIVING IN THE U.S., AND 5 MILLION IN ISRAEL!
UNFORTUNATELY, THE PROMISED LAND IS STILL FAR FROM THE IDYLLIC, PEACEFUL PLACE GOD ONCE PROMISED TO ABRAHAM!

THE CORE OF THE JEWISH FAITH

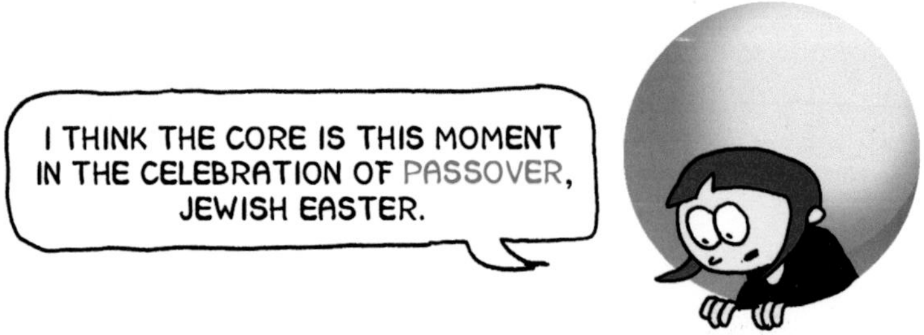
I THINK THE CORE IS THIS MOMENT IN THE CELEBRATION OF PASSOVER, JEWISH EASTER.

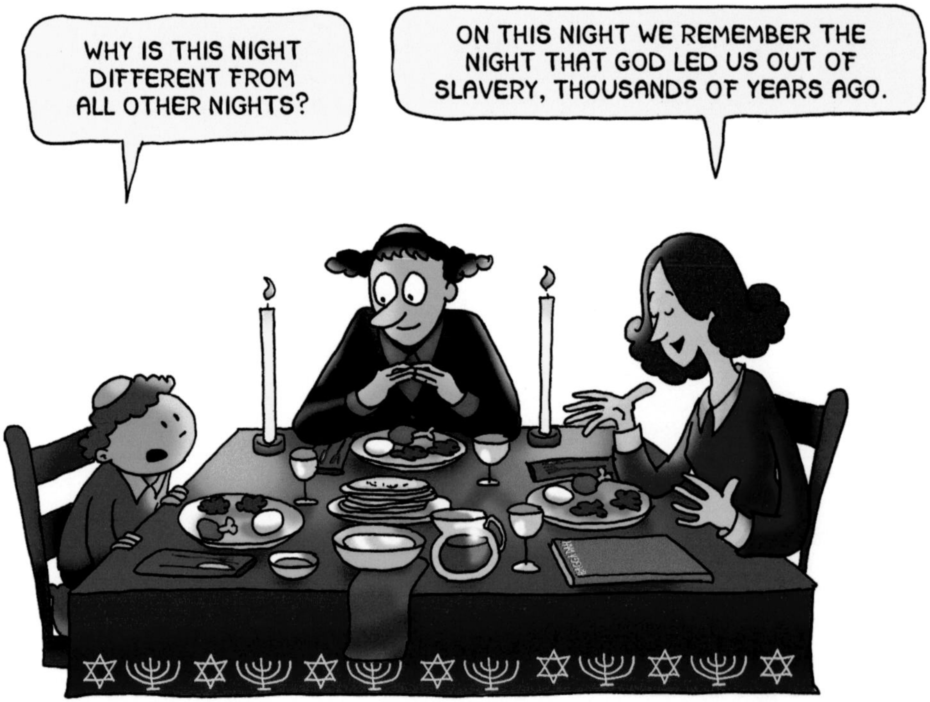
WHY IS THIS NIGHT DIFFERENT FROM ALL OTHER NIGHTS?
ON THIS NIGHT WE REMEMBER THE NIGHT THAT GOD LED US OUT OF SLAVERY, THOUSANDS OF YEARS AGO.

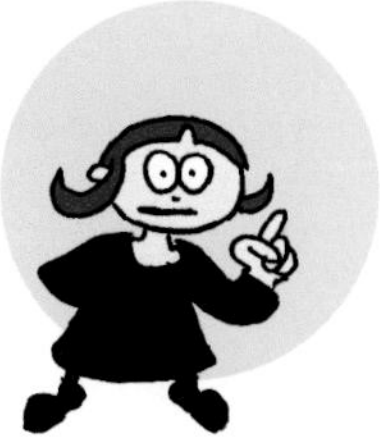

CENTRAL IN JUDAISM ARE THE THEMES OF SUFFERING AND DELIVERANCE FROM SUFFERING, AS WELL AS THE NOTION OF THE CHOSEN PEOPLE.

JUDAISM HAS ELABORATE LAWS ON FOOD – ONLY MEAT FROM RUMINANT ANIMALS WITH CLOVEN HOOVES IS PERMITTED, ALONG WITH POULTRY AND MOST SEAFOOD, EXCEPT FOR SHELLFISH.
THAT WHICH IS IN ACCORDANCE WITH THE LAW IS CALLED KOSHER.

THE MEAL INCLUDES SOMETHING BITTER AND SOMETHING SWEET: TO RECALL THE BITTER TIME IN EGYPT AND THE SWEET LIBERATION.

PASSING ON TRADITION IS VERY IMPORTANT: YOUNG CHILDREN PARTICIPATE IN RITUALS AND ARE ENCOURAGED TO ASK QUESTIONS AND START DEBATES.

THESE ARE MATZOS: UNLEAVENED BREAD THAT WILL KEEP LONGER – THE ISRAELITES BAKED THESE FOR THEIR FLIGHT OUT OF EGYPT.

A LAMB'S BONE IS A SYMBOL FOR THE LAMB SLAUGHTERED THE NIGHT BEFORE THEY LEFT.

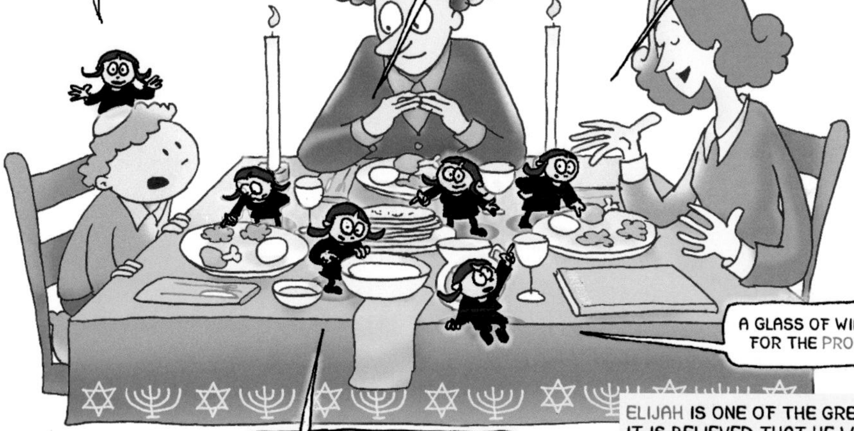

A GLASS OF WINE IS SET OUT FOR THE PROPHET ELIJAH!

ELIJAH IS ONE OF THE GREAT PROPHETS. IT IS BELIEVED THAT HE WILL RETURN TO THE WORLD, JUST BEFORE THE COMING OF THE MESSIAH.

PURIFICATION LAWS PLAY A BIG ROLE IN JEWISH RITUALS, SO HERE'S A HAND WASH BASIN.

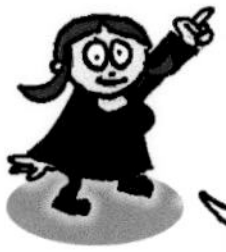

THESE ARE THE SYMBOLS OF JUDAISM: THE STAR OF DAVID AND THE MENORAH, A SEVEN-BRANCHED CANDLE.

ACCORDING TO TRADITION, THE SIX-POINTED STAR STEMS FROM THE TIME OF KING DAVID. FROM THE 15TH CENTURY, IT WAS SEEN AS A SPECIAL JEWISH SIGN. DURING WORLD WAR II JEWS WERE FORCED TO WEAR IT ON THEIR CLOTHES. THIS STAR NOW APPEARS IN THE CENTER OF THE ISRAELI FLAG.

THE BOOKS OF JUDAISM

Ta Na Kh + Talmud

TORAH + NEVI'IM + KETUVIM

COMMENTS ON TANAKH

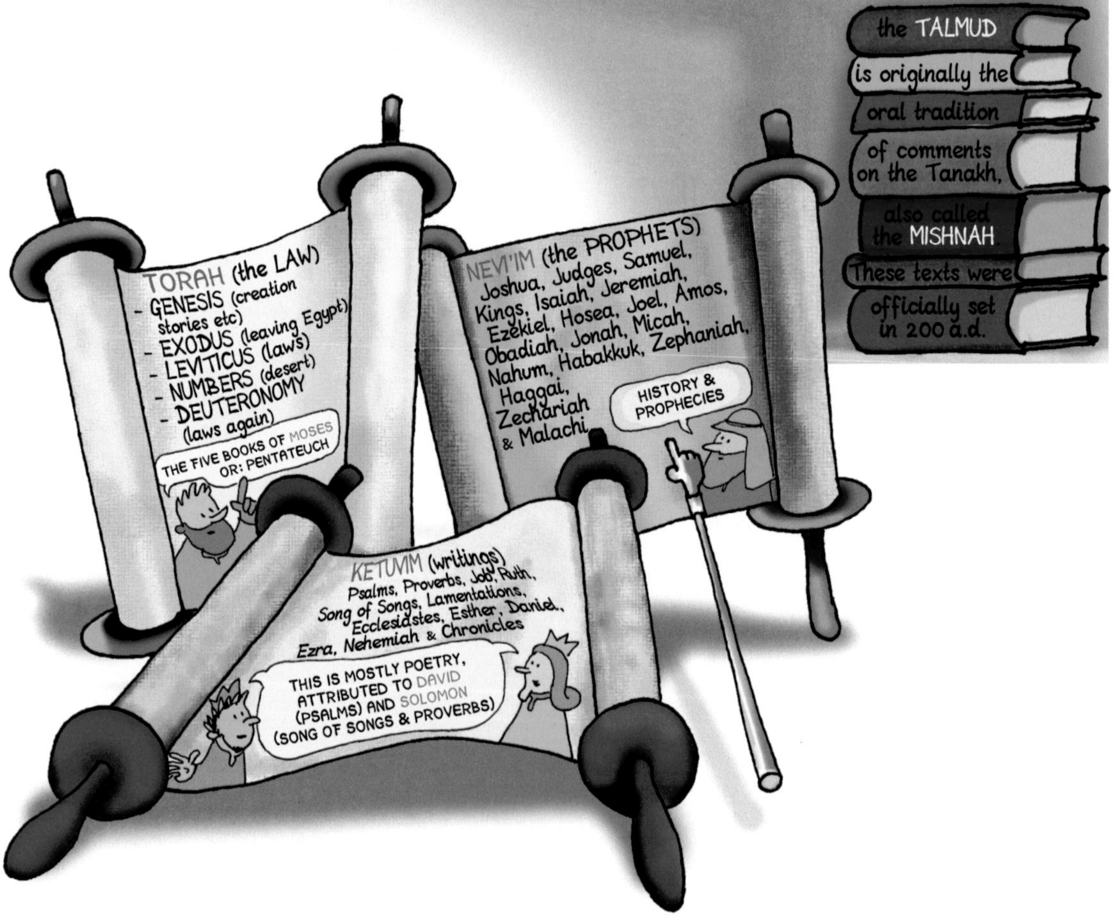

TORAH (the LAW)
- GENESIS (creation stories etc)
- EXODUS (leaving Egypt)
- LEVITICUS (laws)
- NUMBERS (desert)
- DEUTERONOMY (laws again)
THE FIVE BOOKS OF MOSES OR: PENTATEUCH
NEVI'IM (the PROPHETS)
Joshua, Judges, Samuel, Kings, Isaiah, Jeremiah, Ezekiel, Hosea, Joel, Amos, Obadiah, Jonah, Micah, Nahum, Habakkuk, Zephaniah, Haggai, Zechariah & Malachi
HISTORY & PROPHECIES
KETUVIM (writings)
Psalms, Proverbs, Job, Ruth, Song of Songs, Lamentations, Ecclesiastes, Esther, Daniel, Ezra, Nehemiah & Chronicles
THIS IS MOSTLY POETRY, ATTRIBUTED TO DAVID (PSALMS) AND SOLOMON (SONG OF SONGS & PROVERBS)
the TALMUD
is originally the
oral tradition
of comments on the Tanakh,
also called the MISHNAH
These texts were
officially set in 200 a.d.

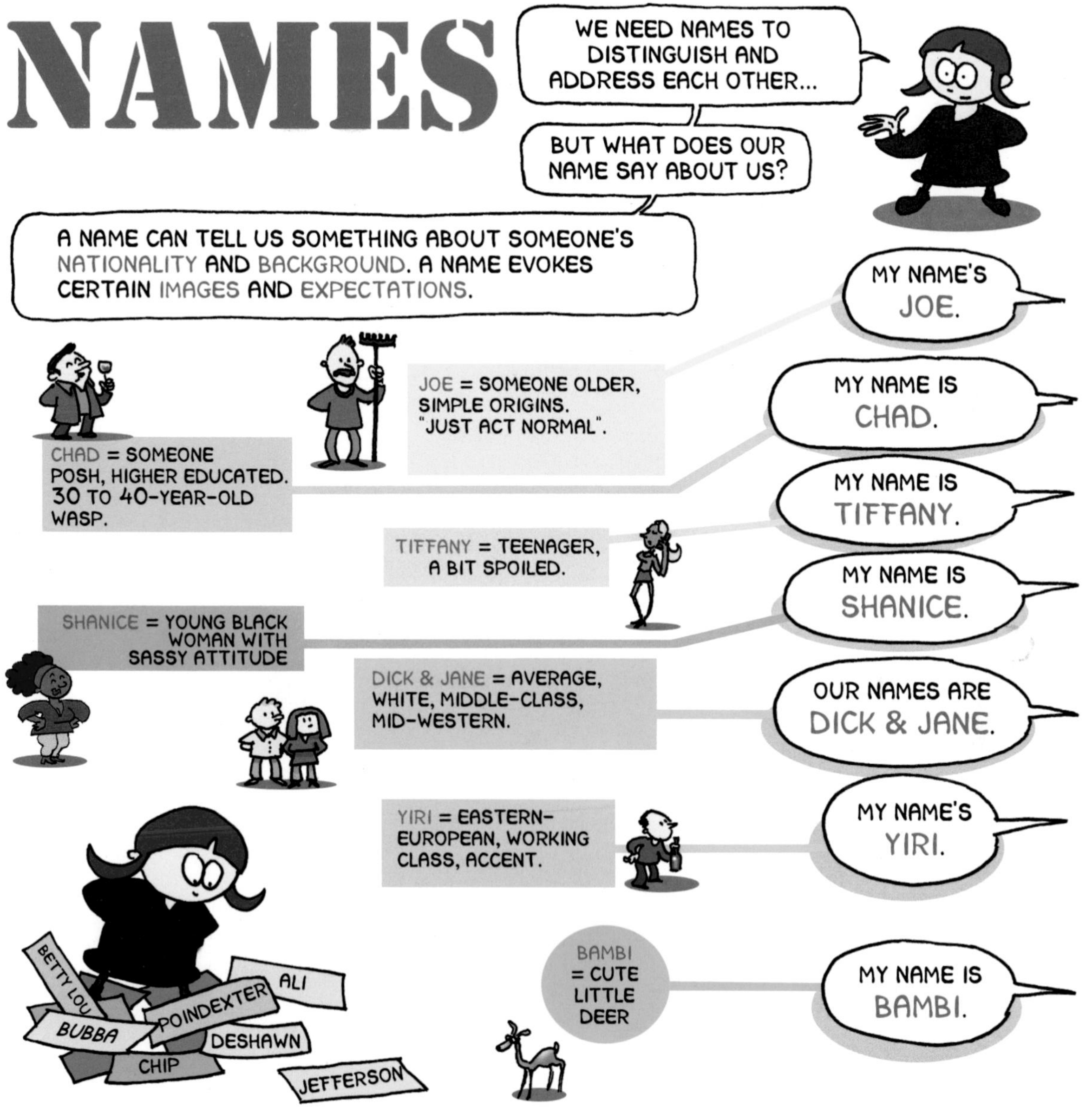
NAMES
WE NEED NAMES TO DISTINGUISH AND ADDRESS EACH OTHER...
BUT WHAT DOES OUR NAME SAY ABOUT US?
A NAME CAN TELL US SOMETHING ABOUT SOMEONE'S NATIONALITY AND BACKGROUND. A NAME EVOKES CERTAIN IMAGES AND EXPECTATIONS.
JOE = SOMEONE OLDER, SIMPLE ORIGINS. "JUST ACT NORMAL".
MY NAME'S JOE.
CHAD = SOMEONE POSH, HIGHER EDUCATED. 30 TO 40-YEAR-OLD WASP.
MY NAME IS CHAD.
TIFFANY = TEENAGER, A BIT SPOILED.
MY NAME IS TIFFANY.
SHANICE = YOUNG BLACK WOMAN WITH SASSY ATTITUDE
MY NAME IS SHANICE.
DICK & JANE = AVERAGE, WHITE, MIDDLE-CLASS, MID-WESTERN.
OUR NAMES ARE DICK & JANE.
YIRI = EASTERN-EUROPEAN, WORKING CLASS, ACCENT.
MY NAME'S YIRI.
BAMBI = CUTE LITTLE DEER
MY NAME IS BAMBI.
BETTY LOU
ALI
POINDEXTER
BUBBA
DESHAWN
CHIP
JEFFERSON

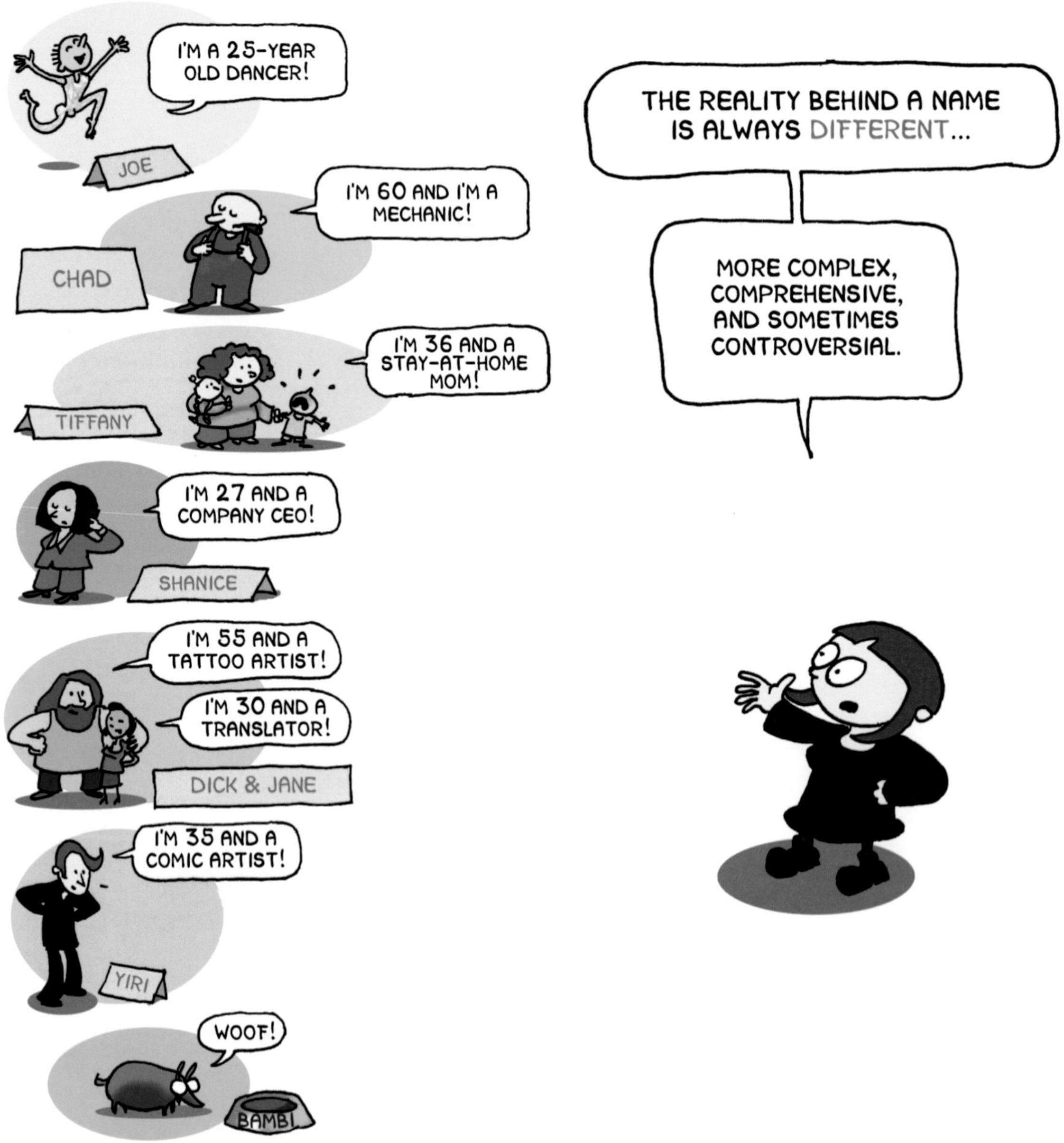
I'M A 25-YEAR OLD DANCER!
JOE
I'M 60 AND I'M A MECHANIC!
CHAD
I'M 36 AND A STAY-AT-HOME MOM!
TIFFANY
I'M 27 AND A COMPANY CEO!
SHANICE
I'M 55 AND A TATTOO ARTIST!
I'M 30 AND A TRANSLATOR!
DICK & JANE
I'M 35 AND A COMIC ARTIST!
YIRI
WOOF!
BAMBI
THE REALITY BEHIND A NAME IS ALWAYS DIFFERENT...
MORE COMPLEX, COMPREHENSIVE, AND SOMETIMES CONTROVERSIAL.

IF NAMES FOR HUMANS CAN BE SO AMBIGUOUS, THEN WHAT ABOUT NAMES FOR GOD?
WHAT SORT OF IMAGES AND EXPECTATIONS DO THOSE EVOKE?
ETERNAL
INFINITE
MY NAME IS GOD
MY NAME IS ALLAH
MY NAME IS ADONAI
MY NAME IS BRAHMA
MY NAME IS JAH
MY NAME IS GAIA
MY NAME IS JEHOVA
FATHER: LOVING & FORGIVING
ALMIGHTY
UNIVERSE
WISE OLD MAN ON A CLOUD
LIFE ENERGY
NATURE
RULES & LAWS
FAIRYTALE FIGURE
SPACE
INSTRUMENT OF POWER
VENGEFUL
LOVE
COMMERCIAL CONCOCTION

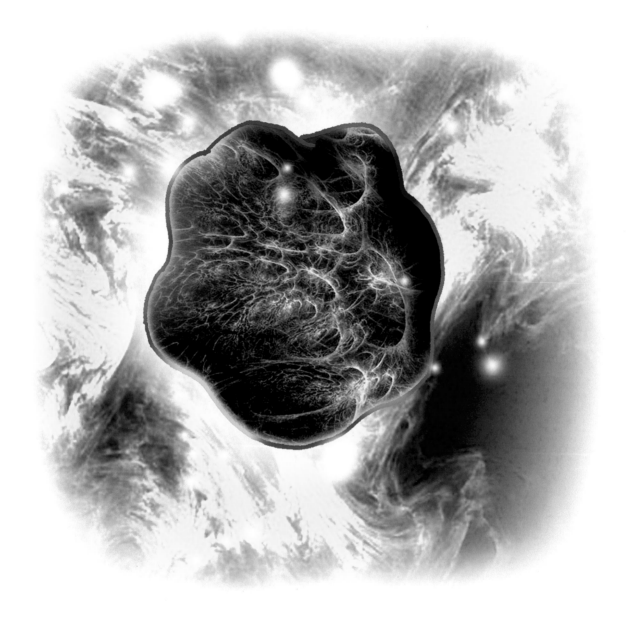

RELIGIOUS JEWS ARE VERY CAREFUL WITH THE NAME OF GOD!
GOD REVEALED HIS NAME TO MOSES, AND HIS NAME IS:
JHWH
THIS CAN MEAN:
I AM
I WILL BE
I CAUSE TO BE
WE DON'T SPEAK THE NAME!
INSTEAD WE SAY ADONAI, WHICH MEANS LORD.
TO SPEAK GOD'S NAME WOULD IMPLY THAT YOU KNOW HIM, AND GOD IS TOO BIG FOR US TO KNOW!

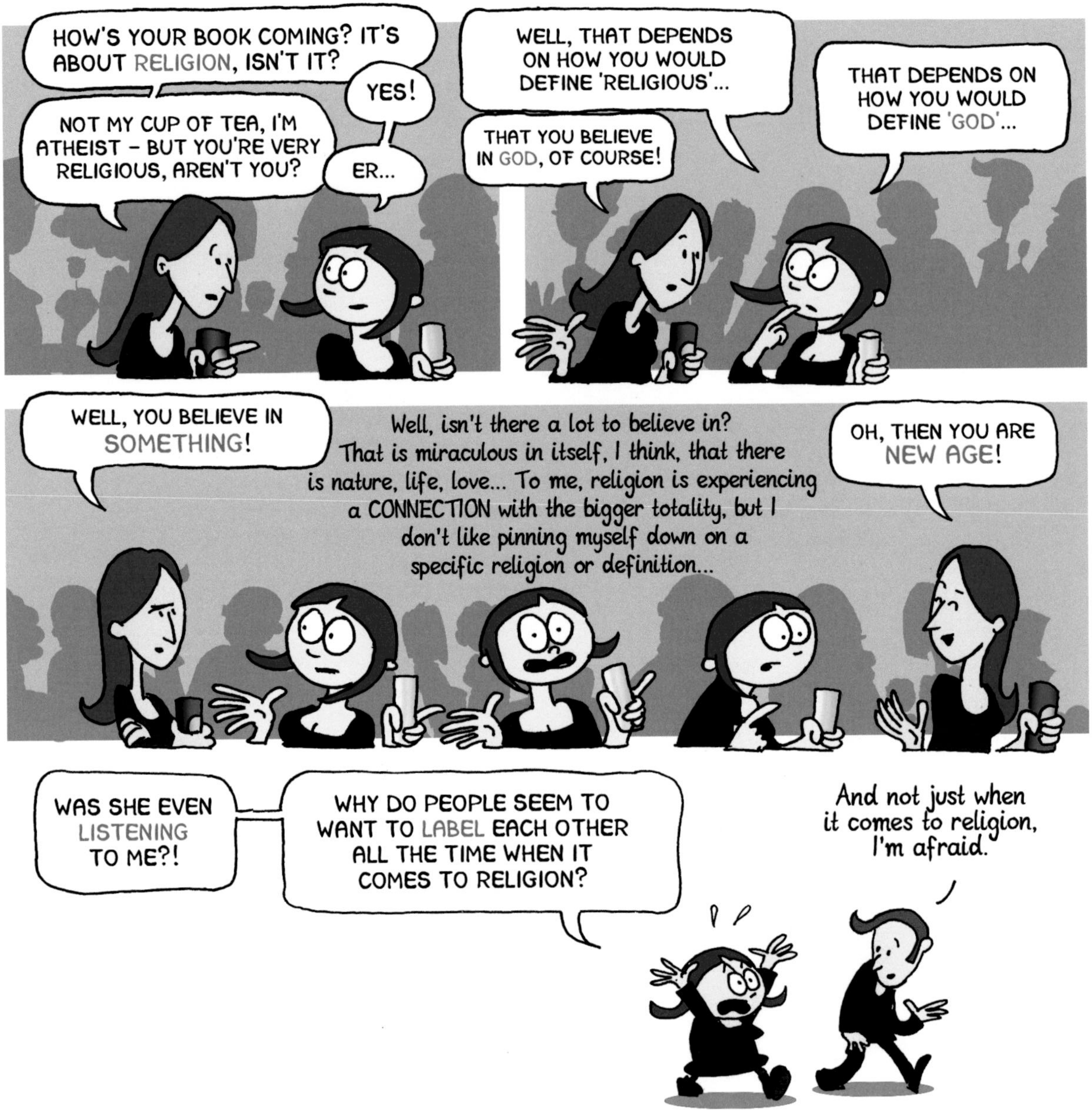
HOW'S YOUR BOOK COMING? IT'S ABOUT RELIGION, ISN'T IT?
YES!
NOT MY CUP OF TEA, I'M ATHEIST – BUT YOU'RE VERY RELIGIOUS, AREN'T YOU?
ER...
WELL, THAT DEPENDS ON HOW YOU WOULD DEFINE 'RELIGIOUS'...
THAT YOU BELIEVE IN GOD, OF COURSE!
THAT DEPENDS ON HOW YOU WOULD DEFINE 'GOD'...
WELL, YOU BELIEVE IN SOMETHING!
Well, isn't there a lot to believe in? That is miraculous in itself, I think, that there is nature, life, love... To me, religion is experiencing a CONNECTION with the bigger totality, but I don't like pinning myself down on a specific religion or definition...
OH, THEN YOU ARE NEW AGE!
WAS SHE EVEN LISTENING TO ME?!
WHY DO PEOPLE SEEM TO WANT TO LABEL EACH OTHER ALL THE TIME WHEN IT COMES TO RELIGION?
And not just when it comes to religion, I'm afraid.

ATHEISTS
VS.
FUNDAMENTALISTS

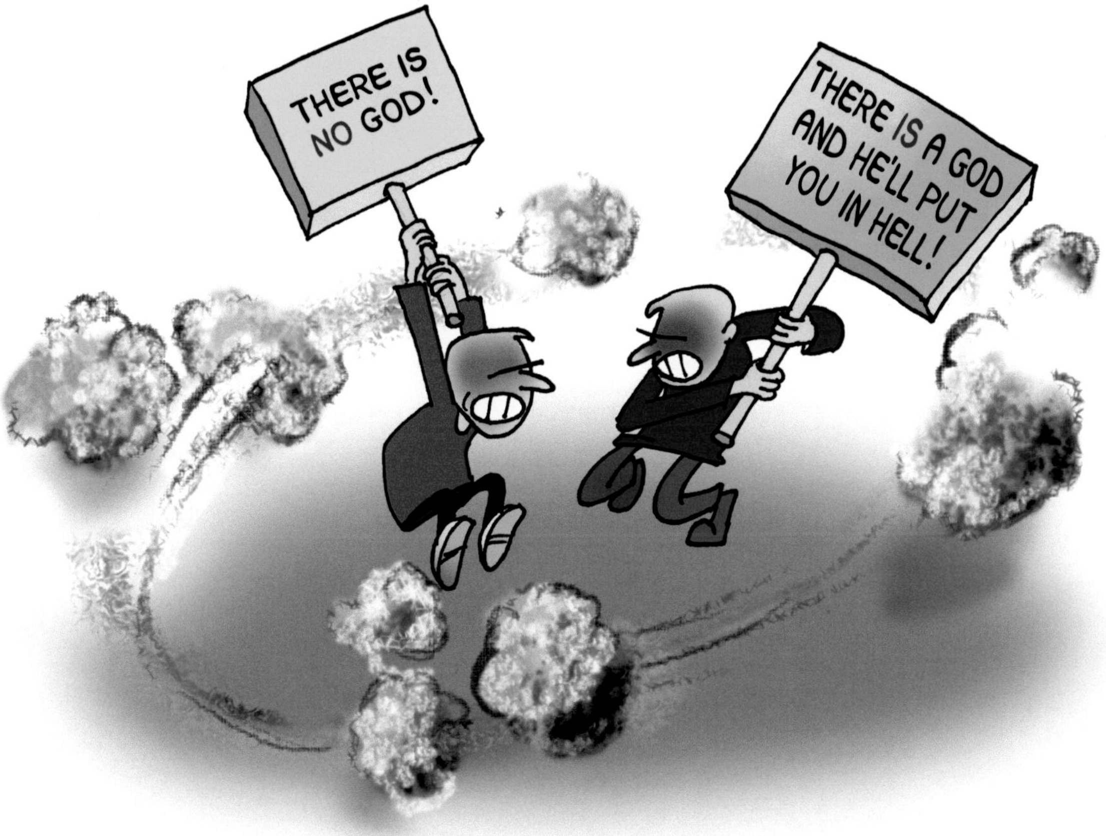
THERE IS NO GOD!
THERE IS A GOD AND HE'LL PUT YOU IN HELL!

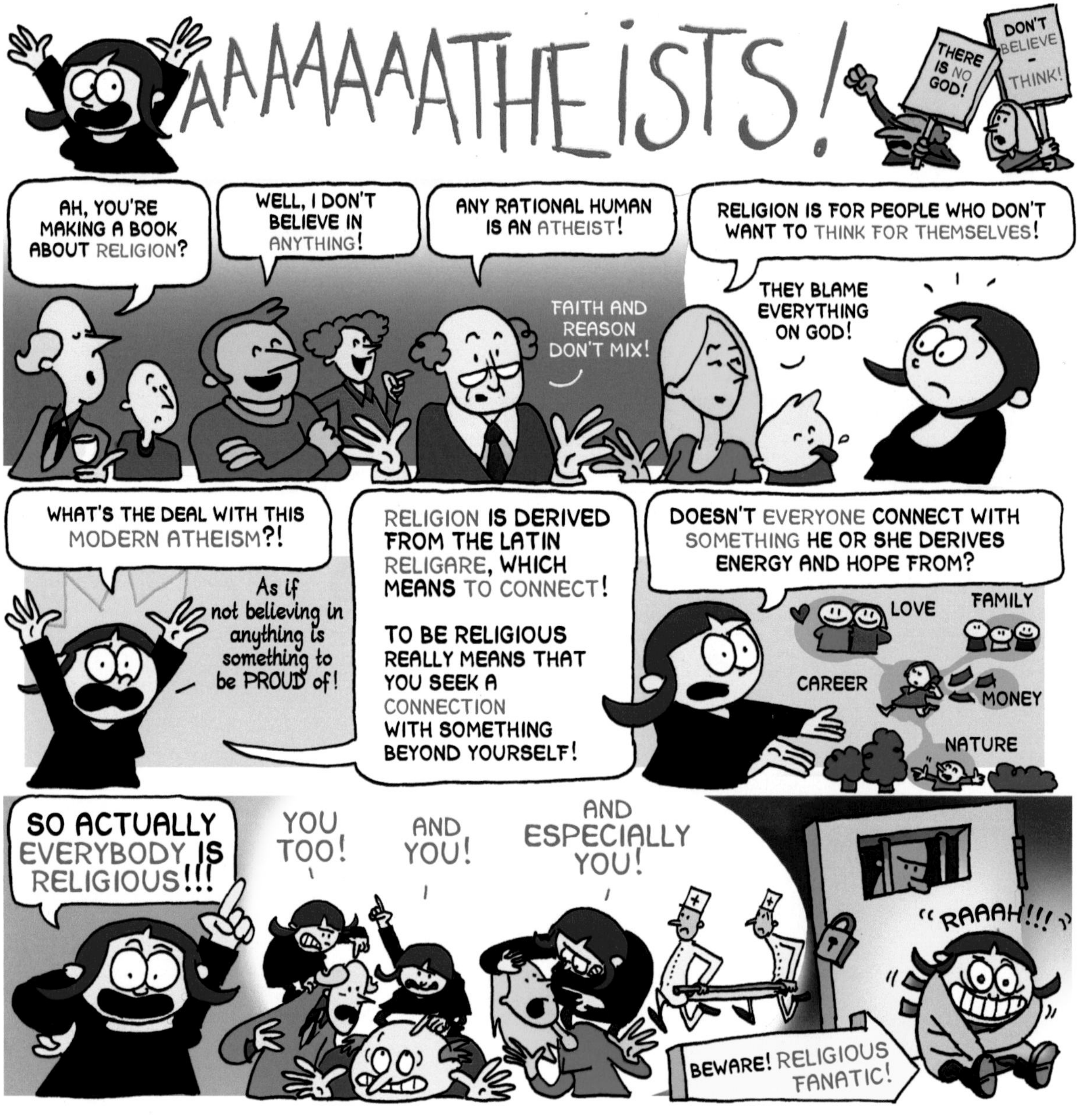
AAAAAAATHEISTS!
THERE IS NO GOD!
DON'T BELIEVE - THINK!
AH, YOU'RE MAKING A BOOK ABOUT RELIGION?
WELL, I DON'T BELIEVE IN ANYTHING!
ANY RATIONAL HUMAN IS AN ATHEIST!
FAITH AND REASON DON'T MIX!
RELIGION IS FOR PEOPLE WHO DON'T WANT TO THINK FOR THEMSELVES!
THEY BLAME EVERYTHING ON GOD!
WHAT'S THE DEAL WITH THIS MODERN ATHEISM?!
As if not believing in anything is something to be PROUD of!
RELIGION IS DERIVED FROM THE LATIN RELIGARE, WHICH MEANS TO CONNECT!
TO BE RELIGIOUS REALLY MEANS THAT YOU SEEK A CONNECTION WITH SOMETHING BEYOND YOURSELF!
DOESN'T EVERYONE CONNECT WITH SOMETHING HE OR SHE DERIVES ENERGY AND HOPE FROM?
LOVE
FAMILY
CAREER
MONEY
NATURE
SO ACTUALLY EVERYBODY IS RELIGIOUS!!!
YOU TOO!
AND YOU!
AND ESPECIALLY YOU!
"RAAAH!!!"
BEWARE! RELIGIOUS FANATIC!

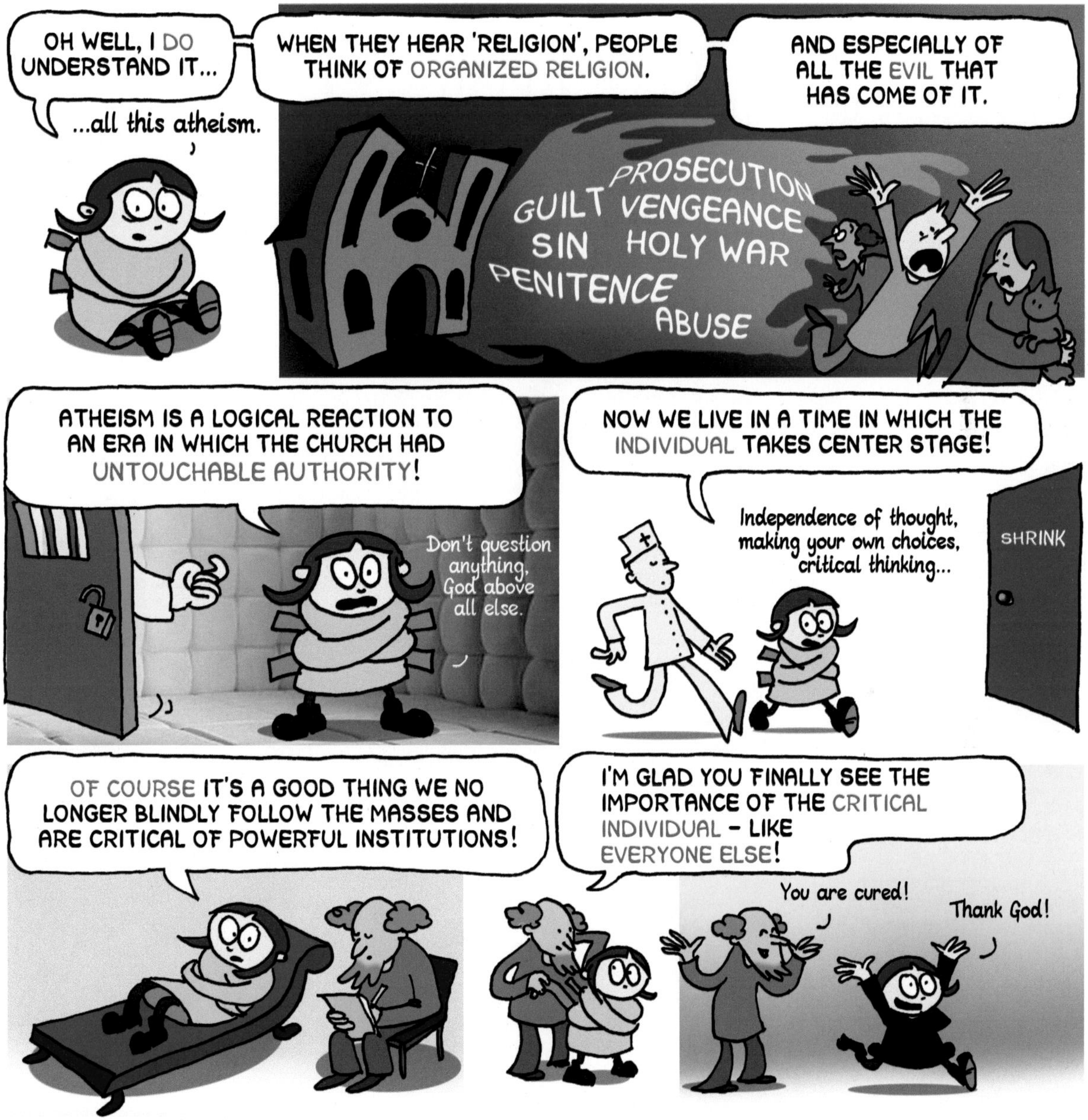
OH WELL, I DO UNDERSTAND IT...
...all this atheism.
WHEN THEY HEAR 'RELIGION', PEOPLE THINK OF ORGANIZED RELIGION.
AND ESPECIALLY OF ALL THE EVIL THAT HAS COME OF IT.
PROSECUTION
GUILT
VENGEANCE
SIN
HOLY WAR
PENITENCE
ABUSE
ATHEISM IS A LOGICAL REACTION TO AN ERA IN WHICH THE CHURCH HAD UNTOUCHABLE AUTHORITY!
Don't question anything, God above all else.
NOW WE LIVE IN A TIME IN WHICH THE INDIVIDUAL TAKES CENTER STAGE!
Independence of thought, making your own choices, critical thinking...
SHRINK
OF COURSE IT'S A GOOD THING WE NO LONGER BLINDLY FOLLOW THE MASSES AND ARE CRITICAL OF POWERFUL INSTITUTIONS!
I'M GLAD YOU FINALLY SEE THE IMPORTANCE OF THE CRITICAL INDIVIDUAL – LIKE EVERYONE ELSE!
You are cured!
Thank God!

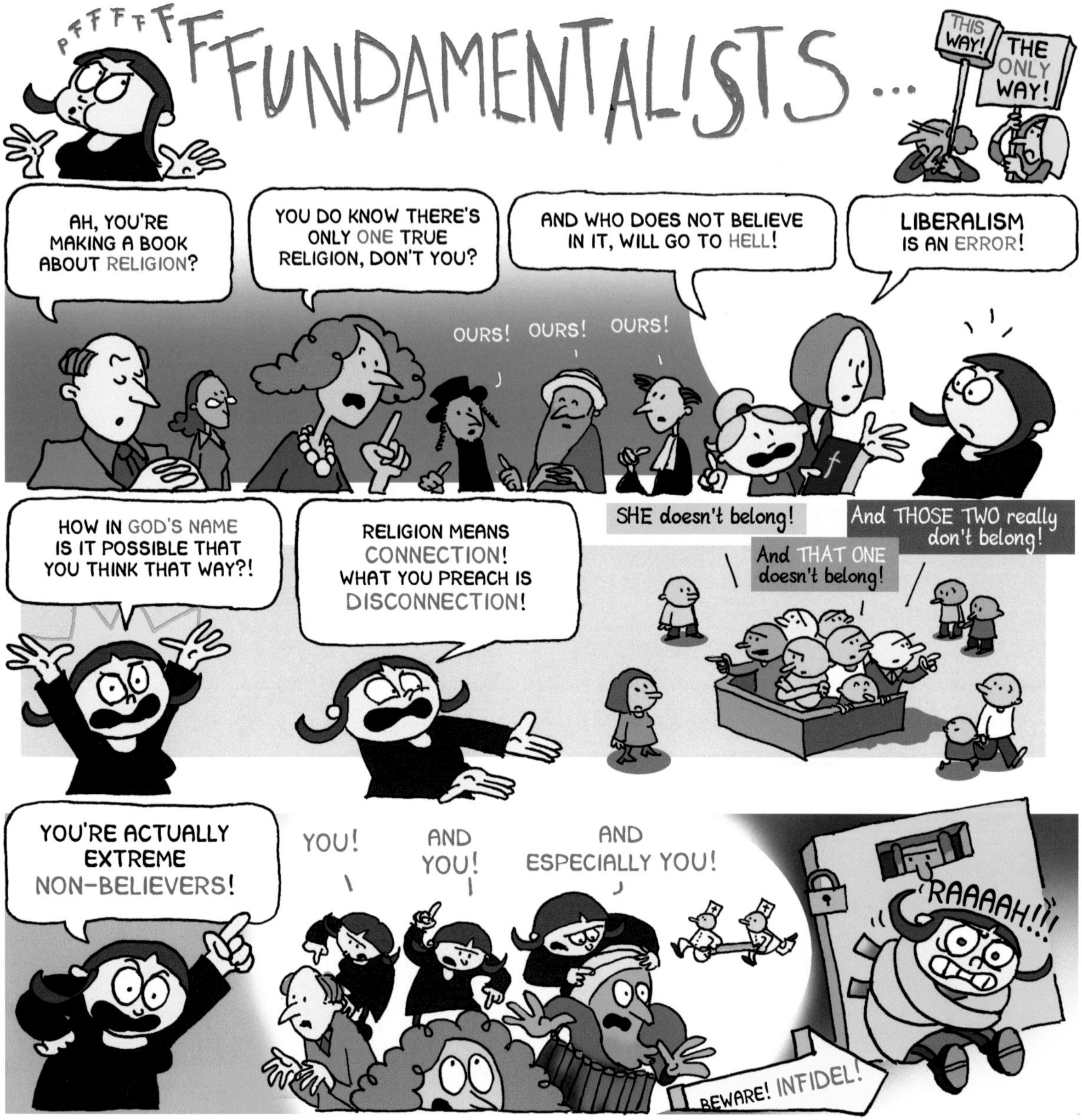
PFFFFFFFUNDAMENTALISTS...
THIS WAY!
THE ONLY WAY!
AH, YOU'RE MAKING A BOOK ABOUT RELIGION?
YOU DO KNOW THERE'S ONLY ONE TRUE RELIGION, DON'T YOU?
OURS!
OURS!
OURS!
AND WHO DOES NOT BELIEVE IN IT, WILL GO TO HELL!
LIBERALISM IS AN ERROR!
HOW IN GOD'S NAME IS IT POSSIBLE THAT YOU THINK THAT WAY?!
RELIGION MEANS CONNECTION! WHAT YOU PREACH IS DISCONNECTION!
SHE doesn't belong!
And THAT ONE doesn't belong!
And THOSE TWO really don't belong!
YOU'RE ACTUALLY EXTREME NON-BELIEVERS!
YOU!
AND YOU!
AND ESPECIALLY YOU!
RAAAAH!!!
BEWARE! INFIDEL!

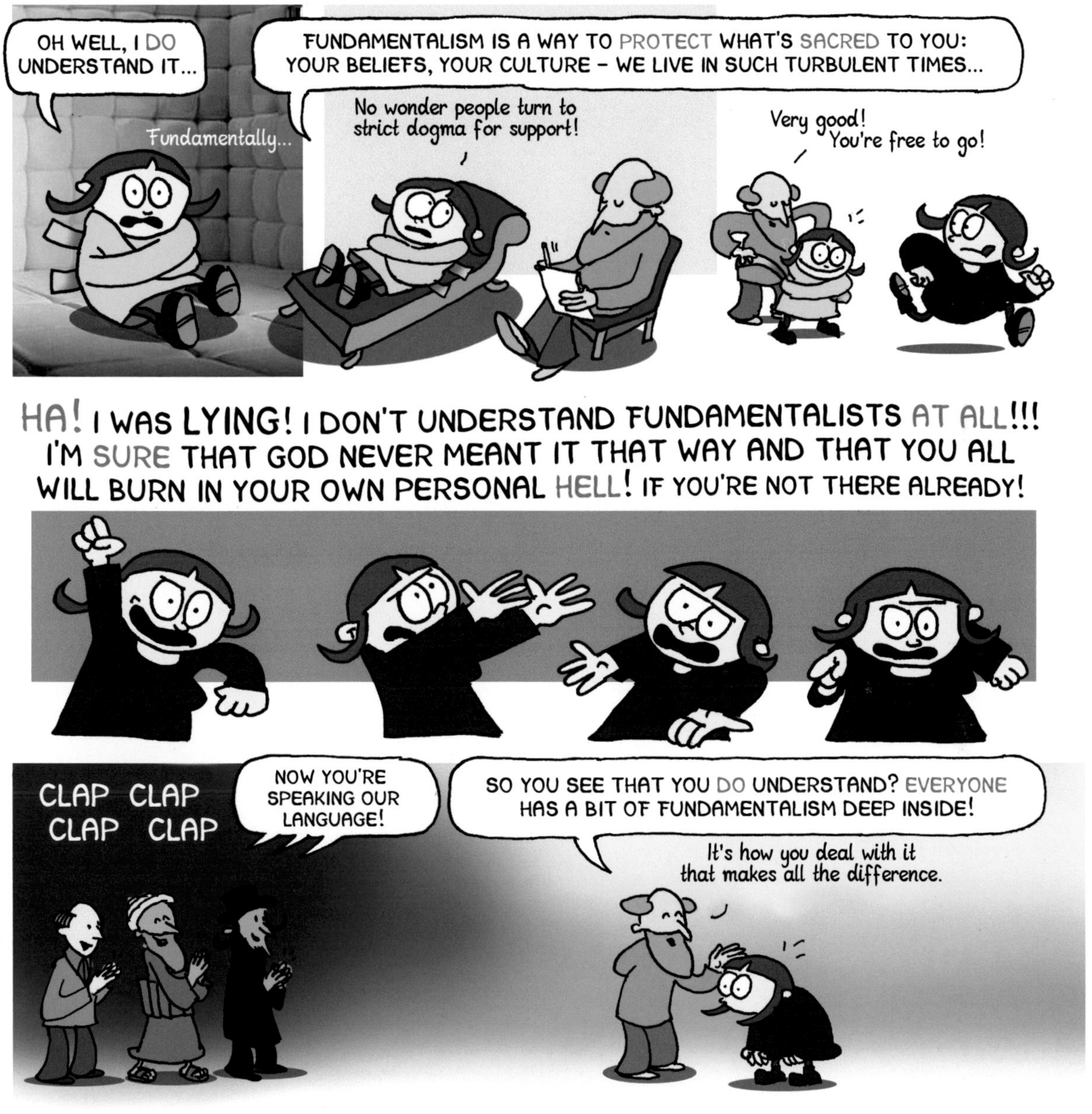
OH WELL, I DO UNDERSTAND IT...
Fundamentally...
FUNDAMENTALISM IS A WAY TO PROTECT WHAT'S SACRED TO YOU: YOUR BELIEFS, YOUR CULTURE – WE LIVE IN SUCH TURBULENT TIMES...
No wonder people turn to strict dogma for support!
Very good! You're free to go!
HA! I WAS LYING! I DON'T UNDERSTAND FUNDAMENTALISTS AT ALL!!! I'M SURE THAT GOD NEVER MEANT IT THAT WAY AND THAT YOU ALL WILL BURN IN YOUR OWN PERSONAL HELL! IF YOU'RE NOT THERE ALREADY!
CLAP CLAP CLAP CLAP
NOW YOU'RE SPEAKING OUR LANGUAGE!
SO YOU SEE THAT YOU DO UNDERSTAND? EVERYONE HAS A BIT OF FUNDAMENTALISM DEEP INSIDE!
It's how you deal with it that makes all the difference.

CHRISTIANITY

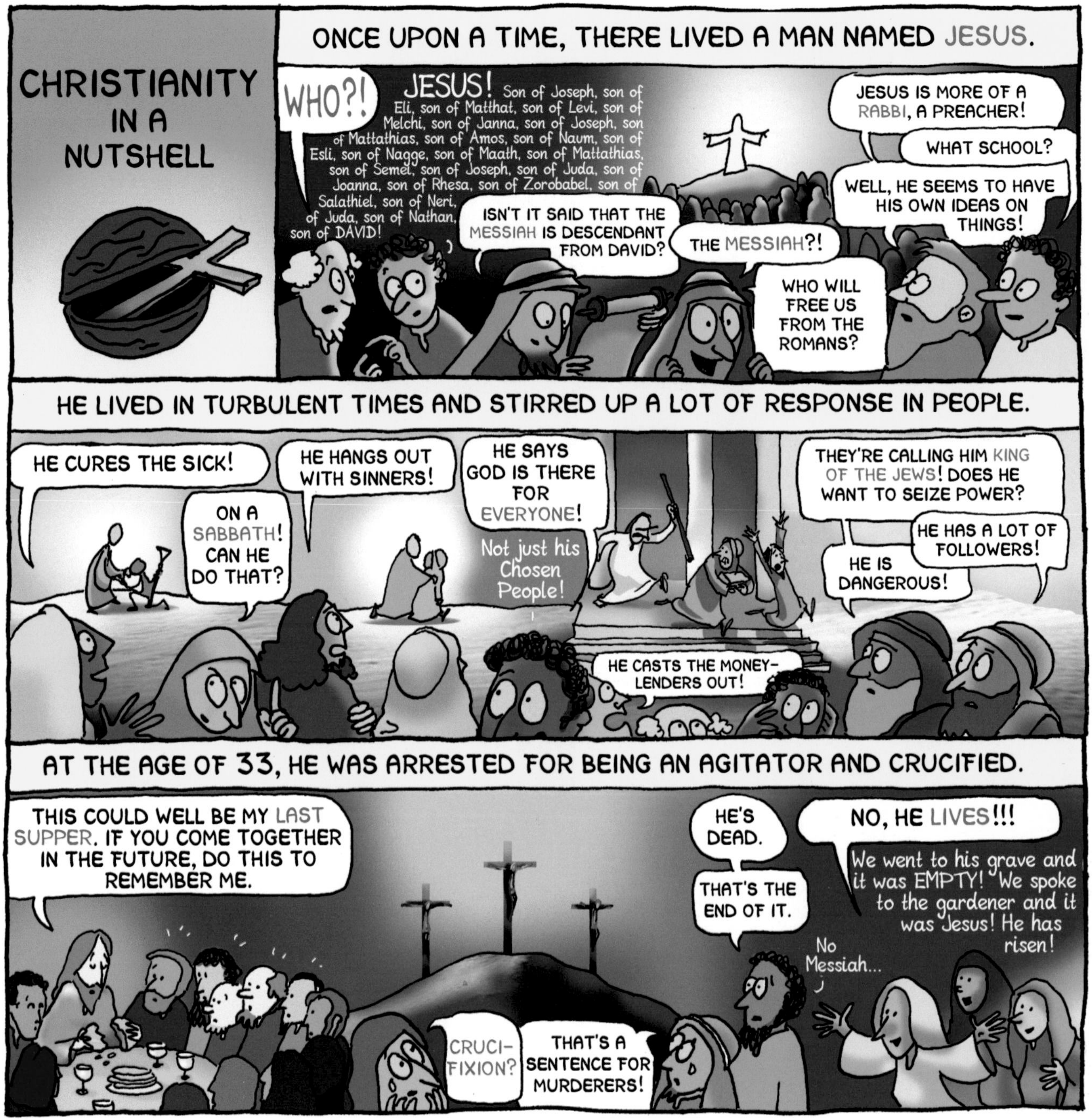
CHRISTIANITY IN A NUTSHELL
ONCE UPON A TIME, THERE LIVED A MAN NAMED JESUS.
WHO?!
JESUS! Son of Joseph, son of Eli, son of Matthat, son of Levi, son of Melchi, son of Janna, son of Joseph, son of Mattathias, son of Amos, son of Naum, son of Esli, son of Nagge, son of Maath, son of Mattathias, son of Semei, son of Joseph, son of Juda, son of Joanna, son of Rhesa, son of Zorobabel, son of Salathiel, son of Neri, of Juda, son of Nathan, son of DAVID!
ISN'T IT SAID THAT THE MESSIAH IS DESCENDANT FROM DAVID?
THE MESSIAH?!
WHO WILL FREE US FROM THE ROMANS?
JESUS IS MORE OF A RABBI, A PREACHER!
WHAT SCHOOL?
WELL, HE SEEMS TO HAVE HIS OWN IDEAS ON THINGS!
HE LIVED IN TURBULENT TIMES AND STIRRED UP A LOT OF RESPONSE IN PEOPLE.
HE CURES THE SICK!
ON A SABBATH! CAN HE DO THAT?
HE HANGS OUT WITH SINNERS!
HE SAYS GOD IS THERE FOR EVERYONE!
Not just his Chosen People!
HE CASTS THE MONEY-LENDERS OUT!
THEY'RE CALLING HIM KING OF THE JEWS! DOES HE WANT TO SEIZE POWER?
HE HAS A LOT OF FOLLOWERS!
HE IS DANGEROUS!
AT THE AGE OF 33, HE WAS ARRESTED FOR BEING AN AGITATOR AND CRUCIFIED.
THIS COULD WELL BE MY LAST SUPPER. IF YOU COME TOGETHER IN THE FUTURE, DO THIS TO REMEMBER ME.
CRUCI-FIXION?
THAT'S A SENTENCE FOR MURDERERS!
HE'S DEAD.
THAT'S THE END OF IT.
No Messiah...
NO, HE LIVES!!!
We went to his grave and it was EMPTY! We spoke to the gardener and it was Jesus! He has risen!

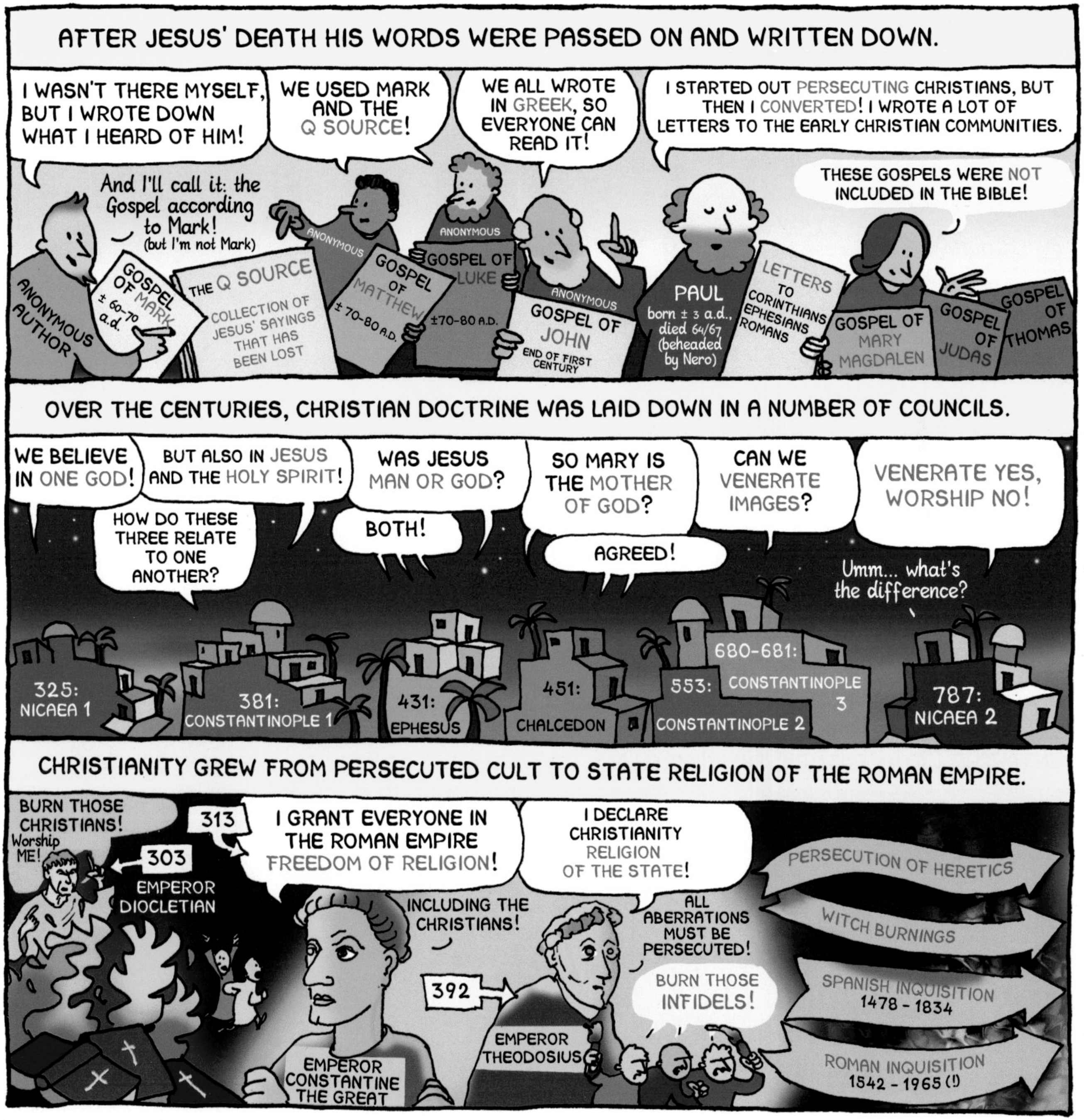

AFTER JESUS' DEATH HIS WORDS WERE PASSED ON AND WRITTEN DOWN.
I WASN'T THERE MYSELF, BUT I WROTE DOWN WHAT I HEARD OF HIM!
And I'll call it: the Gospel according to Mark! (but I'm not Mark)
ANONYMOUS AUTHOR
GOSPEL OF MARK ± 60–70 a.d.
WE USED MARK AND THE Q SOURCE!
THE Q SOURCE
COLLECTION OF JESUS' SAYINGS THAT HAS BEEN LOST
ANONYMOUS
GOSPEL OF MATTHEW ± 70–80 A.D.
ANONYMOUS
GOSPEL OF LUKE ±70–80 A.D.
WE ALL WROTE IN GREEK, SO EVERYONE CAN READ IT!
ANONYMOUS
GOSPEL OF JOHN END OF FIRST CENTURY
I STARTED OUT PERSECUTING CHRISTIANS, BUT THEN I CONVERTED! I WROTE A LOT OF LETTERS TO THE EARLY CHRISTIAN COMMUNITIES.
PAUL born ± 3 a.d., died 64/67 (beheaded by Nero)
LETTERS TO CORINTHIANS EPHESIANS ROMANS
THESE GOSPELS WERE NOT INCLUDED IN THE BIBLE!
GOSPEL OF MARY MAGDALEN
GOSPEL OF JUDAS
GOSPEL OF THOMAS
OVER THE CENTURIES, CHRISTIAN DOCTRINE WAS LAID DOWN IN A NUMBER OF COUNCILS.
WE BELIEVE IN ONE GOD!
BUT ALSO IN JESUS AND THE HOLY SPIRIT!
HOW DO THESE THREE RELATE TO ONE ANOTHER?
WAS JESUS MAN OR GOD?
BOTH!
SO MARY IS THE MOTHER OF GOD?
AGREED!
CAN WE VENERATE IMAGES?
VENERATE YES, WORSHIP NO!
Umm... what's the difference?
325: NICAEA 1
381: CONSTANTINOPLE 1
431: EPHESUS
451: CHALCEDON
553: CONSTANTINOPLE 2
680-681: CONSTANTINOPLE 3
787: NICAEA 2
CHRISTIANITY GREW FROM PERSECUTED CULT TO STATE RELIGION OF THE ROMAN EMPIRE.
BURN THOSE CHRISTIANS!
Worship ME!
303
EMPEROR DIOCLETIAN
313
I GRANT EVERYONE IN THE ROMAN EMPIRE FREEDOM OF RELIGION!
INCLUDING THE CHRISTIANS!
EMPEROR CONSTANTINE THE GREAT
I DECLARE CHRISTIANITY RELIGION OF THE STATE!
ALL ABERRATIONS MUST BE PERSECUTED!
392
EMPEROR THEODOSIUS
BURN THOSE INFIDELS!
PERSECUTION OF HERETICS
WITCH BURNINGS
SPANISH INQUISITION 1478 – 1834
ROMAN INQUISITION 1542 – 1965 (!)

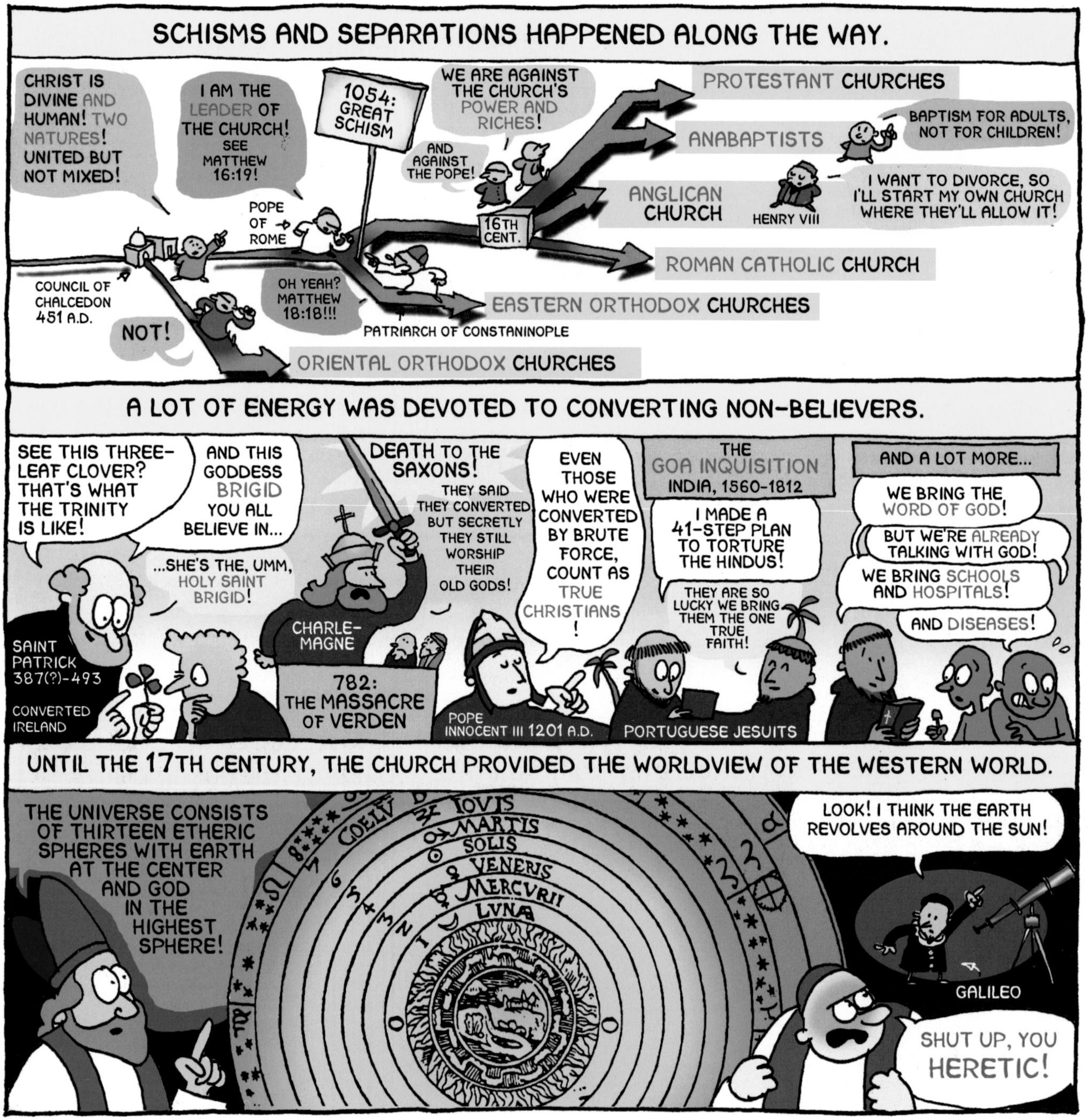
SCHISMS AND SEPARATIONS HAPPENED ALONG THE WAY.
CHRIST IS DIVINE AND HUMAN! TWO NATURES! UNITED BUT NOT MIXED!
COUNCIL OF CHALCEDON 451 A.D.
NOT!
ORIENTAL ORTHODOX CHURCHES
I AM THE LEADER OF THE CHURCH! SEE MATTHEW 16:19!
POPE OF ROME
OH YEAH? MATTHEW 18:18!!!
PATRIARCH OF CONSTANINOPLE
1054: GREAT SCHISM
EASTERN ORTHODOX CHURCHES
AND AGAINST THE POPE!
WE ARE AGAINST THE CHURCH'S POWER AND RICHES!
16TH CENT.
ROMAN CATHOLIC CHURCH
PROTESTANT CHURCHES
ANABAPTISTS
BAPTISM FOR ADULTS, NOT FOR CHILDREN!
ANGLICAN CHURCH
HENRY VIII
I WANT TO DIVORCE, SO I'LL START MY OWN CHURCH WHERE THEY'LL ALLOW IT!
A LOT OF ENERGY WAS DEVOTED TO CONVERTING NON-BELIEVERS.
SEE THIS THREE-LEAF CLOVER? THAT'S WHAT THE TRINITY IS LIKE!
AND THIS GODDESS BRIGID YOU ALL BELIEVE IN...
...SHE'S THE, UMM, HOLY SAINT BRIGID!
SAINT PATRICK 387(?)-493
CONVERTED IRELAND
DEATH TO THE SAXONS!
THEY SAID THEY CONVERTED BUT SECRETLY THEY STILL WORSHIP THEIR OLD GODS!
CHARLE-MAGNE
782: THE MASSACRE OF VERDEN
EVEN THOSE WHO WERE CONVERTED BY BRUTE FORCE, COUNT AS TRUE CHRISTIANS!
POPE INNOCENT III 1201 A.D.
THE GOA INQUISITION
INDIA, 1560-1812
I MADE A 41-STEP PLAN TO TORTURE THE HINDUS!
THEY ARE SO LUCKY WE BRING THEM THE ONE TRUE FAITH!
PORTUGUESE JESUITS
AND A LOT MORE...
WE BRING THE WORD OF GOD!
BUT WE'RE ALREADY TALKING WITH GOD!
WE BRING SCHOOLS AND HOSPITALS!
AND DISEASES!
UNTIL THE 17TH CENTURY, THE CHURCH PROVIDED THE WORLDVIEW OF THE WESTERN WORLD.
THE UNIVERSE CONSISTS OF THIRTEEN ETHERIC SPHERES WITH EARTH AT THE CENTER AND GOD IN THE HIGHEST SPHERE!
COELV
IOVIS
MARTIS
SOLIS
VENERIS
MERCVRII
LVNA
LOOK! I THINK THE EARTH REVOLVES AROUND THE SUN!
GALILEO
SHUT UP, YOU HERETIC!

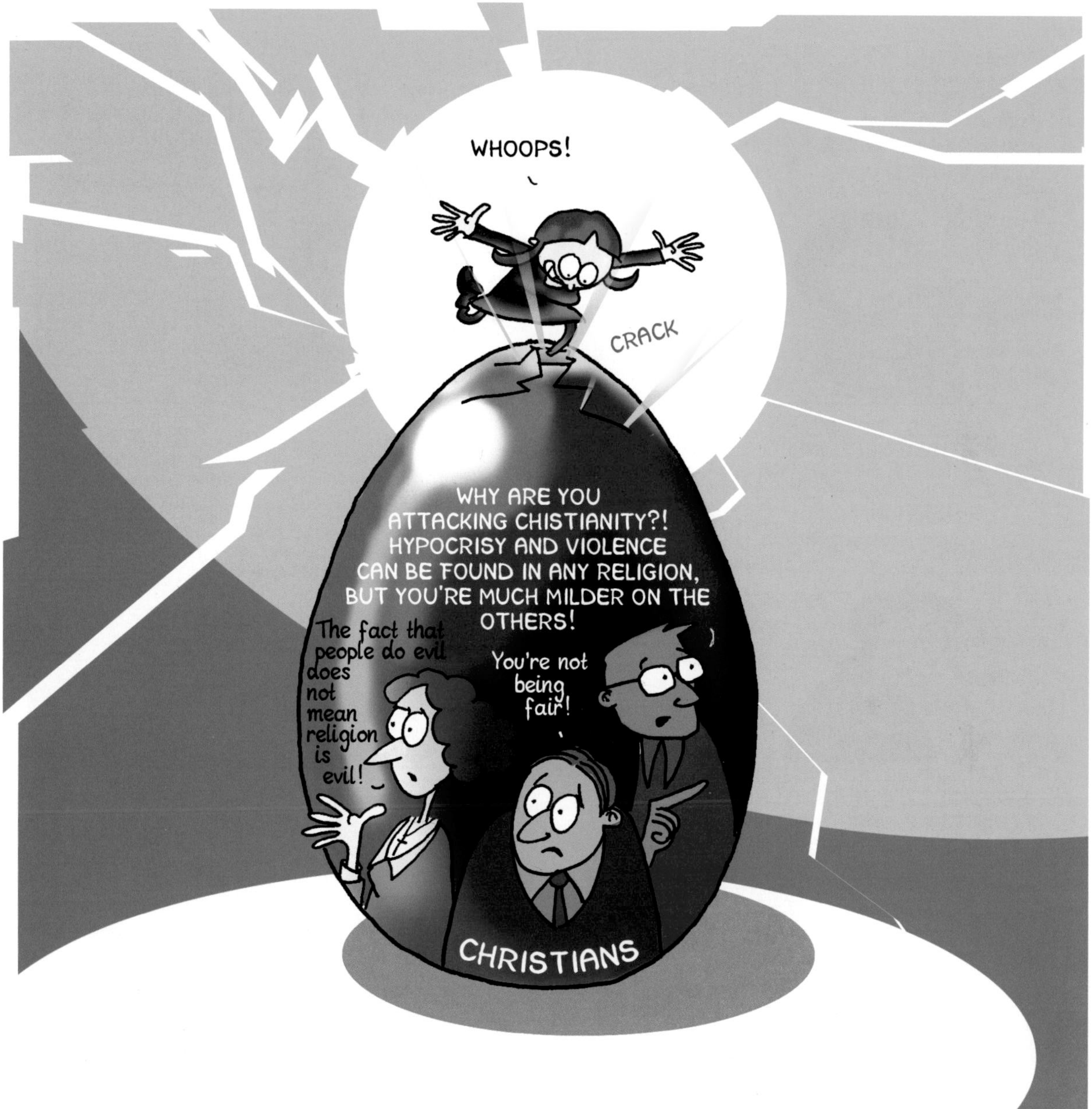
WHOOPS!
CRACK
WHY ARE YOU ATTACKING CHISTIANITY?! HYPOCRISY AND VIOLENCE CAN BE FOUND IN ANY RELIGION, BUT YOU'RE MUCH MILDER ON THE OTHERS!
The fact that people do evil does not mean religion is evil!
You're not being fair!
CHRISTIANS

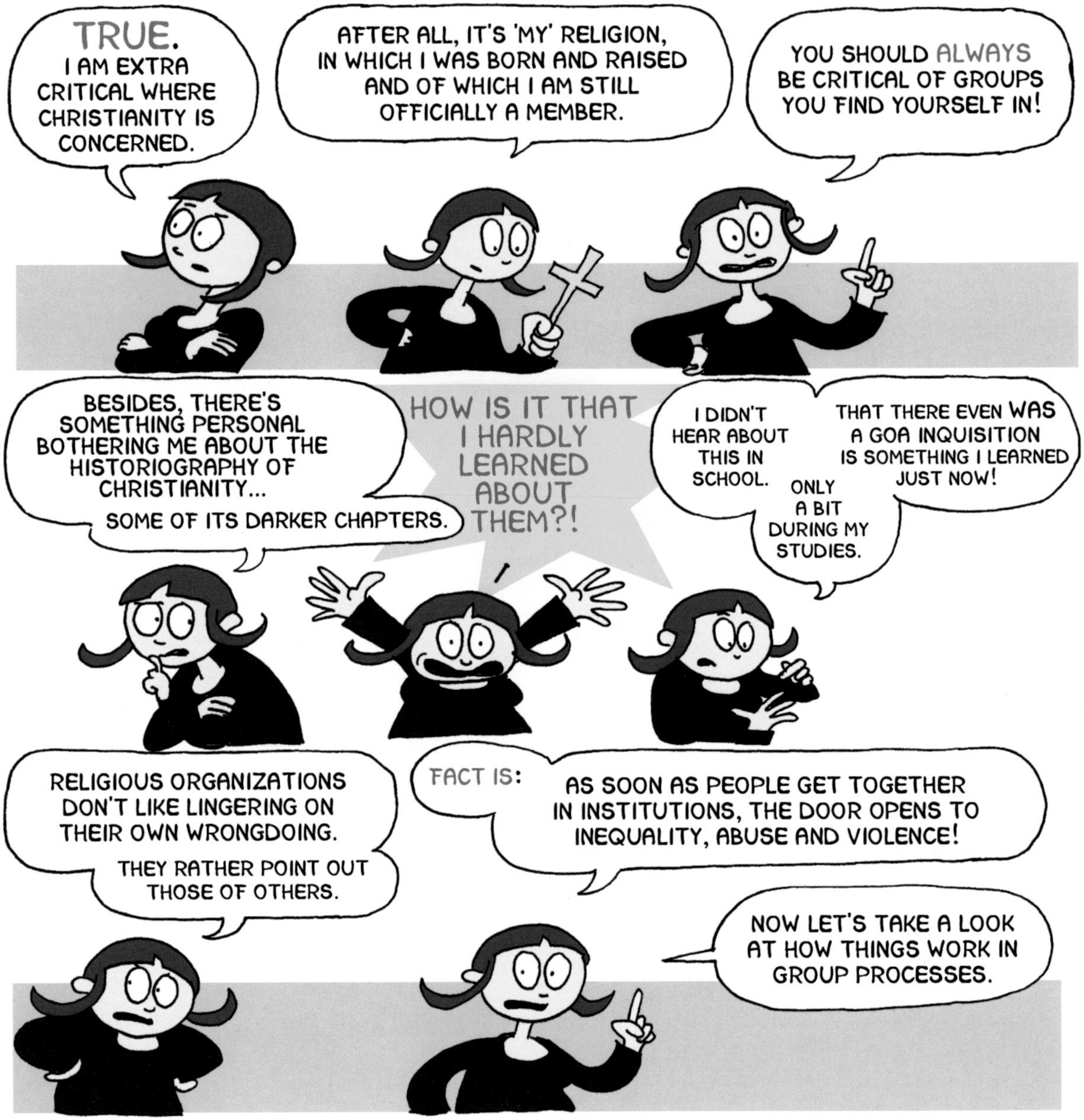
TRUE. I AM EXTRA CRITICAL WHERE CHRISTIANITY IS CONCERNED.
AFTER ALL, IT'S 'MY' RELIGION, IN WHICH I WAS BORN AND RAISED AND OF WHICH I AM STILL OFFICIALLY A MEMBER.
YOU SHOULD ALWAYS BE CRITICAL OF GROUPS YOU FIND YOURSELF IN!
BESIDES, THERE'S SOMETHING PERSONAL BOTHERING ME ABOUT THE HISTORIOGRAPHY OF CHRISTIANITY...
SOME OF ITS DARKER CHAPTERS.
HOW IS IT THAT I HARDLY LEARNED ABOUT THEM?!
I DIDN'T HEAR ABOUT THIS IN SCHOOL.
ONLY A BIT DURING MY STUDIES.
THAT THERE EVEN WAS A GOA INQUISITION IS SOMETHING I LEARNED JUST NOW!
RELIGIOUS ORGANIZATIONS DON'T LIKE LINGERING ON THEIR OWN WRONGDOING.
THEY RATHER POINT OUT THOSE OF OTHERS.
FACT IS:
AS SOON AS PEOPLE GET TOGETHER IN INSTITUTIONS, THE DOOR OPENS TO INEQUALITY, ABUSE AND VIOLENCE!
NOW LET'S TAKE A LOOK AT HOW THINGS WORK IN GROUP PROCESSES.

GROUP PROCESSES

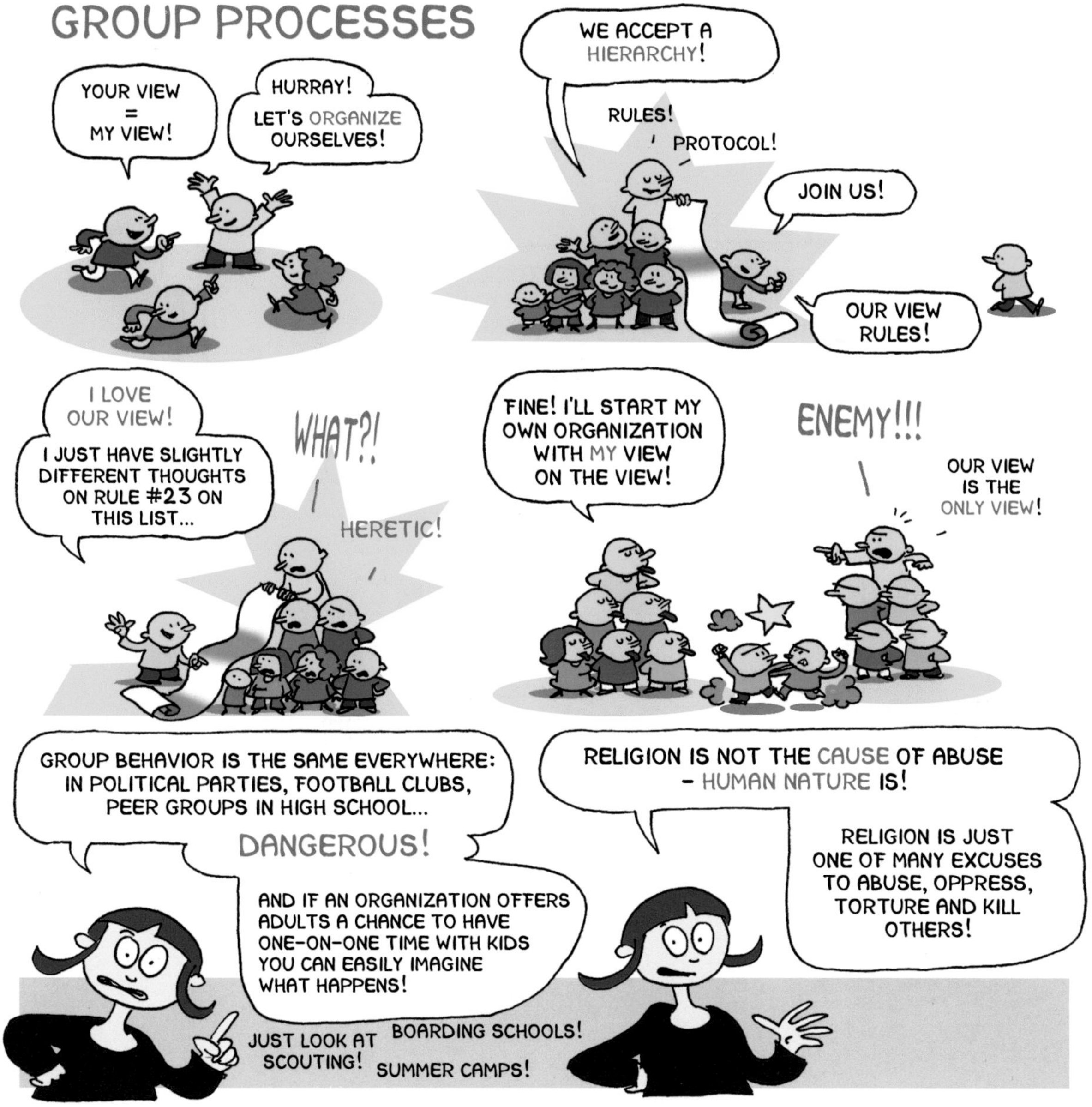

YOUR VIEW = MY VIEW!
HURRAY! LET'S ORGANIZE OURSELVES!
WE ACCEPT A HIERARCHY!
RULES!
PROTOCOL!
JOIN US!
OUR VIEW RULES!
I LOVE OUR VIEW!
I JUST HAVE SLIGHTLY DIFFERENT THOUGHTS ON RULE #23 ON THIS LIST...
WHAT?!
HERETIC!
FINE! I'LL START MY OWN ORGANIZATION WITH MY VIEW ON THE VIEW!
ENEMY!!!
OUR VIEW IS THE ONLY VIEW!
GROUP BEHAVIOR IS THE SAME EVERYWHERE: IN POLITICAL PARTIES, FOOTBALL CLUBS, PEER GROUPS IN HIGH SCHOOL...
DANGEROUS!
AND IF AN ORGANIZATION OFFERS ADULTS A CHANCE TO HAVE ONE-ON-ONE TIME WITH KIDS YOU CAN EASILY IMAGINE WHAT HAPPENS!
JUST LOOK AT SCOUTING!
BOARDING SCHOOLS!
SUMMER CAMPS!
RELIGION IS NOT THE CAUSE OF ABUSE – HUMAN NATURE IS!
RELIGION IS JUST ONE OF MANY EXCUSES TO ABUSE, OPPRESS, TORTURE AND KILL OTHERS!

THE CORE OF THE CHRISTIAN FAITH

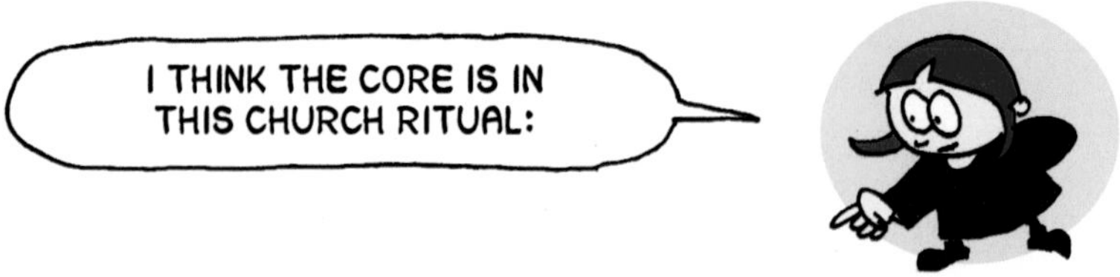
I THINK THE CORE IS IN THIS CHURCH RITUAL:

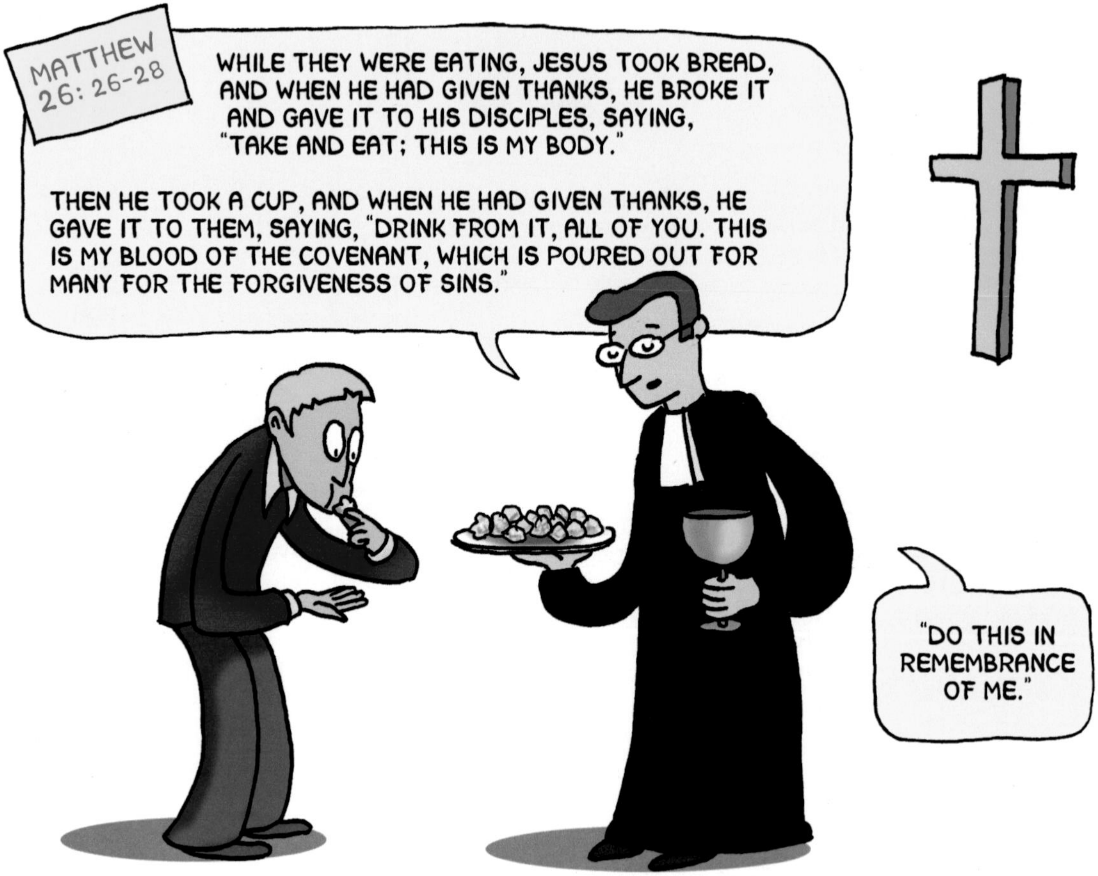
MATTHEW 26: 26-28
WHILE THEY WERE EATING, JESUS TOOK BREAD, AND WHEN HE HAD GIVEN THANKS, HE BROKE IT AND GAVE IT TO HIS DISCIPLES, SAYING, "TAKE AND EAT; THIS IS MY BODY."
THEN HE TOOK A CUP, AND WHEN HE HAD GIVEN THANKS, HE GAVE IT TO THEM, SAYING, "DRINK FROM IT, ALL OF YOU. THIS IS MY BLOOD OF THE COVENANT, WHICH IS POURED OUT FOR MANY FOR THE FORGIVENESS OF SINS."
"DO THIS IN REMEMBRANCE OF ME."

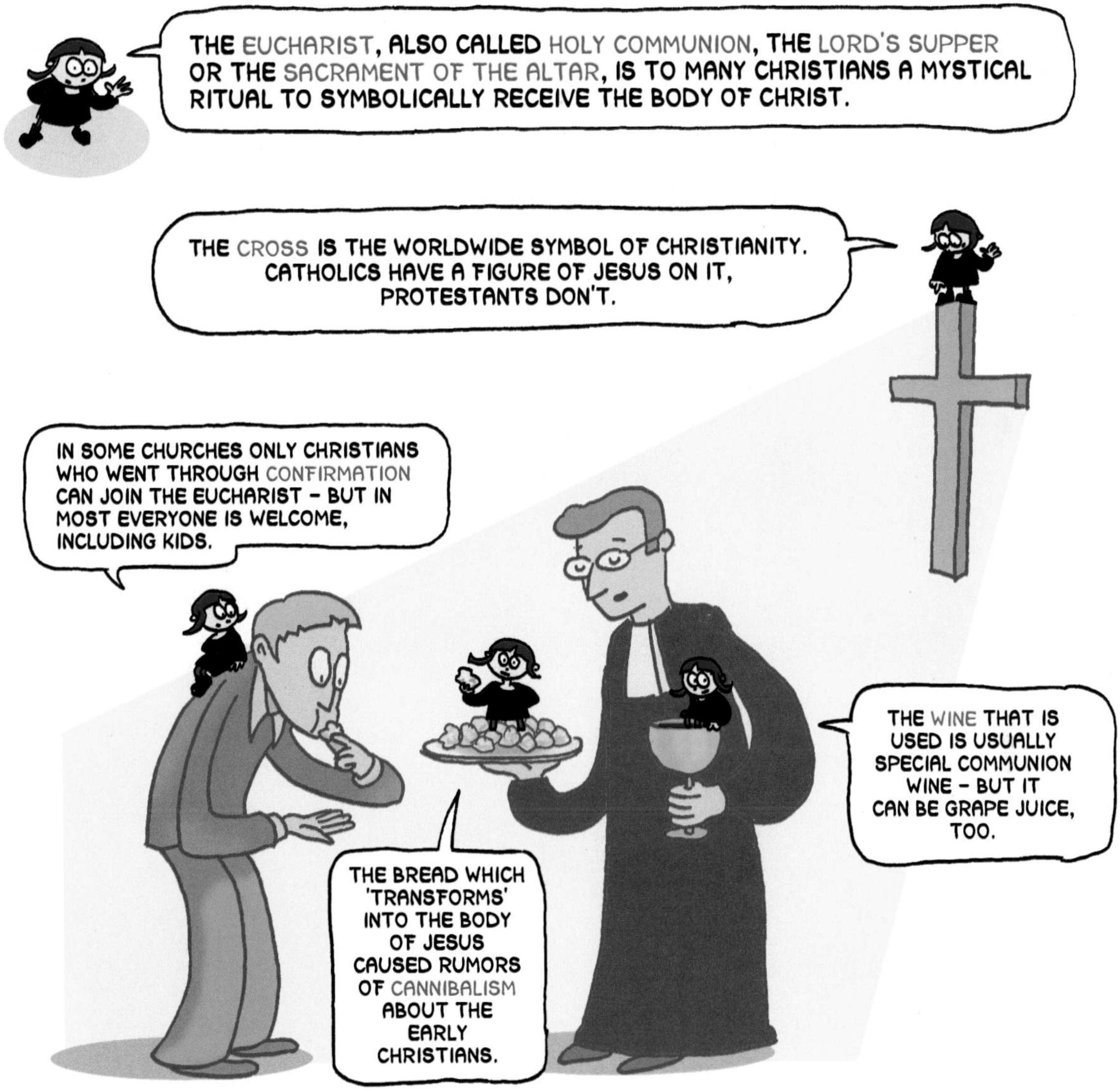
THE EUCHARIST, ALSO CALLED HOLY COMMUNION, THE LORD'S SUPPER OR THE SACRAMENT OF THE ALTAR, IS TO MANY CHRISTIANS A MYSTICAL RITUAL TO SYMBOLICALLY RECEIVE THE BODY OF CHRIST.
THE CROSS IS THE WORLDWIDE SYMBOL OF CHRISTIANITY. CATHOLICS HAVE A FIGURE OF JESUS ON IT, PROTESTANTS DON'T.
IN SOME CHURCHES ONLY CHRISTIANS WHO WENT THROUGH CONFIRMATION CAN JOIN THE EUCHARIST - BUT IN MOST EVERYONE IS WELCOME, INCLUDING KIDS.
THE BREAD WHICH 'TRANSFORMS' INTO THE BODY OF JESUS CAUSED RUMORS OF CANNIBALISM ABOUT THE EARLY CHRISTIANS.
THE WINE THAT IS USED IS USUALLY SPECIAL COMMUNION WINE - BUT IT CAN BE GRAPE JUICE, TOO.

THE BOOKS OF CHRISTIANITY

BIBLE MEANS 'BOOKS'

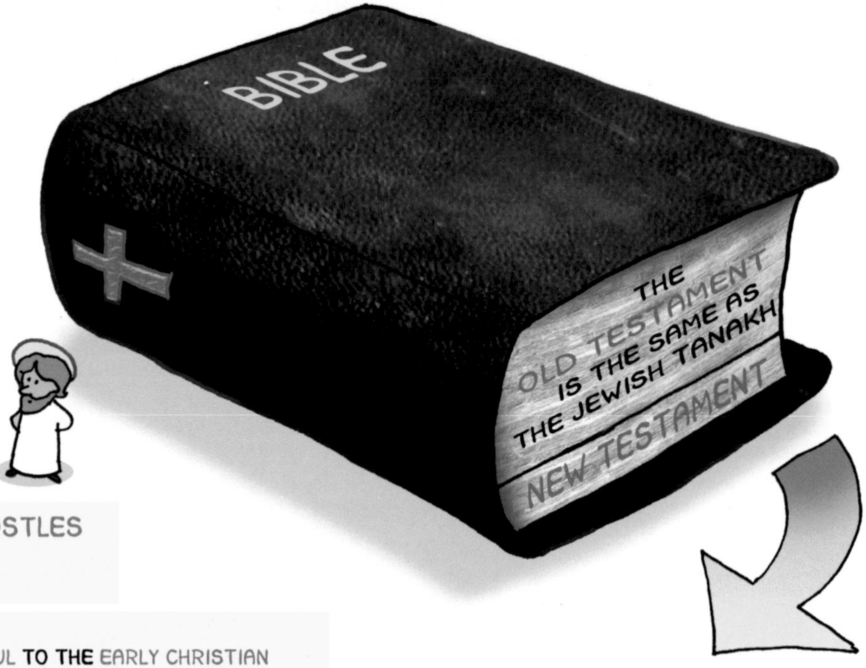

BIBLE
THE OLD TESTAMENT IS THE SAME AS THE JEWISH TANAKH
NEW TESTAMENT

THE NEW TESTAMENT:

- **GOSPELS**
  ABOUT THE LIFE OF JESUS CHRIST

  MATTHEW, MARK, LUKE & JOHN

- **ACTS OF THE APOSTLES**
  ABOUT THE EARLY MISSIONARY WORK

- **LETTERS**
  MAINLY WRITTEN BY PAUL TO THE EARLY CHRISTIAN COMMUNITIES HE HAD VISITED ON HIS TRAVELS

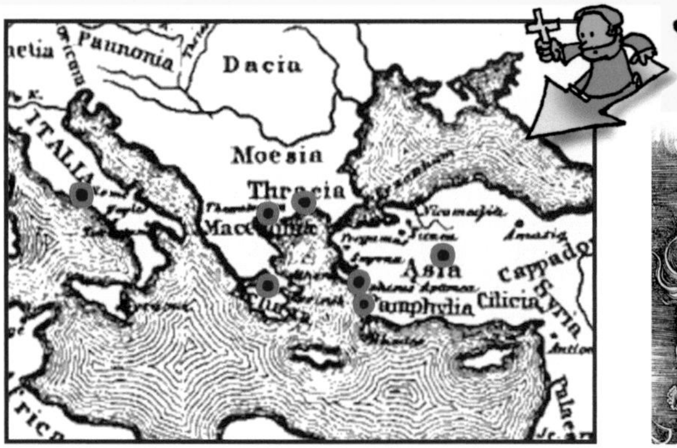

Pannonia
Dacia
Moesia
Cilicia

- **BOOK OF REVELATION**
  DESCRIPTION OF A VISION ABOUT THE APOCALYPSE

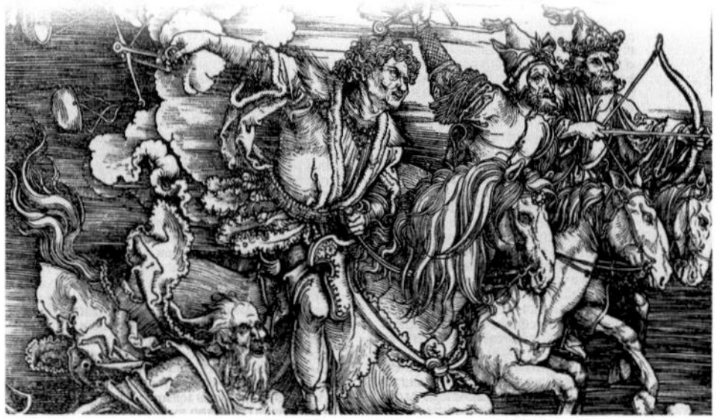

The Four Horsemen of the Apocalypse
Albrecht Dürer, 1498 A.D.

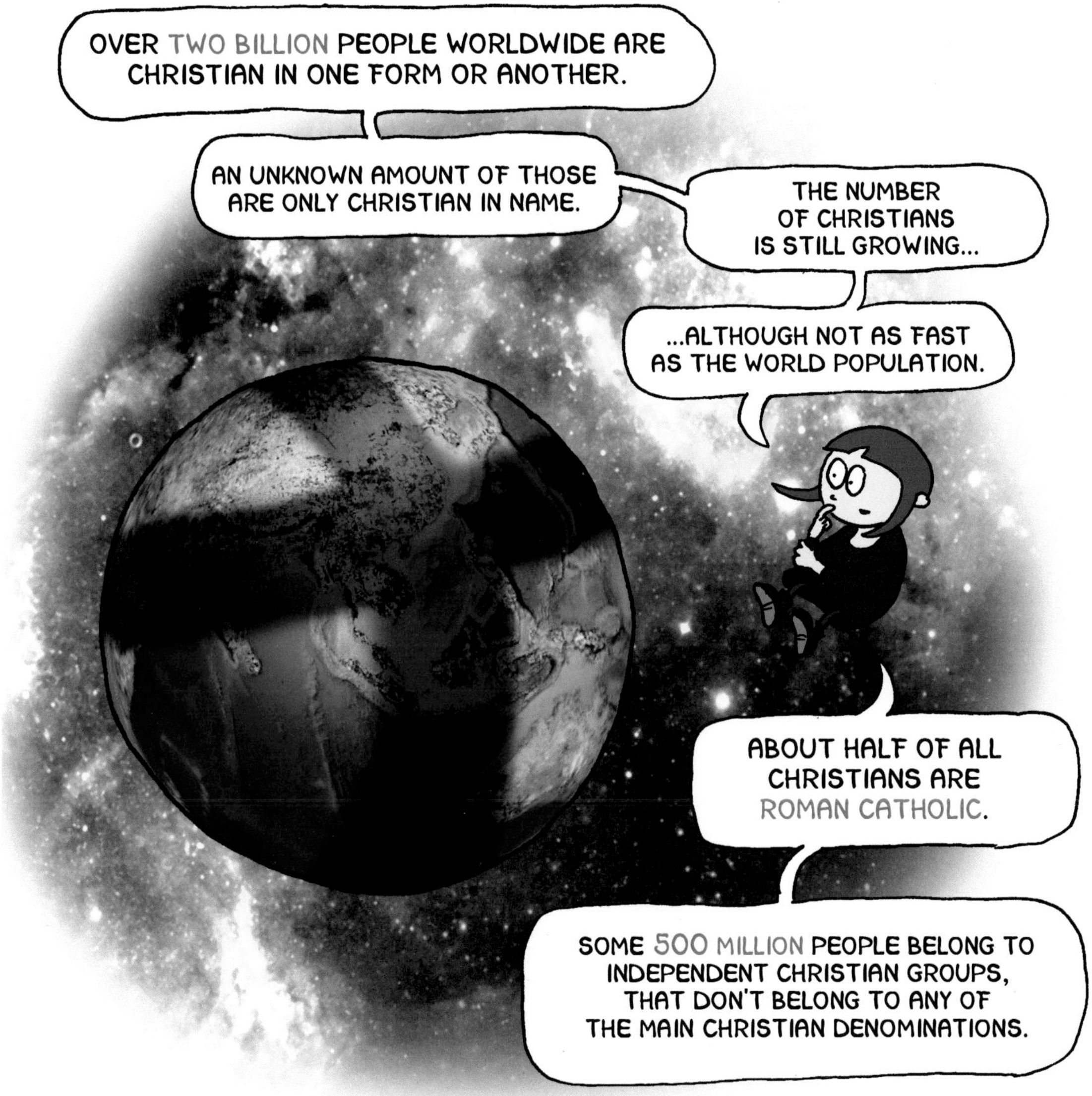
OVER TWO BILLION PEOPLE WORLDWIDE ARE CHRISTIAN IN ONE FORM OR ANOTHER.
AN UNKNOWN AMOUNT OF THOSE ARE ONLY CHRISTIAN IN NAME.
THE NUMBER OF CHRISTIANS IS STILL GROWING...
...ALTHOUGH NOT AS FAST AS THE WORLD POPULATION.
ABOUT HALF OF ALL CHRISTIANS ARE ROMAN CATHOLIC.
SOME 500 MILLION PEOPLE BELONG TO INDEPENDENT CHRISTIAN GROUPS, THAT DON'T BELONG TO ANY OF THE MAIN CHRISTIAN DENOMINATIONS.

ISLAM

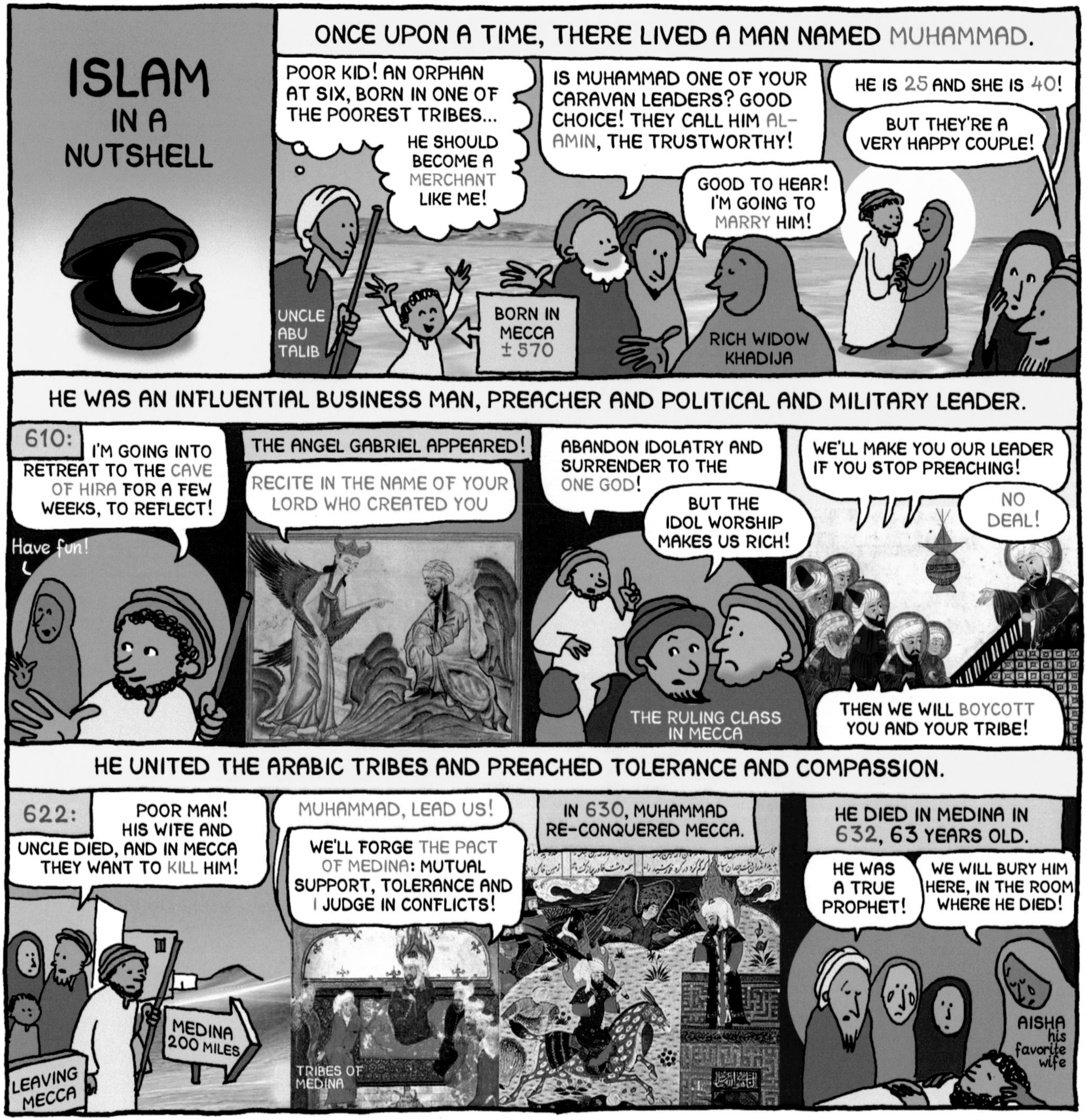

ISLAM IN A NUTSHELL
ONCE UPON A TIME, THERE LIVED A MAN NAMED MUHAMMAD.
POOR KID! AN ORPHAN AT SIX, BORN IN ONE OF THE POOREST TRIBES...
HE SHOULD BECOME A MERCHANT LIKE ME!
UNCLE ABU TALIB
BORN IN MECCA ± 570
IS MUHAMMAD ONE OF YOUR CARAVAN LEADERS? GOOD CHOICE! THEY CALL HIM AL-AMIN, THE TRUSTWORTHY!
GOOD TO HEAR! I'M GOING TO MARRY HIM!
RICH WIDOW KHADIJA
HE IS 25 AND SHE IS 40!
BUT THEY'RE A VERY HAPPY COUPLE!
HE WAS AN INFLUENTIAL BUSINESS MAN, PREACHER AND POLITICAL AND MILITARY LEADER.
610:
I'M GOING INTO RETREAT TO THE CAVE OF HIRA FOR A FEW WEEKS, TO REFLECT!
Have fun!
THE ANGEL GABRIEL APPEARED!
RECITE IN THE NAME OF YOUR LORD WHO CREATED YOU
ABANDON IDOLATRY AND SURRENDER TO THE ONE GOD!
BUT THE IDOL WORSHIP MAKES US RICH!
THE RULING CLASS IN MECCA
WE'LL MAKE YOU OUR LEADER IF YOU STOP PREACHING!
NO DEAL!
THEN WE WILL BOYCOTT YOU AND YOUR TRIBE!
HE UNITED THE ARABIC TRIBES AND PREACHED TOLERANCE AND COMPASSION.
622:
POOR MAN! HIS WIFE AND UNCLE DIED, AND IN MECCA THEY WANT TO KILL HIM!
LEAVING MECCA
MEDINA 200 MILES
MUHAMMAD, LEAD US!
WE'LL FORGE THE PACT OF MEDINA: MUTUAL SUPPORT, TOLERANCE AND I JUDGE IN CONFLICTS!
TRIBES OF MEDINA
IN 630, MUHAMMAD RE-CONQUERED MECCA.
HE DIED IN MEDINA IN 632, 63 YEARS OLD.
HE WAS A TRUE PROPHET!
WE WILL BURY HIM HERE, IN THE ROOM WHERE HE DIED!
AISHA his favorite wife

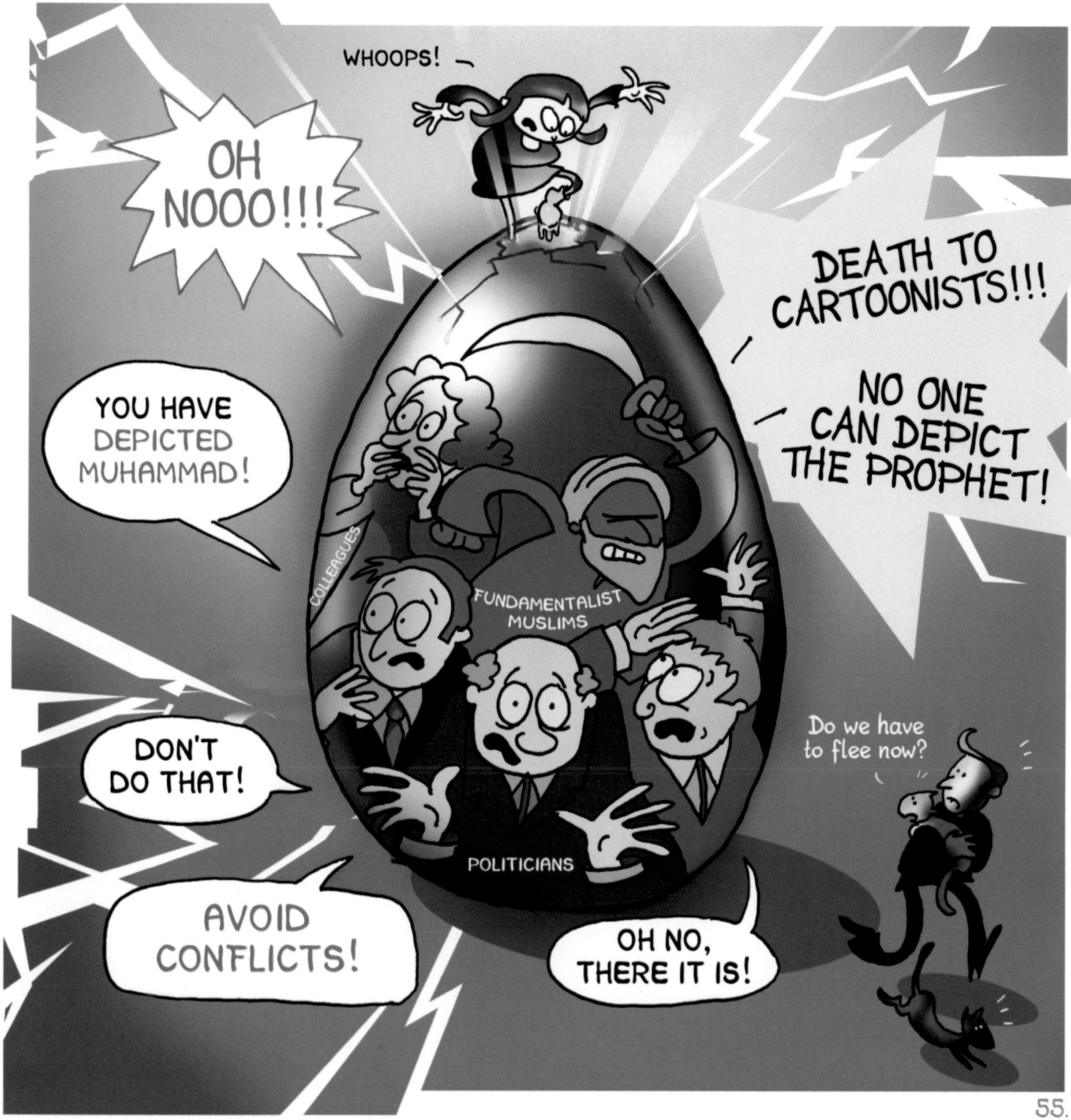
WHOOPS!
OH NOOO!!!
DEATH TO CARTOONISTS!!!
NO ONE CAN DEPICT THE PROPHET!
YOU HAVE DEPICTED MUHAMMAD!
COLLEAGUES
FUNDAMENTALIST MUSLIMS
POLITICIANS
DON'T DO THAT!
Do we have to flee now?
AVOID CONFLICTS!
OH NO, THERE IT IS!

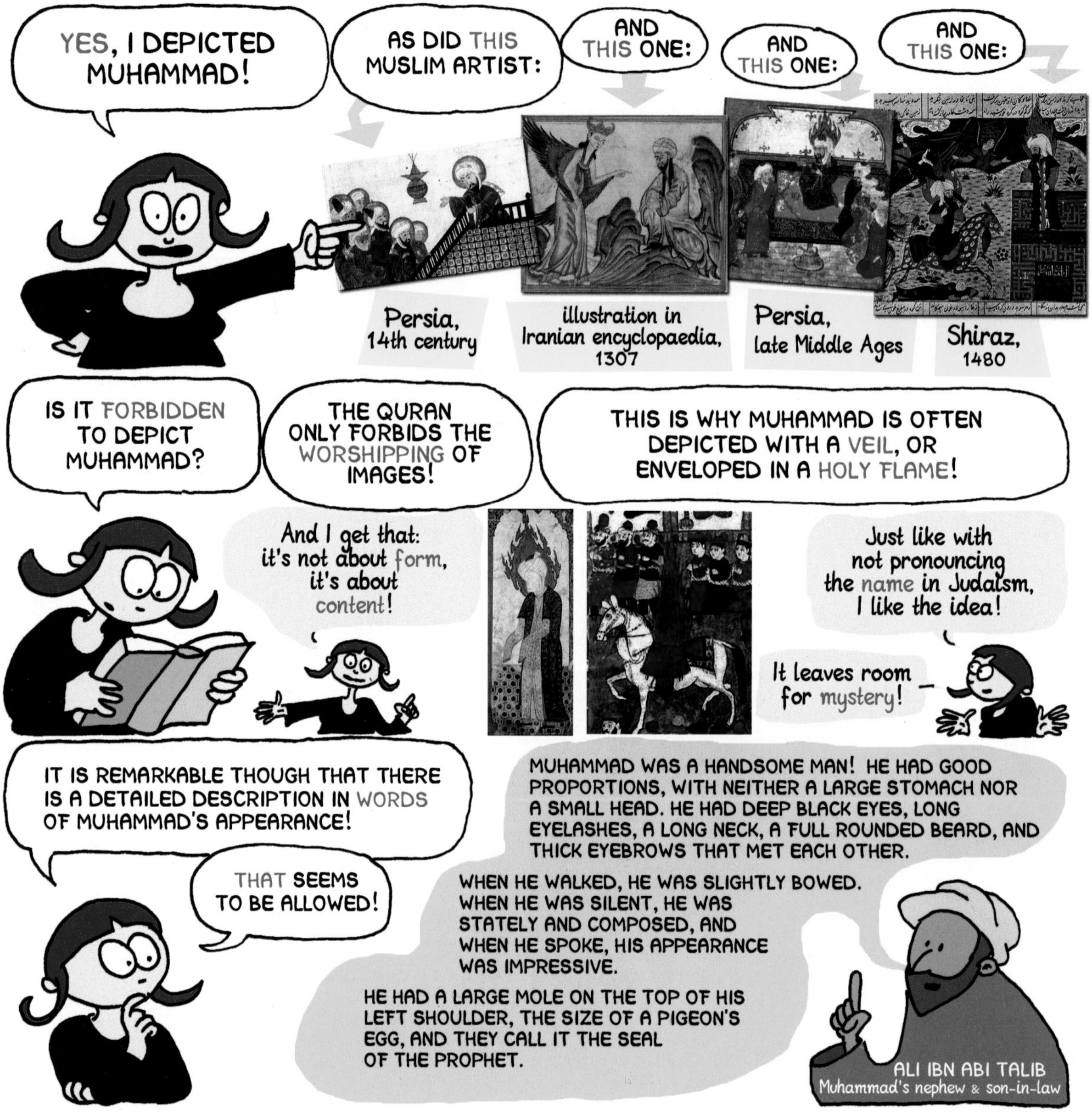

YES, I DEPICTED MUHAMMAD!
AS DID THIS MUSLIM ARTIST:
AND THIS ONE:
AND THIS ONE:
AND THIS ONE:
Persia, 14th century
illustration in Iranian encyclopaedia, 1307
Persia, late Middle Ages
Shiraz, 1480
IS IT FORBIDDEN TO DEPICT MUHAMMAD?
THE QURAN ONLY FORBIDS THE WORSHIPPING OF IMAGES!
THIS IS WHY MUHAMMAD IS OFTEN DEPICTED WITH A VEIL, OR ENVELOPED IN A HOLY FLAME!
And I get that: it's not about form, it's about content!
Just like with not pronouncing the name in Judaism, I like the idea!
It leaves room for mystery!
IT IS REMARKABLE THOUGH THAT THERE IS A DETAILED DESCRIPTION IN WORDS OF MUHAMMAD'S APPEARANCE!
THAT SEEMS TO BE ALLOWED!
MUHAMMAD WAS A HANDSOME MAN! HE HAD GOOD PROPORTIONS, WITH NEITHER A LARGE STOMACH NOR A SMALL HEAD. HE HAD DEEP BLACK EYES, LONG EYELASHES, A LONG NECK, A FULL ROUNDED BEARD, AND THICK EYEBROWS THAT MET EACH OTHER.
WHEN HE WALKED, HE WAS SLIGHTLY BOWED. WHEN HE WAS SILENT, HE WAS STATELY AND COMPOSED, AND WHEN HE SPOKE, HIS APPEARANCE WAS IMPRESSIVE.
HE HAD A LARGE MOLE ON THE TOP OF HIS LEFT SHOULDER, THE SIZE OF A PIGEON'S EGG, AND THEY CALL IT THE SEAL OF THE PROPHET.
ALI IBN ABI TALIB
Muhammad's nephew & son-in-law

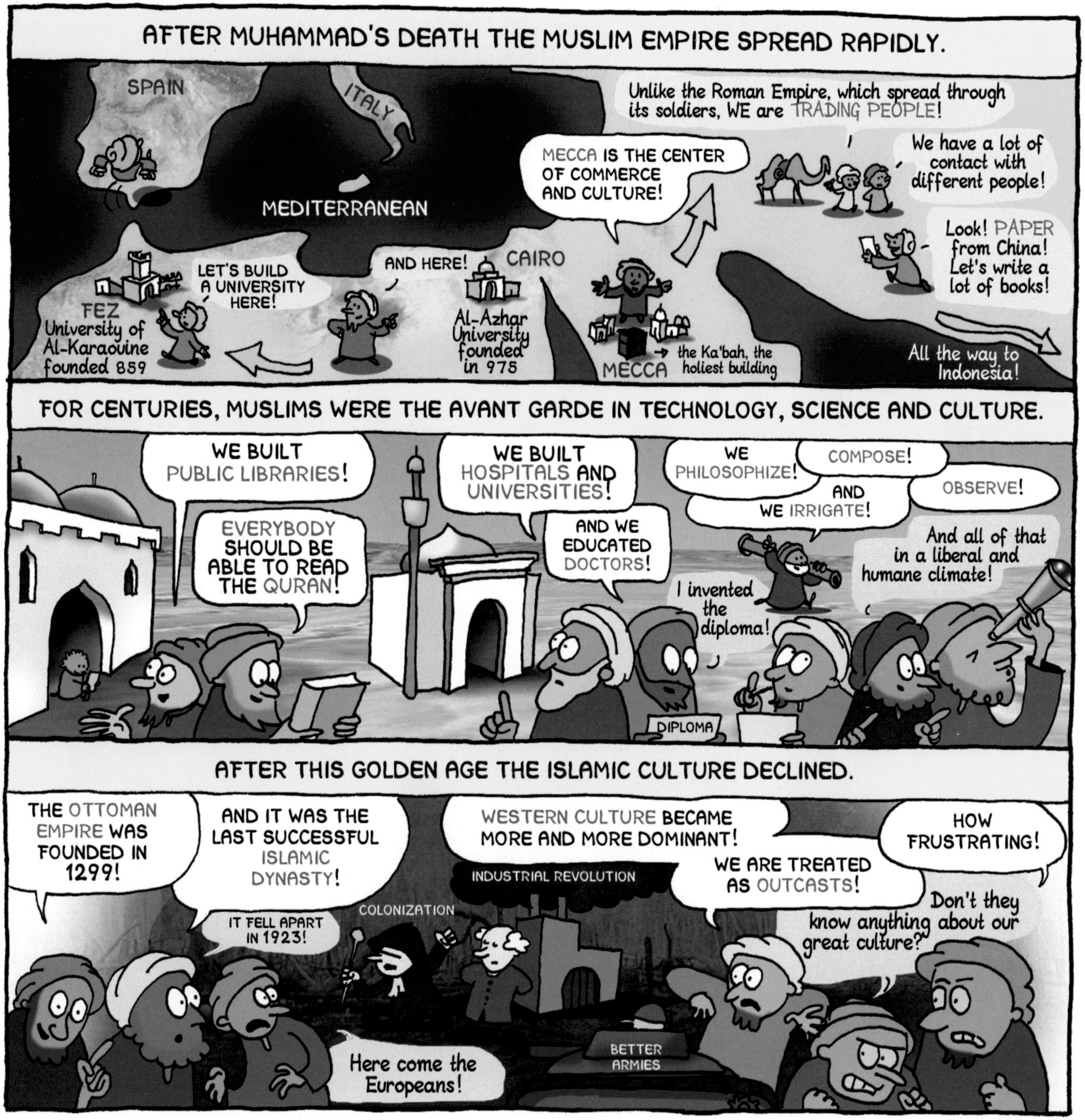
AFTER MUHAMMAD'S DEATH THE MUSLIM EMPIRE SPREAD RAPIDLY.
SPAIN
ITALY
MEDITERRANEAN
Unlike the Roman Empire, which spread through its soldiers, WE are TRADING PEOPLE!
We have a lot of contact with different people!
MECCA IS THE CENTER OF COMMERCE AND CULTURE!
Look! PAPER from China! Let's write a lot of books!
LET'S BUILD A UNIVERSITY HERE!
AND HERE!
CAIRO
FEZ
University of Al-Karaouine founded 859
Al-Azhar University founded in 975
MECCA
the Ka'bah, the holiest building
All the way to Indonesia!
FOR CENTURIES, MUSLIMS WERE THE AVANT GARDE IN TECHNOLOGY, SCIENCE AND CULTURE.
WE BUILT PUBLIC LIBRARIES!
EVERYBODY SHOULD BE ABLE TO READ THE QURAN!
WE BUILT HOSPITALS AND UNIVERSITIES!
AND WE EDUCATED DOCTORS!
WE PHILOSOPHIZE!
COMPOSE!
OBSERVE!
AND WE IRRIGATE!
And all of that in a liberal and humane climate!
I invented the diploma!
DIPLOMA
AFTER THIS GOLDEN AGE THE ISLAMIC CULTURE DECLINED.
THE OTTOMAN EMPIRE WAS FOUNDED IN 1299!
AND IT WAS THE LAST SUCCESSFUL ISLAMIC DYNASTY!
IT FELL APART IN 1923!
WESTERN CULTURE BECAME MORE AND MORE DOMINANT!
HOW FRUSTRATING!
WE ARE TREATED AS OUTCASTS!
Don't they know anything about our great culture?
INDUSTRIAL REVOLUTION
COLONIZATION
BETTER ARMIES
Here come the Europeans!

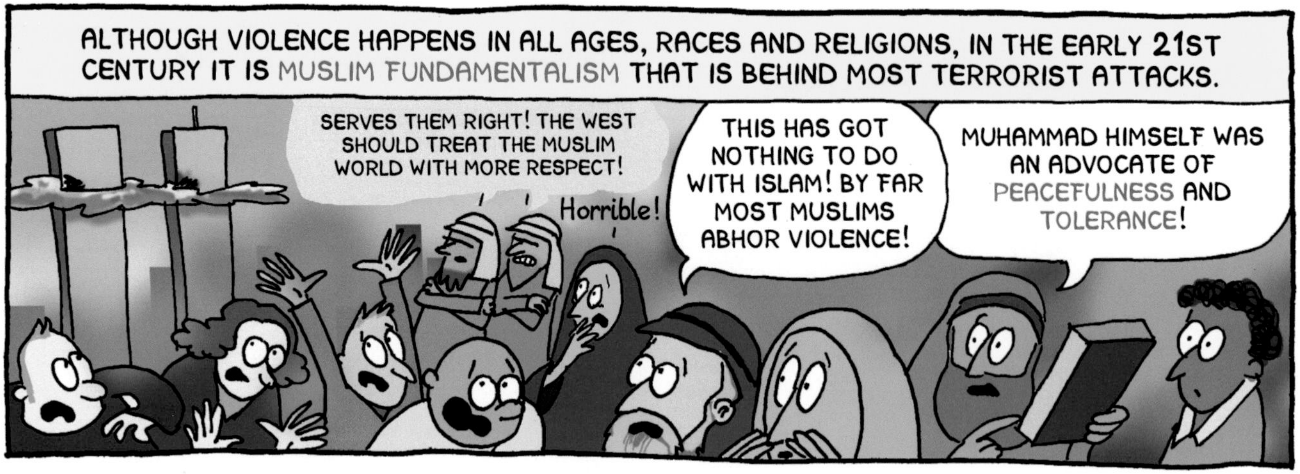
ALTHOUGH VIOLENCE HAPPENS IN ALL AGES, RACES AND RELIGIONS, IN THE EARLY 21ST CENTURY IT IS MUSLIM FUNDAMENTALISM THAT IS BEHIND MOST TERRORIST ATTACKS.
SERVES THEM RIGHT! THE WEST SHOULD TREAT THE MUSLIM WORLD WITH MORE RESPECT!
Horrible!
THIS HAS GOT NOTHING TO DO WITH ISLAM! BY FAR MOST MUSLIMS ABHOR VIOLENCE!
MUHAMMAD HIMSELF WAS AN ADVOCATE OF PEACEFULNESS AND TOLERANCE!

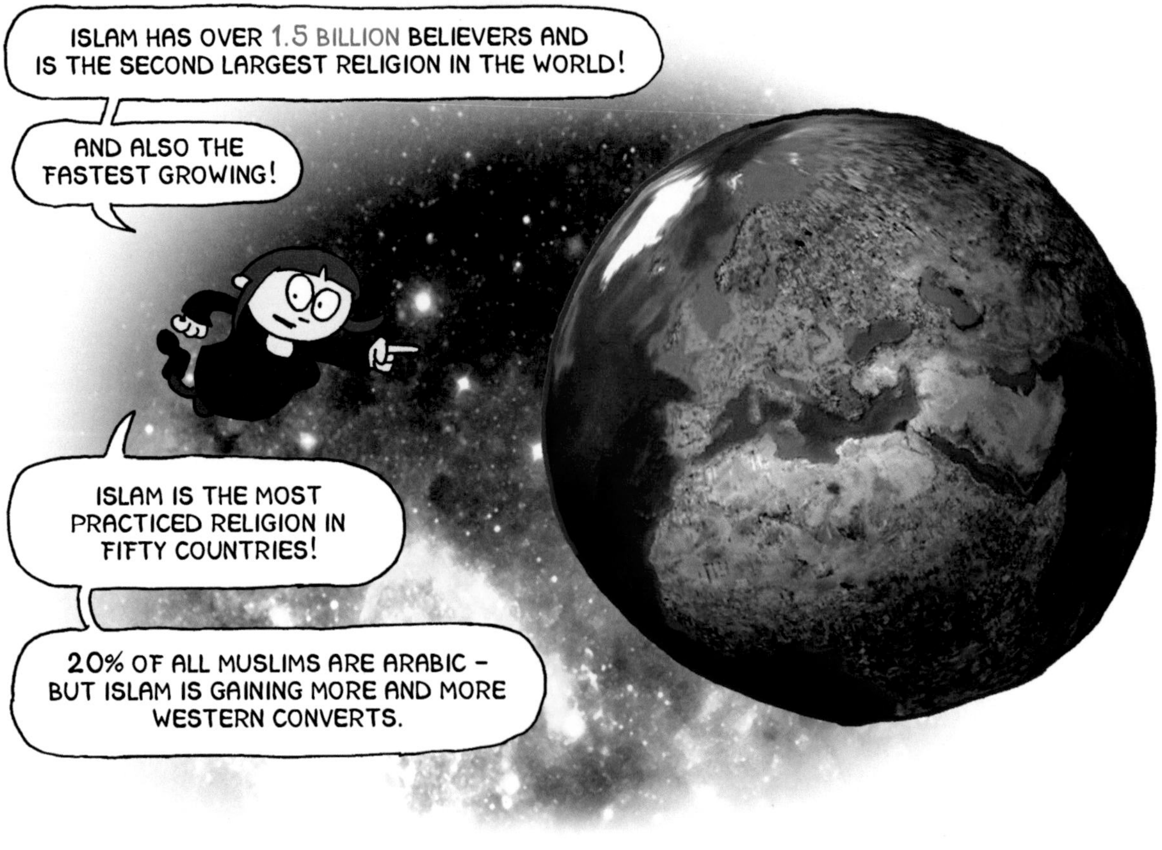
ISLAM HAS OVER 1.5 BILLION BELIEVERS AND IS THE SECOND LARGEST RELIGION IN THE WORLD!
AND ALSO THE FASTEST GROWING!
ISLAM IS THE MOST PRACTICED RELIGION IN FIFTY COUNTRIES!
20% OF ALL MUSLIMS ARE ARABIC – BUT ISLAM IS GAINING MORE AND MORE WESTERN CONVERTS.

THE KA'BAH

THE KA'BAH ("CUBE") IN MECCA IS THE CENTRAL HOLY SPOT IN ISLAM. EVERY MUSLIM MUST, IF HE OR SHE CAN, MAKE A PILGRIMAGE TO MECCA ONCE IN LIFE, AND CIRCLE THE KA'BAH SEVEN TIMES.

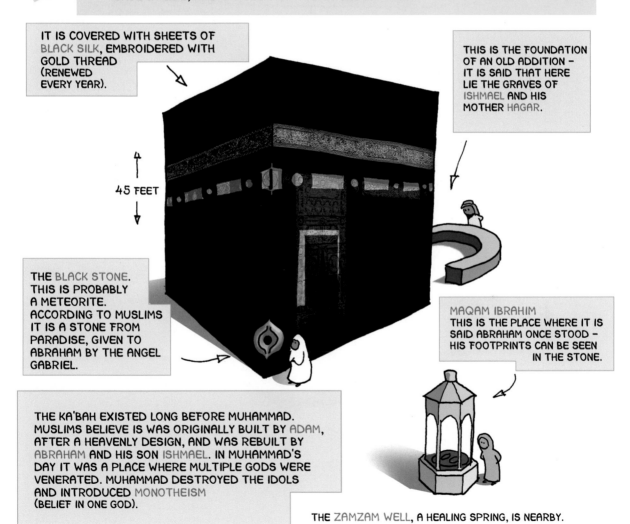

IT IS COVERED WITH SHEETS OF BLACK SILK, EMBROIDERED WITH GOLD THREAD (RENEWED EVERY YEAR).

THIS IS THE FOUNDATION OF AN OLD ADDITION – IT IS SAID THAT HERE LIE THE GRAVES OF ISHMAEL AND HIS MOTHER HAGAR.

45 FEET

THE BLACK STONE. THIS IS PROBABLY A METEORITE. ACCORDING TO MUSLIMS IT IS A STONE FROM PARADISE, GIVEN TO ABRAHAM BY THE ANGEL GABRIEL.

MAQAM IBRAHIM THIS IS THE PLACE WHERE IT IS SAID ABRAHAM ONCE STOOD – HIS FOOTPRINTS CAN BE SEEN IN THE STONE.

THE KA'BAH EXISTED LONG BEFORE MUHAMMAD. MUSLIMS BELIEVE IS WAS ORIGINALLY BUILT BY ADAM, AFTER A HEAVENLY DESIGN, AND WAS REBUILT BY ABRAHAM AND HIS SON ISHMAEL. IN MUHAMMAD'S DAY IT WAS A PLACE WHERE MULTIPLE GODS WERE VENERATED. MUHAMMAD DESTROYED THE IDOLS AND INTRODUCED MONOTHEISM (BELIEF IN ONE GOD).

THE ZAMZAM WELL, A HEALING SPRING, IS NEARBY.

59.

THE CORE OF ISLAM

I THINK THE CORE OF ISLAM IS THE SALAT – THE RITUAL PRAYER MUSLIMS PERFORM FIVE TIMES A DAY.

ASH-HADU AN LAA ILAAHA ILLALLAH WA ASH-HADU ANNA MUHAMMADAN RASULULLAH!

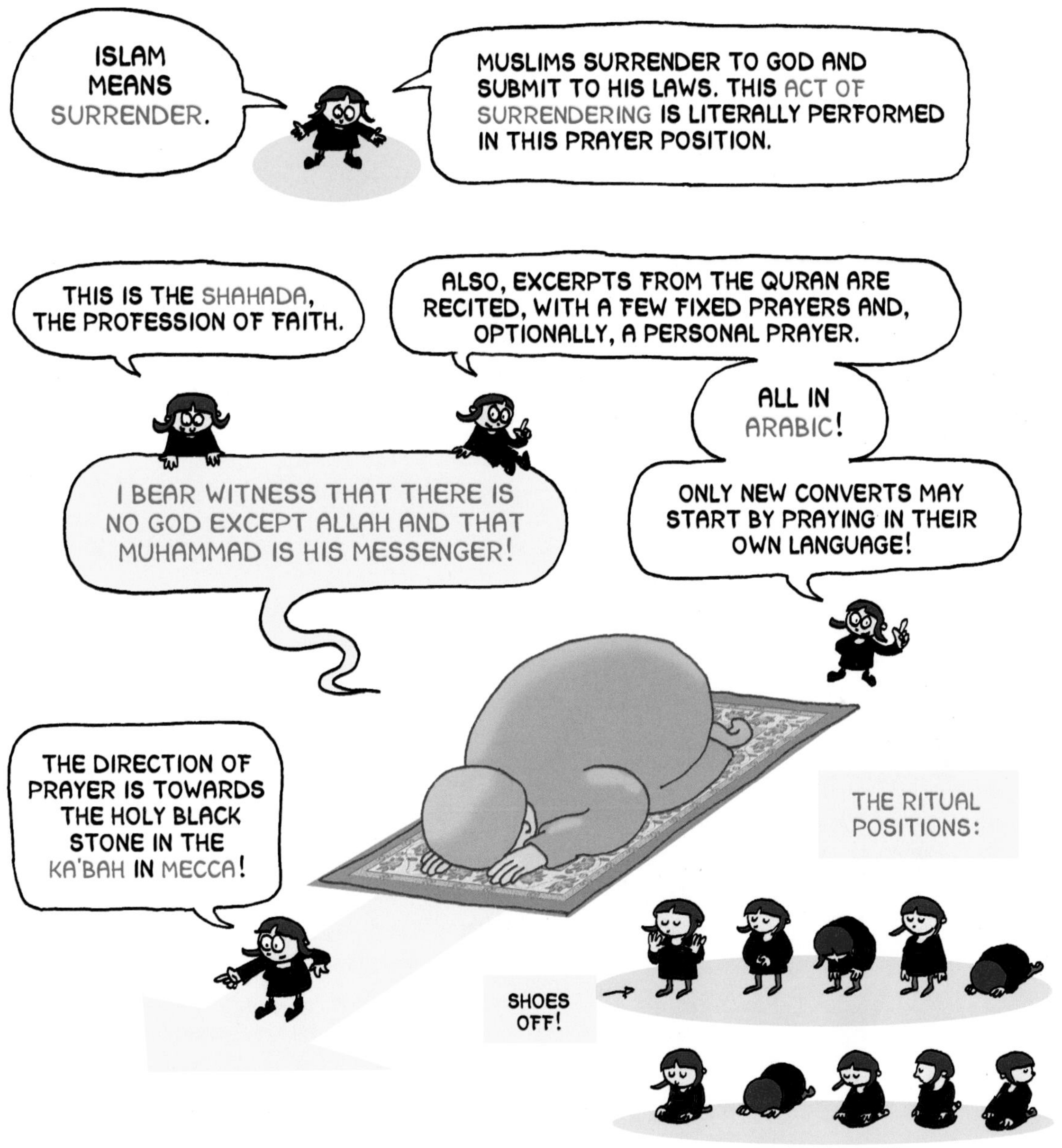
ISLAM MEANS SURRENDER.
MUSLIMS SURRENDER TO GOD AND SUBMIT TO HIS LAWS. THIS ACT OF SURRENDERING IS LITERALLY PERFORMED IN THIS PRAYER POSITION.
THIS IS THE SHAHADA, THE PROFESSION OF FAITH.
ALSO, EXCERPTS FROM THE QURAN ARE RECITED, WITH A FEW FIXED PRAYERS AND, OPTIONALLY, A PERSONAL PRAYER.
ALL IN ARABIC!
I BEAR WITNESS THAT THERE IS NO GOD EXCEPT ALLAH AND THAT MUHAMMAD IS HIS MESSENGER!
ONLY NEW CONVERTS MAY START BY PRAYING IN THEIR OWN LANGUAGE!
THE DIRECTION OF PRAYER IS TOWARDS THE HOLY BLACK STONE IN THE KA'BAH IN MECCA!
THE RITUAL POSITIONS:
SHOES OFF!

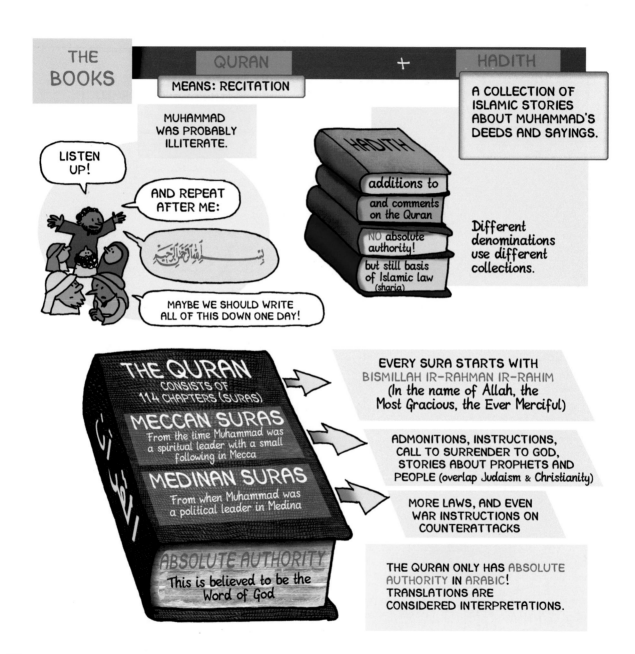

THE BOOKS

QURAN + HADITH

MEANS: RECITATION

A COLLECTION OF ISLAMIC STORIES ABOUT MUHAMMAD'S DEEDS AND SAYINGS.

MUHAMMAD WAS PROBABLY ILLITERATE.

LISTEN UP!

AND REPEAT AFTER ME:

MAYBE WE SHOULD WRITE ALL OF THIS DOWN ONE DAY!

HADITH

additions to

and comments on the Quran

NO absolute authority!

but still basis of Islamic law (sharia)

Different denominations use different collections.

THE QURAN CONSISTS OF 114 CHAPTERS (SURAS)

EVERY SURA STARTS WITH BISMILLAH IR-RAHMAN IR-RAHIM (In the name of Allah, the Most Gracious, the Ever Merciful)

MECCAN SURAS
From the time Muhammad was a spiritual leader with a small following in Mecca

ADMONITIONS, INSTRUCTIONS, CALL TO SURRENDER TO GOD, STORIES ABOUT PROPHETS AND PEOPLE (overlap Judaism & Christianity)

MEDINAN SURAS
From when Muhammad was a political leader in Medina

MORE LAWS, AND EVEN WAR INSTRUCTIONS ON COUNTERATTACKS

ABSOLUTE AUTHORITY
This is believed to be the Word of God

THE QURAN ONLY HAS ABSOLUTE AUTHORITY IN ARABIC! TRANSLATIONS ARE CONSIDERED INTERPRETATIONS.

JUDAISM, CHRISTIANITY AND ISLAM ARE CALLED ABRAHAMIC RELIGIONS, BECAUSE THEY ALL HAVE ABRAHAM AS THEIR PATRIARCH.

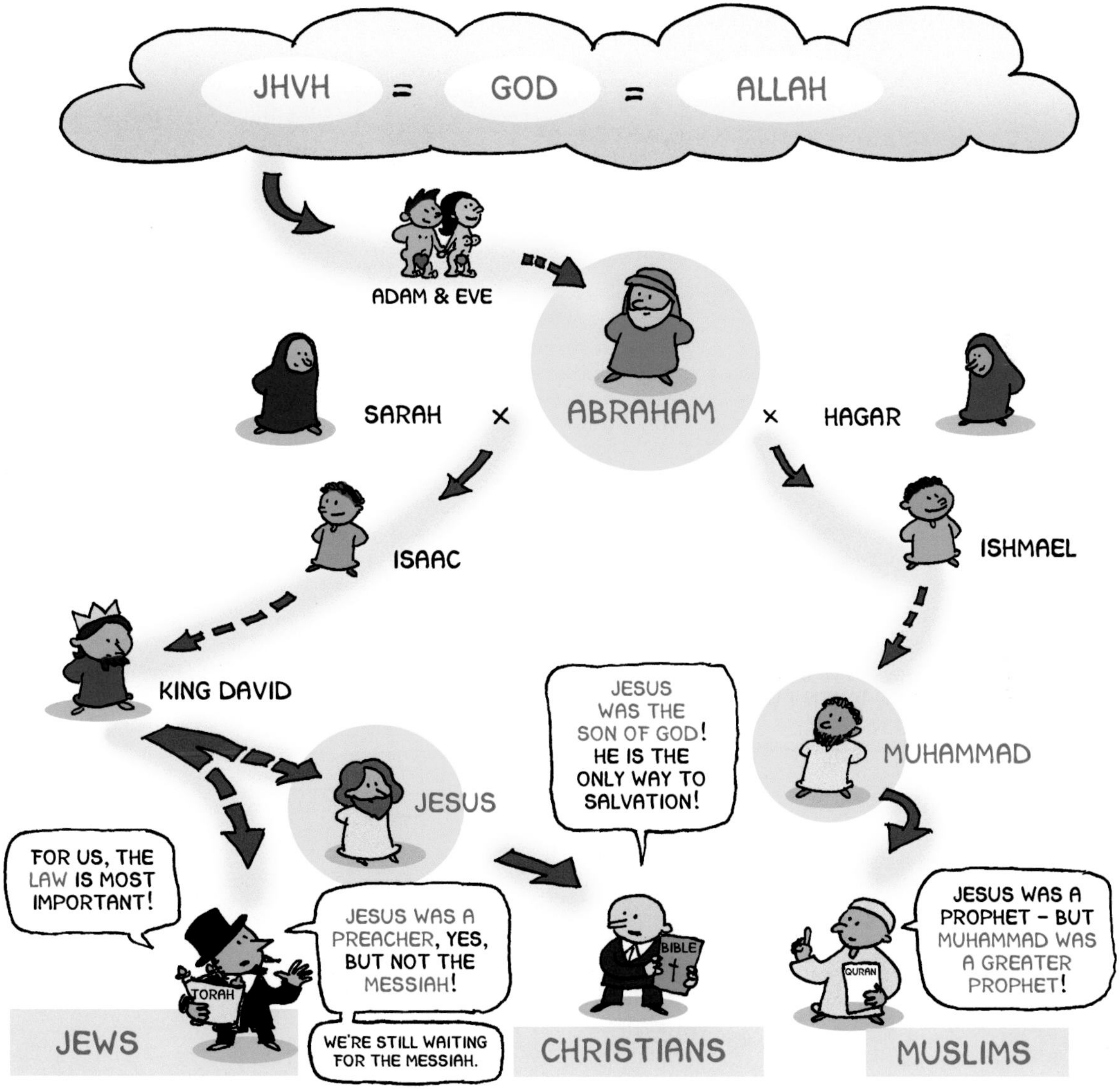

I DIDN'T REALLY REBEL THAT MUCH AGAINST MY CHRISTIAN UPBRINGING WHEN I WAS A TEENAGER...

...BUT I WAS INCREASINGLY BOTHERED BY THE LANGUAGE THAT I HEARD IN CHURCH.

OUR FATHER * WHO ART IN HEAVEN, * HALLOWED BE THY NAME. *
THY KINGDOM COME. THY WILL BE DONE * ON EARTH AS IT IS IN HEAVEN.
GIVE US THIS DAY OUR DAILY BREAD, AND FORGIVE US OUR TRESPASSES, *
AS WE FORGIVE THOSE WHO TRESPASS AGAINST US,
AND LEAD US NOT INTO TEMPTATION, * BUT DELIVER US FROM EVIL. *
FOR THINE IS THE KINGDOM, AND THE POWER, AND THE GLORY, FOR EVER AND EVER. AMEN.
* FATHER? WHY NOT MOTHER?
* IN HEAVEN? BUT ISN'T GOD EVERYWHERE?
* NAME? BUT ISN'T IT ABOUT WHAT GOD IS, NOT HIS NAME?
* IT ALL SOUNDS SO PASSIVE!
* ALWAYS THIS EMPHASIS ON GUILT!
* DELIVER US? AS IF WE'RE NOT RESPONSIBLE FOR EVIL OURSELVES!

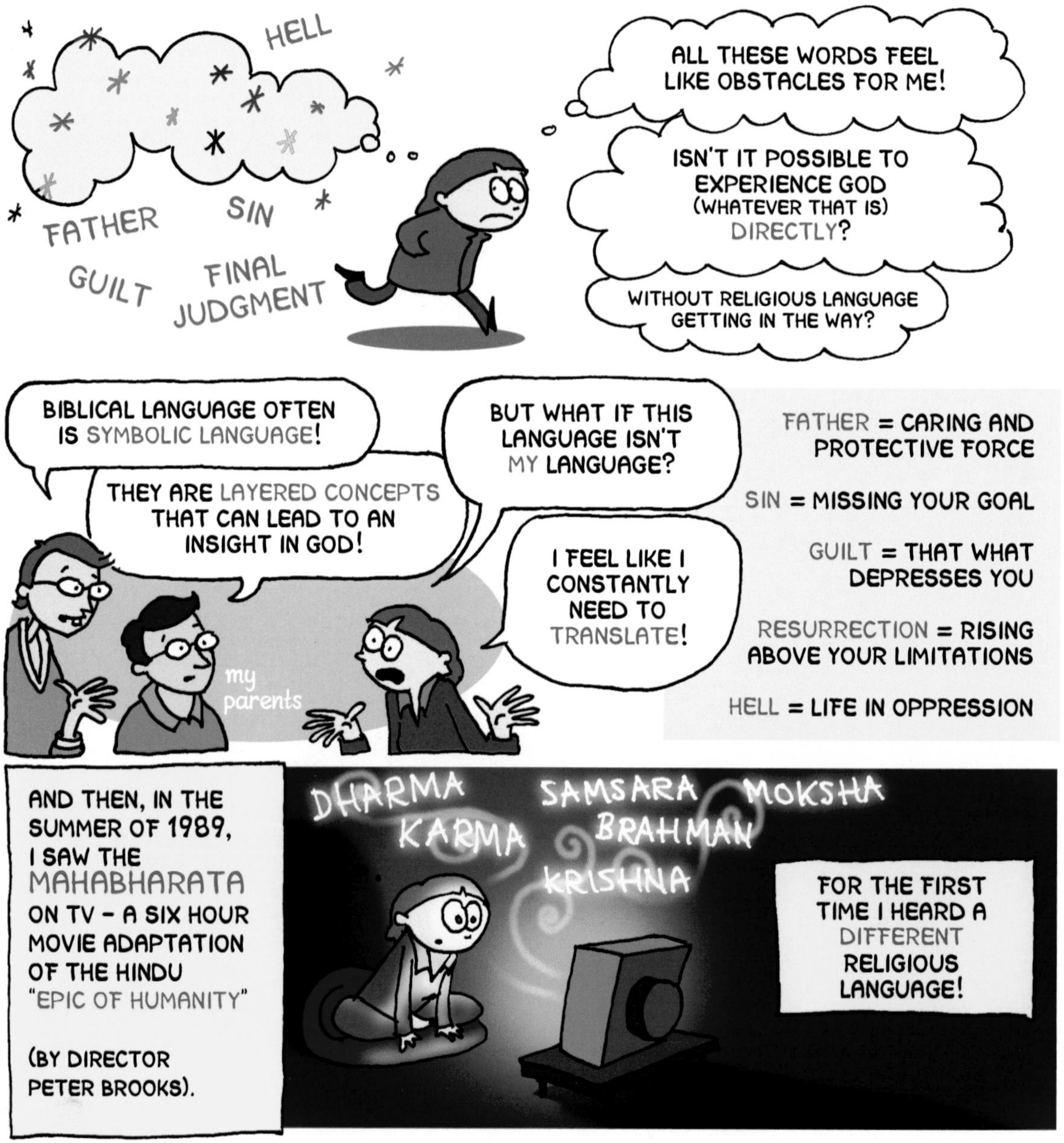
HELL
FATHER
SIN
GUILT
FINAL JUDGMENT
ALL THESE WORDS FEEL LIKE OBSTACLES FOR ME!
ISN'T IT POSSIBLE TO EXPERIENCE GOD (WHATEVER THAT IS) DIRECTLY?
WITHOUT RELIGIOUS LANGUAGE GETTING IN THE WAY?
BIBLICAL LANGUAGE OFTEN IS SYMBOLIC LANGUAGE!
THEY ARE LAYERED CONCEPTS THAT CAN LEAD TO AN INSIGHT IN GOD!
BUT WHAT IF THIS LANGUAGE ISN'T MY LANGUAGE?
I FEEL LIKE I CONSTANTLY NEED TO TRANSLATE!
my parents
FATHER = CARING AND PROTECTIVE FORCE
SIN = MISSING YOUR GOAL
GUILT = THAT WHAT DEPRESSES YOU
RESURRECTION = RISING ABOVE YOUR LIMITATIONS
HELL = LIFE IN OPPRESSION
AND THEN, IN THE SUMMER OF 1989, I SAW THE MAHABHARATA ON TV – A SIX HOUR MOVIE ADAPTATION OF THE HINDU "EPIC OF HUMANITY"
(BY DIRECTOR PETER BROOKS).
DHARMA
SAMSARA
MOKSHA
KARMA
BRAHMAN
KRISHNA
FOR THE FIRST TIME I HEARD A DIFFERENT RELIGIOUS LANGUAGE!

HINDUISM

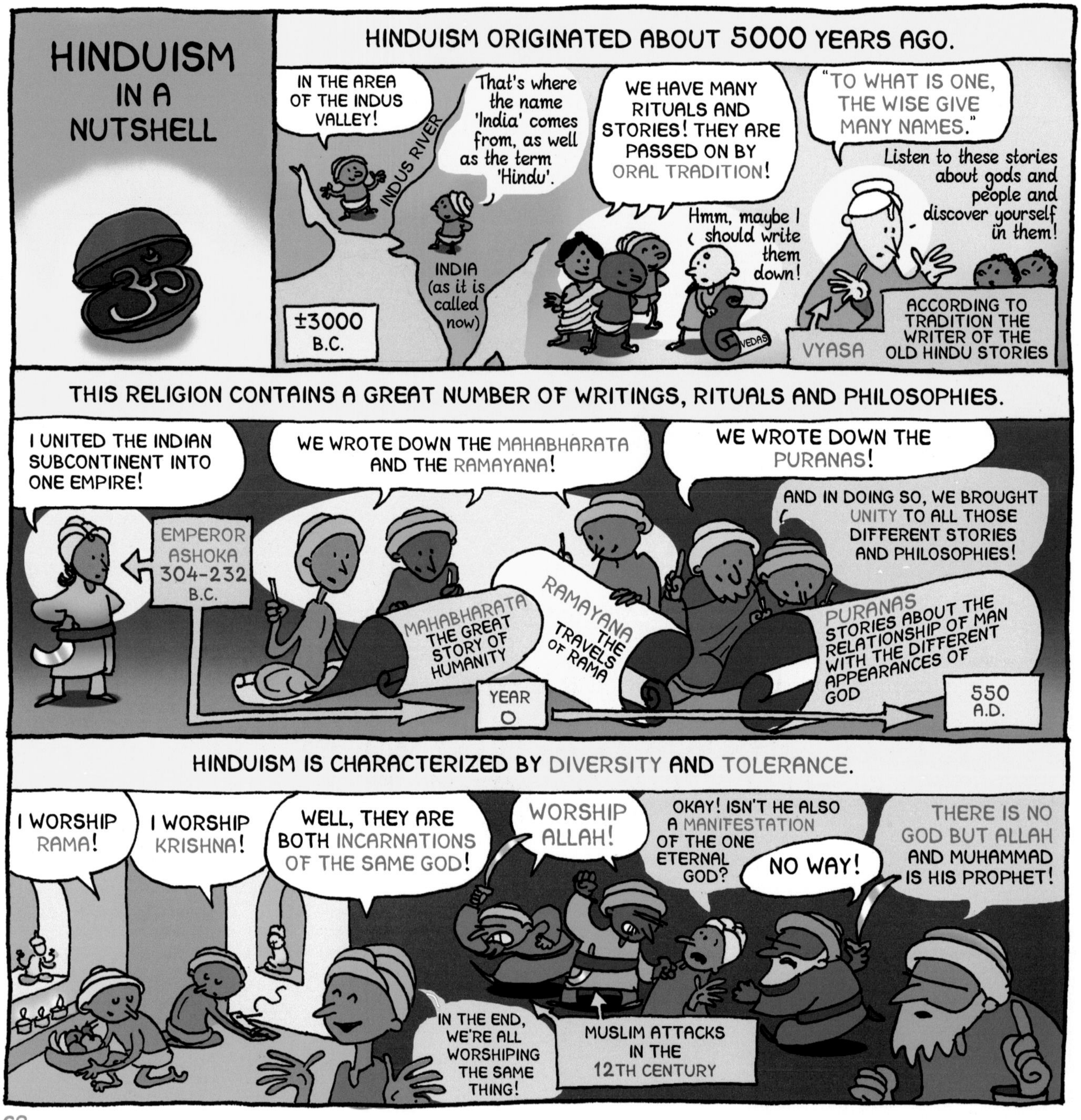
HINDUISM IN A NUTSHELL
HINDUISM ORIGINATED ABOUT 5000 YEARS AGO.
IN THE AREA OF THE INDUS VALLEY!
INDUS RIVER
That's where the name 'India' comes from, as well as the term 'Hindu'.
INDIA (as it is called now)
±3000 B.C.
WE HAVE MANY RITUALS AND STORIES! THEY ARE PASSED ON BY ORAL TRADITION!
Hmm, maybe I should write them down!
VEDAS
"TO WHAT IS ONE, THE WISE GIVE MANY NAMES."
Listen to these stories about gods and people and discover yourself in them!
VYASA
ACCORDING TO TRADITION THE WRITER OF THE OLD HINDU STORIES
THIS RELIGION CONTAINS A GREAT NUMBER OF WRITINGS, RITUALS AND PHILOSOPHIES.
I UNITED THE INDIAN SUBCONTINENT INTO ONE EMPIRE!
EMPEROR ASHOKA 304-232 B.C.
WE WROTE DOWN THE MAHABHARATA AND THE RAMAYANA!
WE WROTE DOWN THE PURANAS!
AND IN DOING SO, WE BROUGHT UNITY TO ALL THOSE DIFFERENT STORIES AND PHILOSOPHIES!
MAHABHARATA THE GREAT STORY OF HUMANITY
RAMAYANA THE TRAVELS OF RAMA
PURANAS STORIES ABOUT THE RELATIONSHIP OF MAN WITH THE DIFFERENT APPEARANCES OF GOD
YEAR 0
550 A.D.
HINDUISM IS CHARACTERIZED BY DIVERSITY AND TOLERANCE.
I WORSHIP RAMA!
I WORSHIP KRISHNA!
WELL, THEY ARE BOTH INCARNATIONS OF THE SAME GOD!
IN THE END, WE'RE ALL WORSHIPING THE SAME THING!
WORSHIP ALLAH!
OKAY! ISN'T HE ALSO A MANIFESTATION OF THE ONE ETERNAL GOD?
NO WAY!
THERE IS NO GOD BUT ALLAH AND MUHAMMAD IS HIS PROPHET!
MUSLIM ATTACKS IN THE 12TH CENTURY

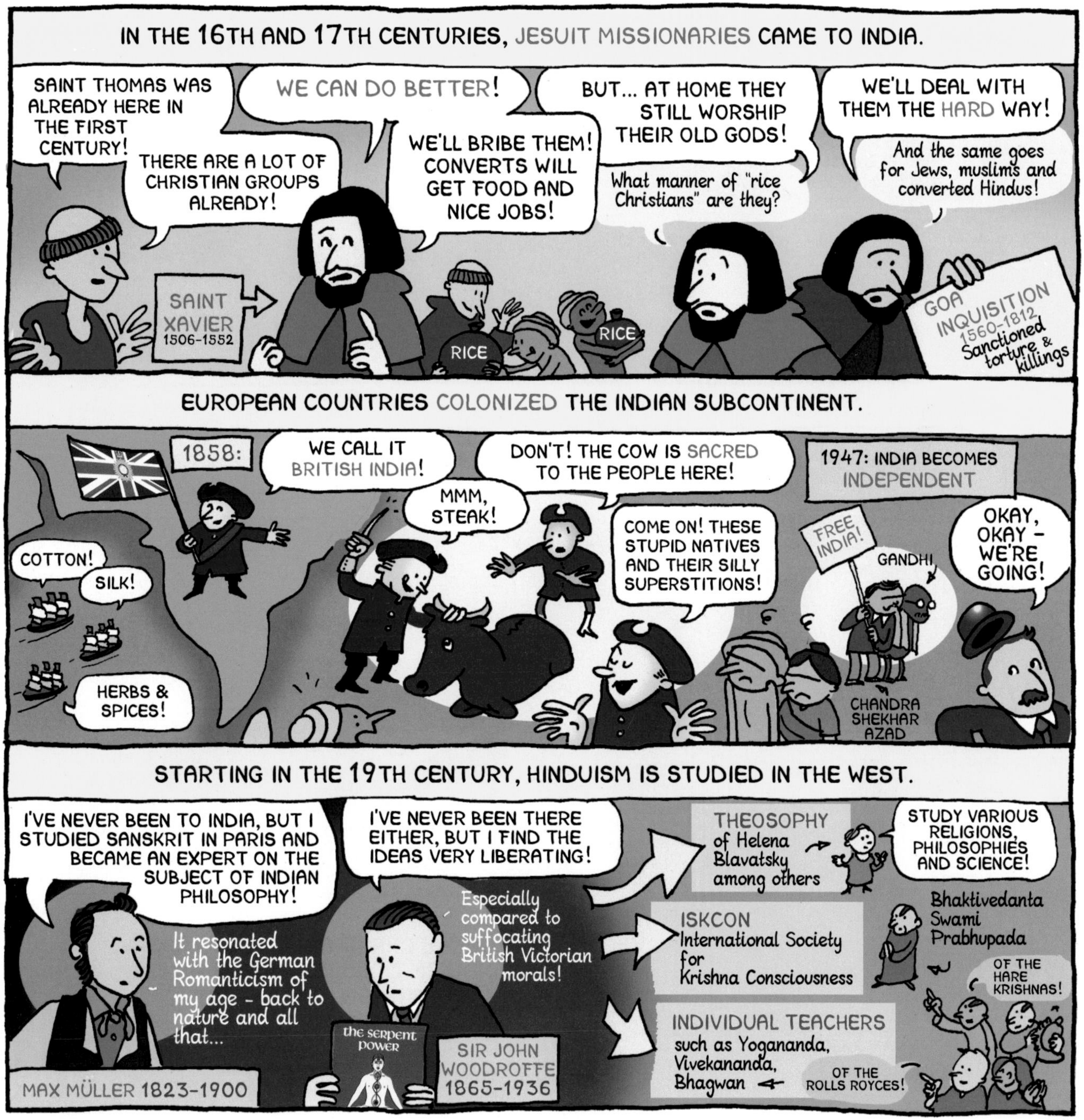
IN THE 16TH AND 17TH CENTURIES, JESUIT MISSIONARIES CAME TO INDIA.
SAINT THOMAS WAS ALREADY HERE IN THE FIRST CENTURY!
THERE ARE A LOT OF CHRISTIAN GROUPS ALREADY!
SAINT XAVIER 1506–1552
WE CAN DO BETTER!
WE'LL BRIBE THEM! CONVERTS WILL GET FOOD AND NICE JOBS!
RICE
RICE
BUT... AT HOME THEY STILL WORSHIP THEIR OLD GODS!
What manner of "rice Christians" are they?
WE'LL DEAL WITH THEM THE HARD WAY!
And the same goes for Jews, muslims and converted Hindus!
GOA INQUISITION 1560–1812 Sanctioned torture & killings
EUROPEAN COUNTRIES COLONIZED THE INDIAN SUBCONTINENT.
1858:
WE CALL IT BRITISH INDIA!
COTTON!
SILK!
HERBS & SPICES!
MMM, STEAK!
DON'T! THE COW IS SACRED TO THE PEOPLE HERE!
COME ON! THESE STUPID NATIVES AND THEIR SILLY SUPERSTITIONS!
1947: INDIA BECOMES INDEPENDENT
FREE INDIA!
GANDHI
CHANDRA SHEKHAR AZAD
OKAY, OKAY – WE'RE GOING!
STARTING IN THE 19TH CENTURY, HINDUISM IS STUDIED IN THE WEST.
I'VE NEVER BEEN TO INDIA, BUT I STUDIED SANSKRIT IN PARIS AND BECAME AN EXPERT ON THE SUBJECT OF INDIAN PHILOSOPHY!
It resonated with the German Romanticism of my age – back to nature and all that...
MAX MÜLLER 1823–1900
I'VE NEVER BEEN THERE EITHER, BUT I FIND THE IDEAS VERY LIBERATING!
Especially compared to suffocating British Victorian morals!
the serpent power
SIR JOHN WOODROFFE 1865–1936
THEOSOPHY of Helena Blavatsky among others
STUDY VARIOUS RELIGIONS, PHILOSOPHIES AND SCIENCE!
ISKCON International Society for Krishna Consciousness
Bhaktivedanta Swami Prabhupada
OF THE HARE KRISHNAS!
INDIVIDUAL TEACHERS such as Yogananda, Vivekananda, Bhagwan
OF THE ROLLS ROYCES!

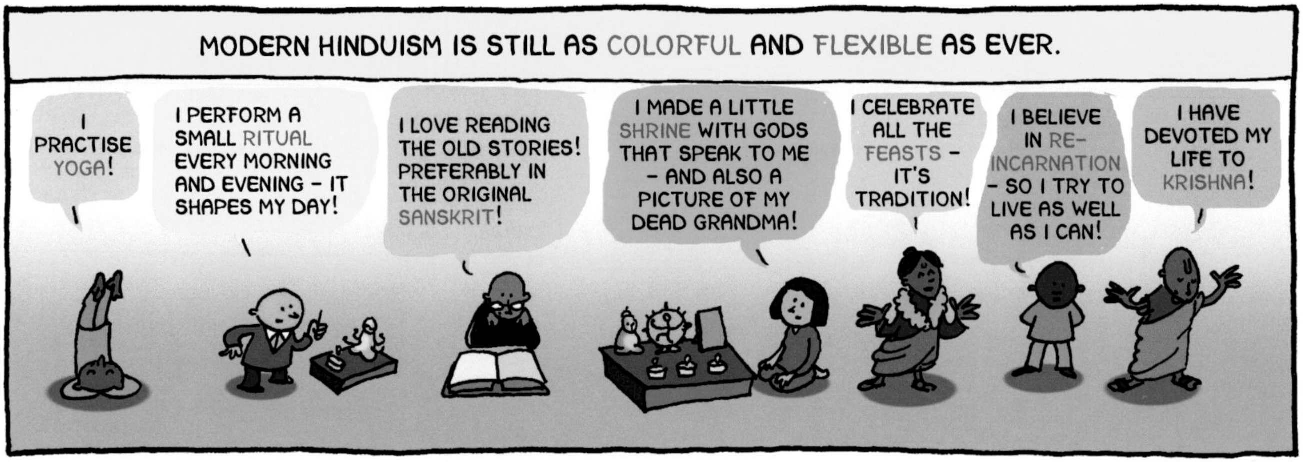
MODERN HINDUISM IS STILL AS COLORFUL AND FLEXIBLE AS EVER.
I PRACTISE YOGA!
I PERFORM A SMALL RITUAL EVERY MORNING AND EVENING – IT SHAPES MY DAY!
I LOVE READING THE OLD STORIES! PREFERABLY IN THE ORIGINAL SANSKRIT!
I MADE A LITTLE SHRINE WITH GODS THAT SPEAK TO ME – AND ALSO A PICTURE OF MY DEAD GRANDMA!
I CELEBRATE ALL THE FEASTS – IT'S TRADITION!
I BELIEVE IN RE-INCARNATION – SO I TRY TO LIVE AS WELL AS I CAN!
I HAVE DEVOTED MY LIFE TO KRISHNA!

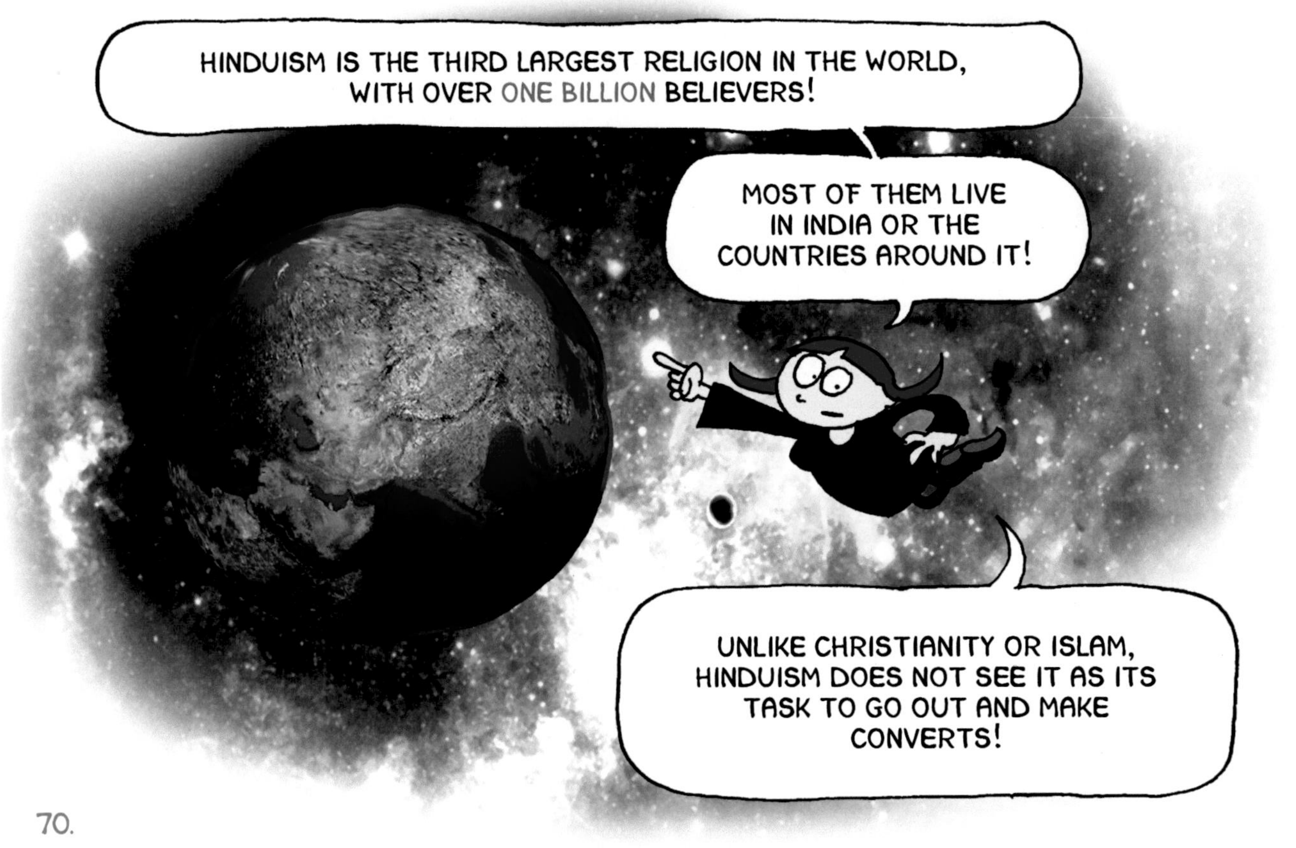
HINDUISM IS THE THIRD LARGEST RELIGION IN THE WORLD, WITH OVER ONE BILLION BELIEVERS!
MOST OF THEM LIVE IN INDIA OR THE COUNTRIES AROUND IT!
UNLIKE CHRISTIANITY OR ISLAM, HINDUISM DOES NOT SEE IT AS ITS TASK TO GO OUT AND MAKE CONVERTS!

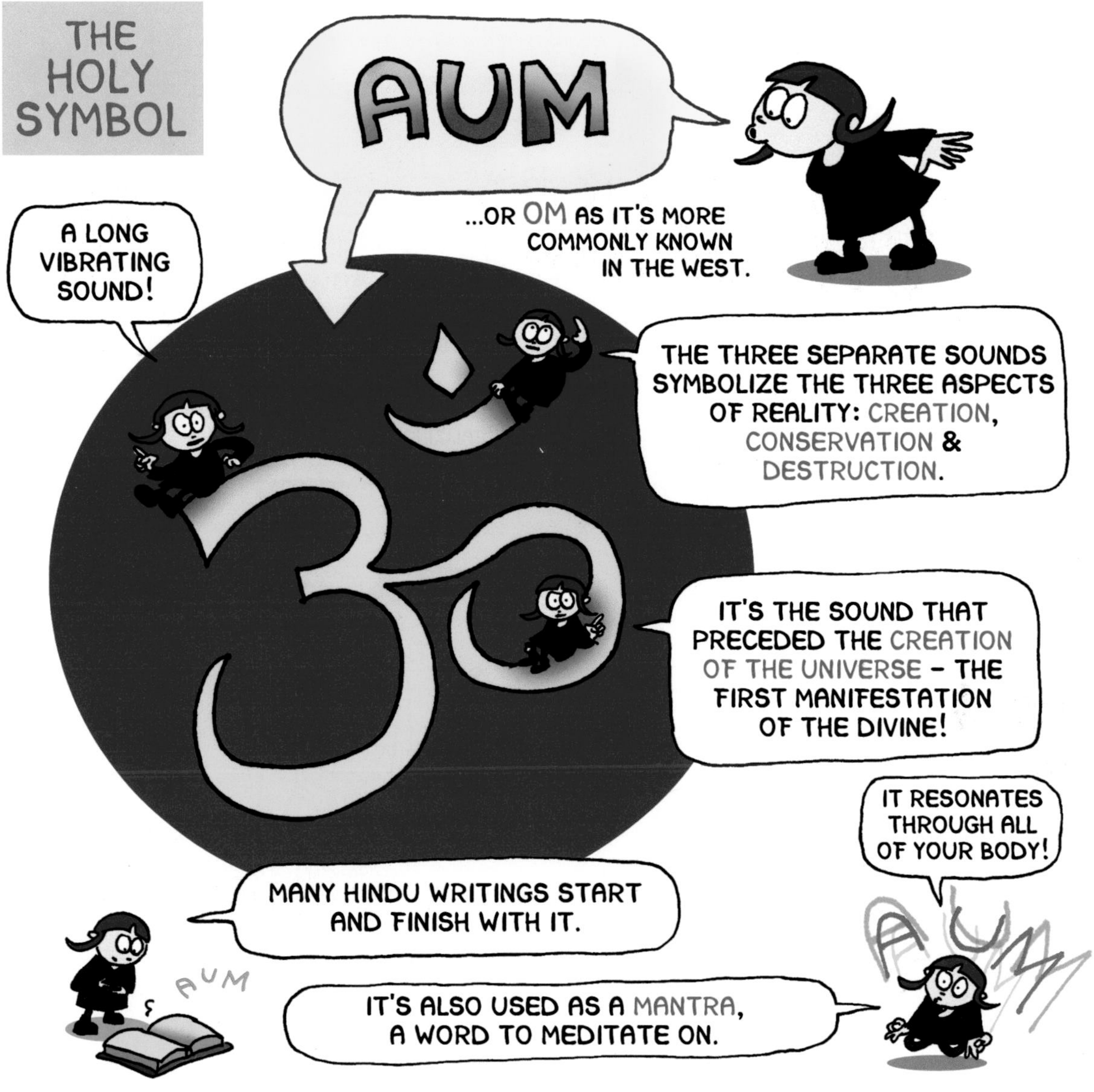
THE HOLY SYMBOL
AUM
...OR OM AS IT'S MORE COMMONLY KNOWN IN THE WEST.
A LONG VIBRATING SOUND!
THE THREE SEPARATE SOUNDS SYMBOLIZE THE THREE ASPECTS OF REALITY: CREATION, CONSERVATION & DESTRUCTION.
IT'S THE SOUND THAT PRECEDED THE CREATION OF THE UNIVERSE – THE FIRST MANIFESTATION OF THE DIVINE!
IT RESONATES THROUGH ALL OF YOUR BODY!
MANY HINDU WRITINGS START AND FINISH WITH IT.
AUM
AUM
IT'S ALSO USED AS A MANTRA, A WORD TO MEDITATE ON.

THE CORE OF BUDDHISM

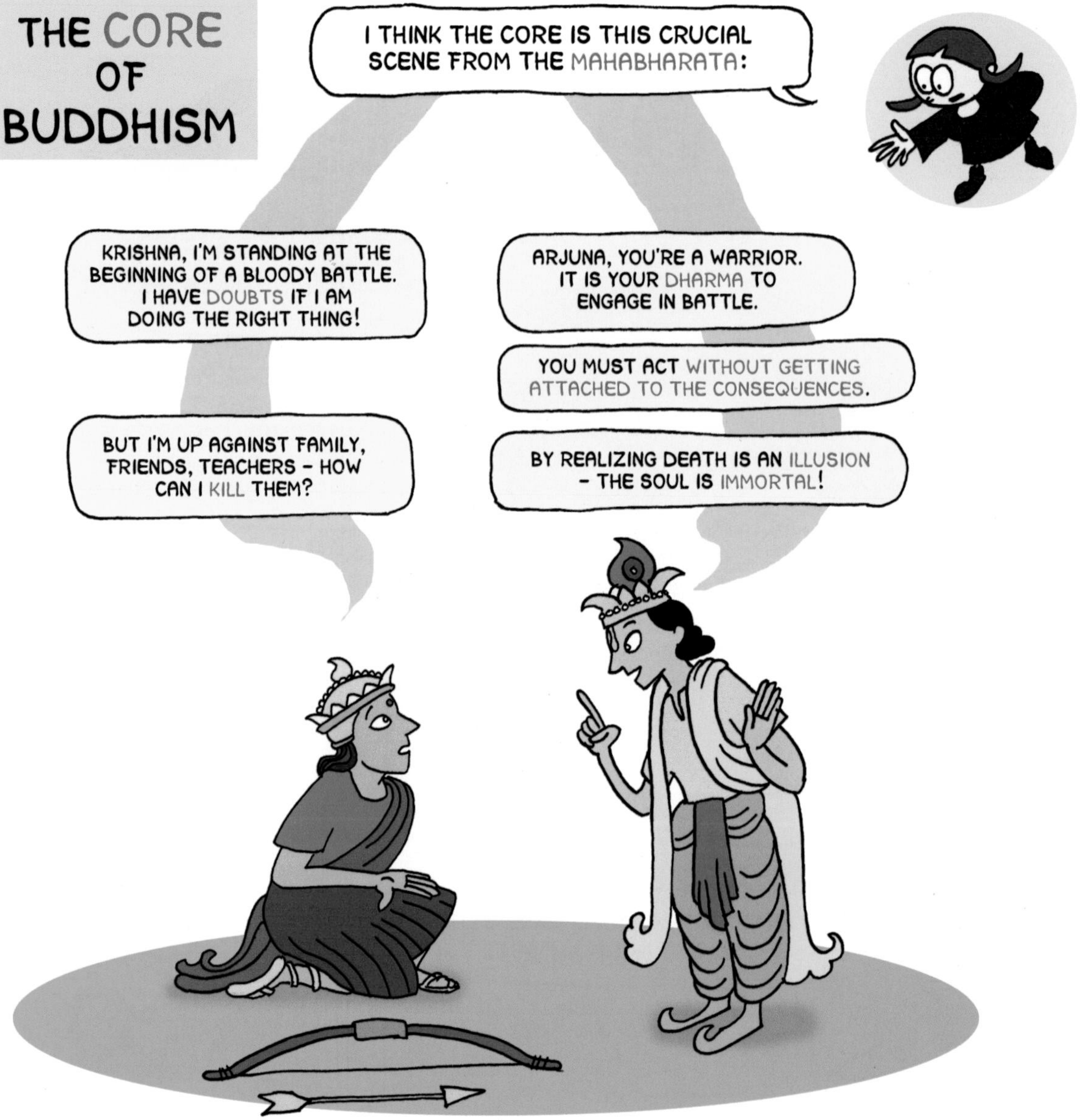
I THINK THE CORE IS THIS CRUCIAL SCENE FROM THE MAHABHARATA:
KRISHNA, I'M STANDING AT THE BEGINNING OF A BLOODY BATTLE. I HAVE DOUBTS IF I AM DOING THE RIGHT THING!
ARJUNA, YOU'RE A WARRIOR. IT IS YOUR DHARMA TO ENGAGE IN BATTLE.
YOU MUST ACT WITHOUT GETTING ATTACHED TO THE CONSEQUENCES.
BUT I'M UP AGAINST FAMILY, FRIENDS, TEACHERS – HOW CAN I KILL THEM?
BY REALIZING DEATH IS AN ILLUSION – THE SOUL IS IMMORTAL!

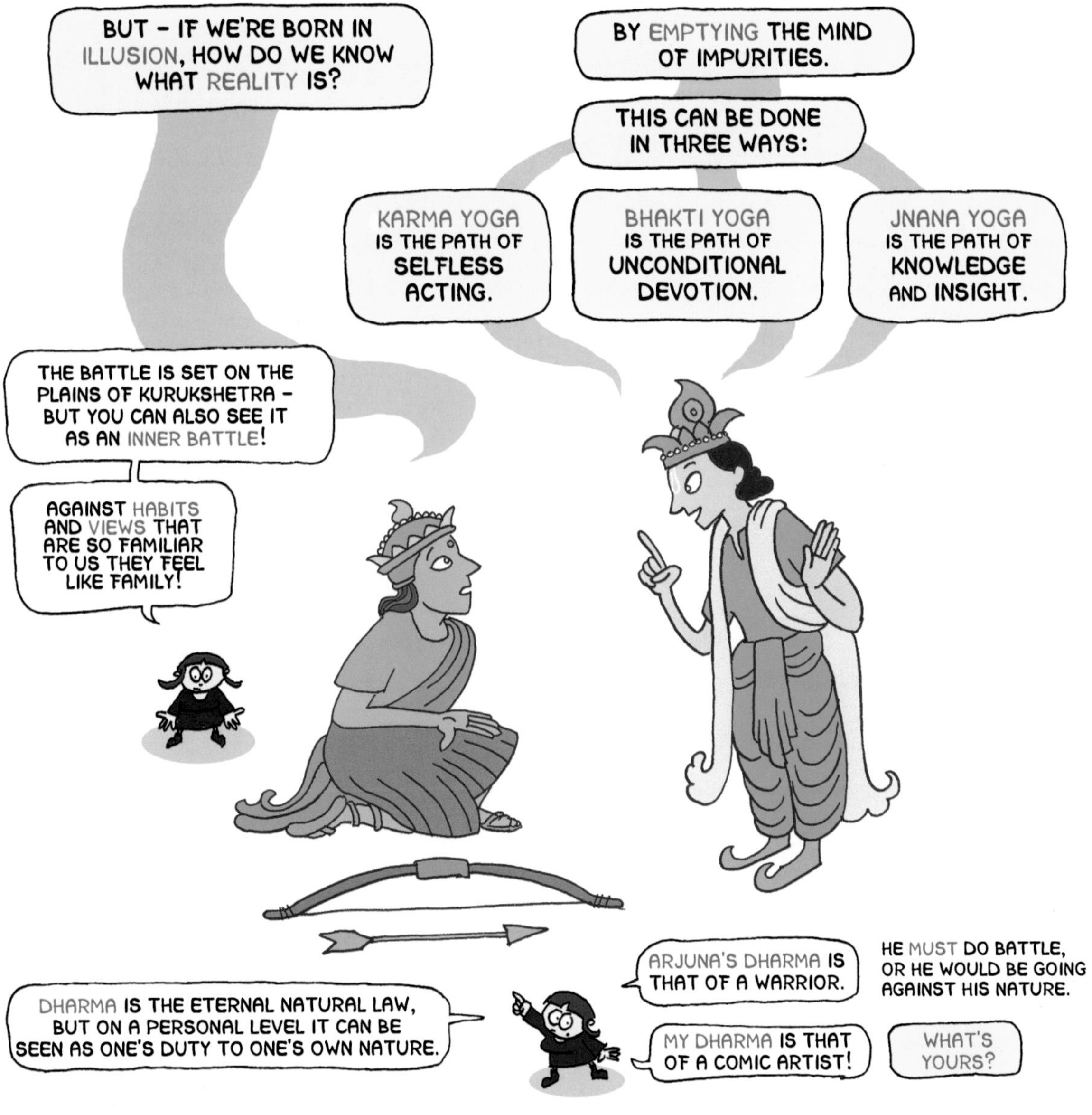
BUT - IF WE'RE BORN IN ILLUSION, HOW DO WE KNOW WHAT REALITY IS?
BY EMPTYING THE MIND OF IMPURITIES.
THIS CAN BE DONE IN THREE WAYS:
KARMA YOGA IS THE PATH OF SELFLESS ACTING.
BHAKTI YOGA IS THE PATH OF UNCONDITIONAL DEVOTION.
JNANA YOGA IS THE PATH OF KNOWLEDGE AND INSIGHT.
THE BATTLE IS SET ON THE PLAINS OF KURUKSHETRA - BUT YOU CAN ALSO SEE IT AS AN INNER BATTLE!
AGAINST HABITS AND VIEWS THAT ARE SO FAMILIAR TO US THEY FEEL LIKE FAMILY!
DHARMA IS THE ETERNAL NATURAL LAW, BUT ON A PERSONAL LEVEL IT CAN BE SEEN AS ONE'S DUTY TO ONE'S OWN NATURE.
ARJUNA'S DHARMA IS THAT OF A WARRIOR.
HE MUST DO BATTLE, OR HE WOULD BE GOING AGAINST HIS NATURE.
MY DHARMA IS THAT OF A COMIC ARTIST!
WHAT'S YOURS?

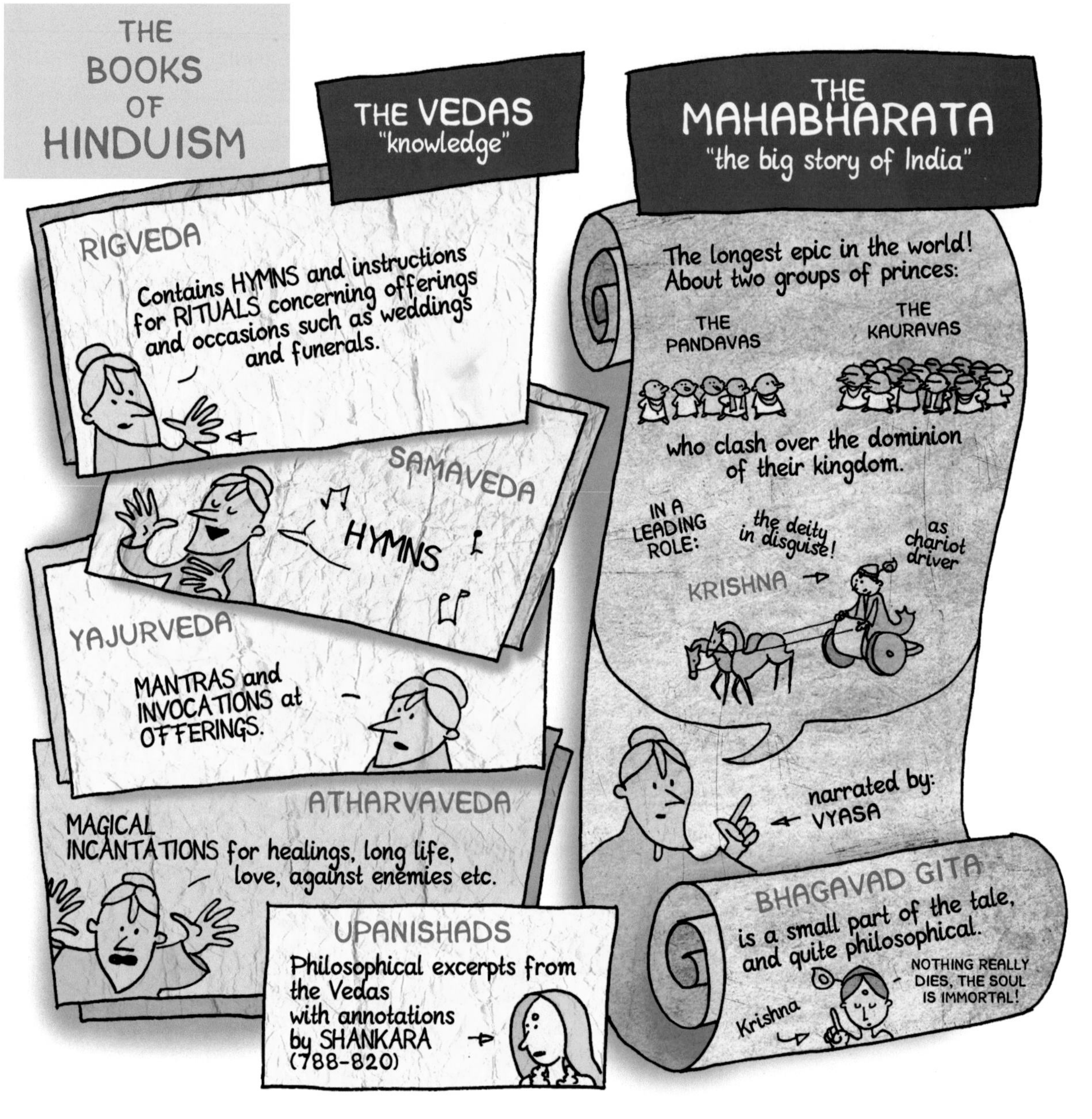
THE BOOKS OF HINDUISM
THE VEDAS "knowledge"
RIGVEDA
Contains HYMNS and instructions for RITUALS concerning offerings and occasions such as weddings and funerals.
SAMAVEDA
HYMNS
YAJURVEDA
MANTRAS and INVOCATIONS at OFFERINGS.
ATHARVAVEDA
MAGICAL INCANTATIONS for healings, long life, love, against enemies etc.
UPANISHADS
Philosophical excerpts from the Vedas with annotations by SHANKARA (788-820)
THE MAHABHARATA "the big story of India"
The longest epic in the world! About two groups of princes:
THE PANDAVAS
THE KAURAVAS
who clash over the dominion of their kingdom.
IN A LEADING ROLE:
the deity in disguise!
as chariot driver
KRISHNA
narrated by: VYASA
BHAGAVAD GITA
is a small part of the tale, and quite philosophical.
Krishna
NOTHING REALLY DIES, THE SOUL IS IMMORTAL!

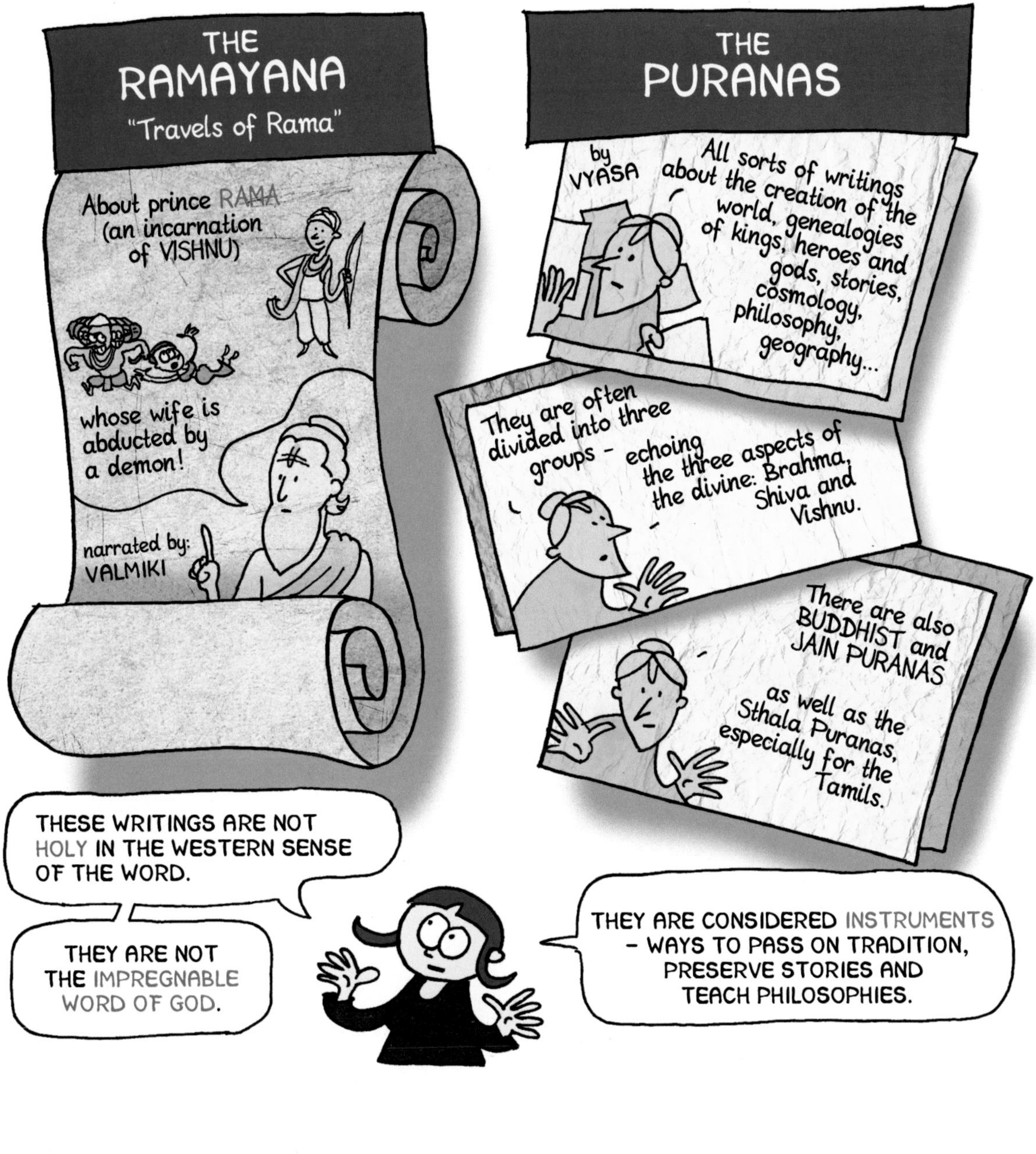

THE RAMAYANA
"Travels of Rama"
About prince RAMA (an incarnation of VISHNU)
whose wife is abducted by a demon!
narrated by: VALMIKI
THE PURANAS
by VYASA
All sorts of writings about the creation of the world, genealogies of kings, heroes and gods, stories, cosmology, philosophy, geography...
They are often divided into three groups - echoing the three aspects of the divine: Brahma, Shiva and Vishnu.
There are also BUDDHIST and JAIN PURANAS
as well as the Sthala Puranas, especially for the Tamils.
THESE WRITINGS ARE NOT HOLY IN THE WESTERN SENSE OF THE WORD.
THEY ARE NOT THE IMPREGNABLE WORD OF GOD.
THEY ARE CONSIDERED INSTRUMENTS - WAYS TO PASS ON TRADITION, PRESERVE STORIES AND TEACH PHILOSOPHIES.

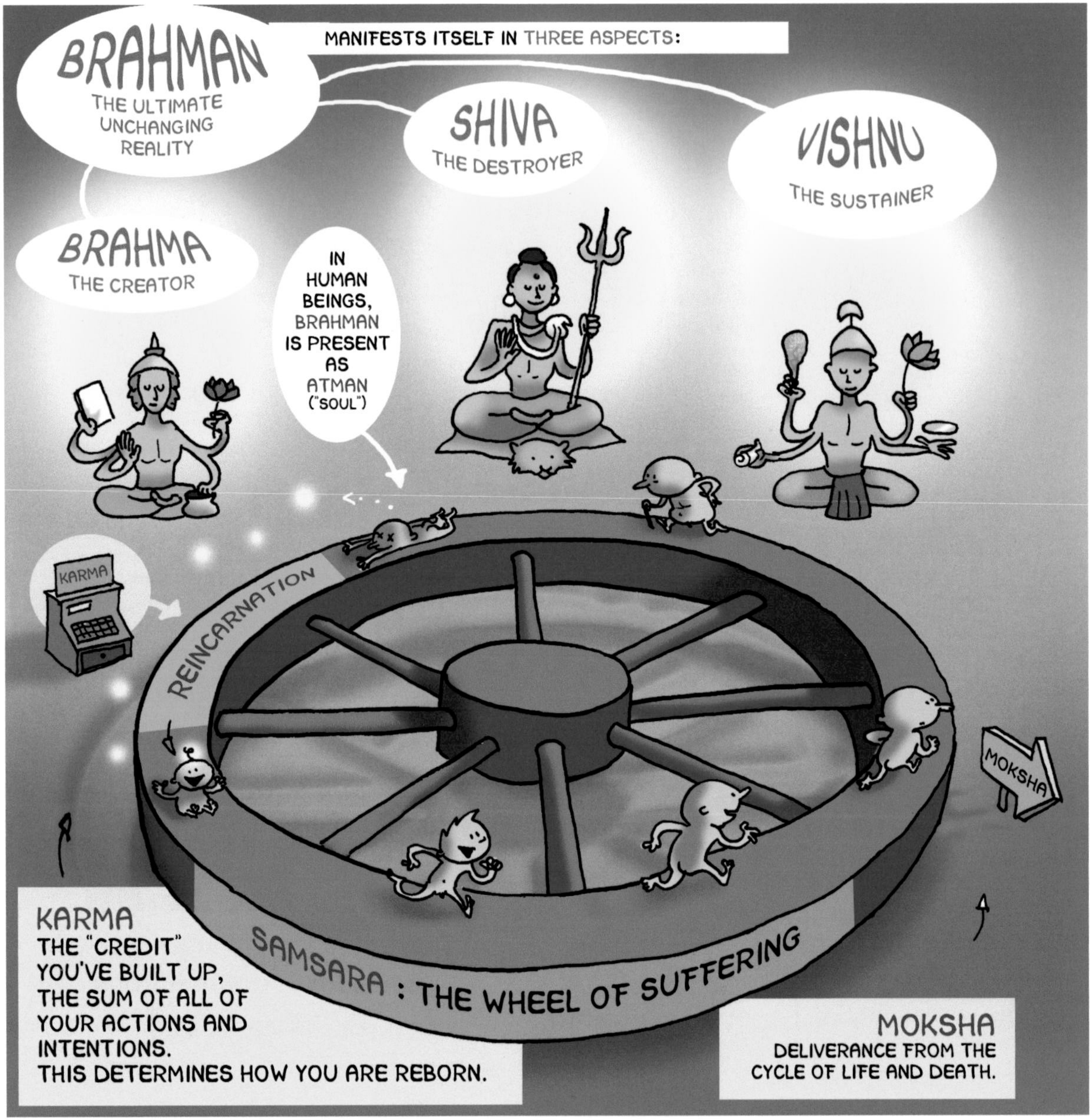
BRAHMAN
THE ULTIMATE UNCHANGING REALITY
MANIFESTS ITSELF IN THREE ASPECTS:
SHIVA
THE DESTROYER
VISHNU
THE SUSTAINER
BRAHMA
THE CREATOR
IN HUMAN BEINGS, BRAHMAN IS PRESENT AS ATMAN ("SOUL")
KARMA
REINCARNATION
MOKSHA
SAMSARA : THE WHEEL OF SUFFERING
KARMA
THE "CREDIT" YOU'VE BUILT UP, THE SUM OF ALL OF YOUR ACTIONS AND INTENTIONS.
THIS DETERMINES HOW YOU ARE REBORN.
MOKSHA
DELIVERANCE FROM THE CYCLE OF LIFE AND DEATH.

THIS IS MORE OR LESS THE HINDU VIEW OF THE WORLD!

WELL...

... IT'S ALL A BIT MORE SUBTLE THAN THAT, REALLY!

THE PROBLEM IS THAT YOU WESTERNERS HAVE A WAY DIFFERENT FRAME OF THOUGHT THAN WE DO!

TAKE SHIVA FOR INSTANCE.

THE GOD OF CHANGE THROUGH DESTRUCTION.

THAT DOES NOT MERELY MEAN DEATH

– THE WAY YOU DEPICTED HIM –

BUT ALSO

DISCARDING OLD HABITS, DETACHMENT, SHEDDING YOUR OLD LIFE, GETTING LIBERATED, LEAVING THE OLD BEHIND!

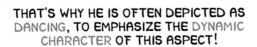

THAT'S WHY HE IS OFTEN DEPICTED AS DANCING, TO EMPHASIZE THE DYNAMIC CHARACTER OF THIS ASPECT!

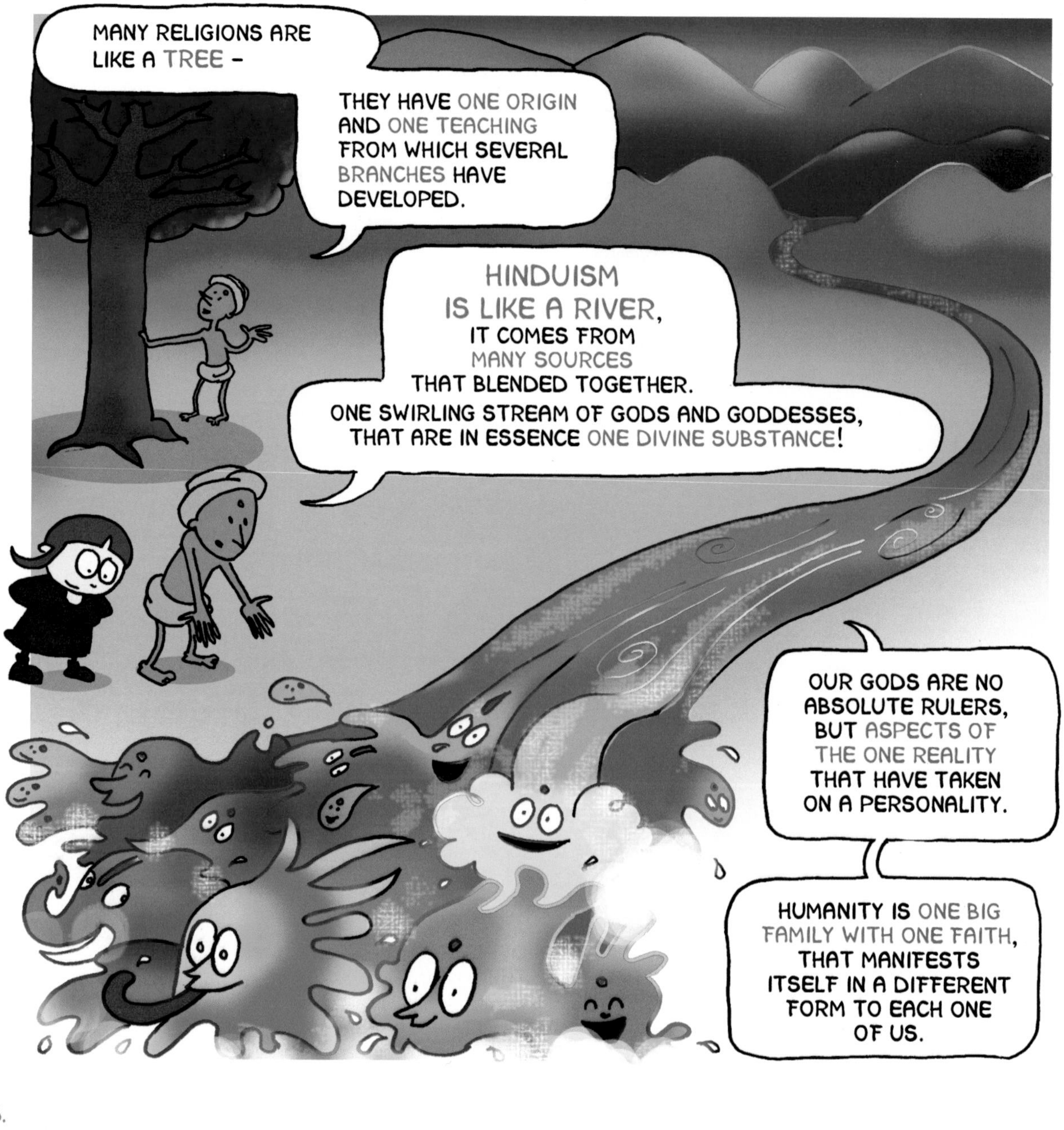
MANY RELIGIONS ARE LIKE A TREE –
THEY HAVE ONE ORIGIN AND ONE TEACHING FROM WHICH SEVERAL BRANCHES HAVE DEVELOPED.
HINDUISM IS LIKE A RIVER, IT COMES FROM MANY SOURCES THAT BLENDED TOGETHER. ONE SWIRLING STREAM OF GODS AND GODDESSES, THAT ARE IN ESSENCE ONE DIVINE SUBSTANCE!
OUR GODS ARE NO ABSOLUTE RULERS, BUT ASPECTS OF THE ONE REALITY THAT HAVE TAKEN ON A PERSONALITY.
HUMANITY IS ONE BIG FAMILY WITH ONE FAITH, THAT MANIFESTS ITSELF IN A DIFFERENT FORM TO EACH ONE OF US.

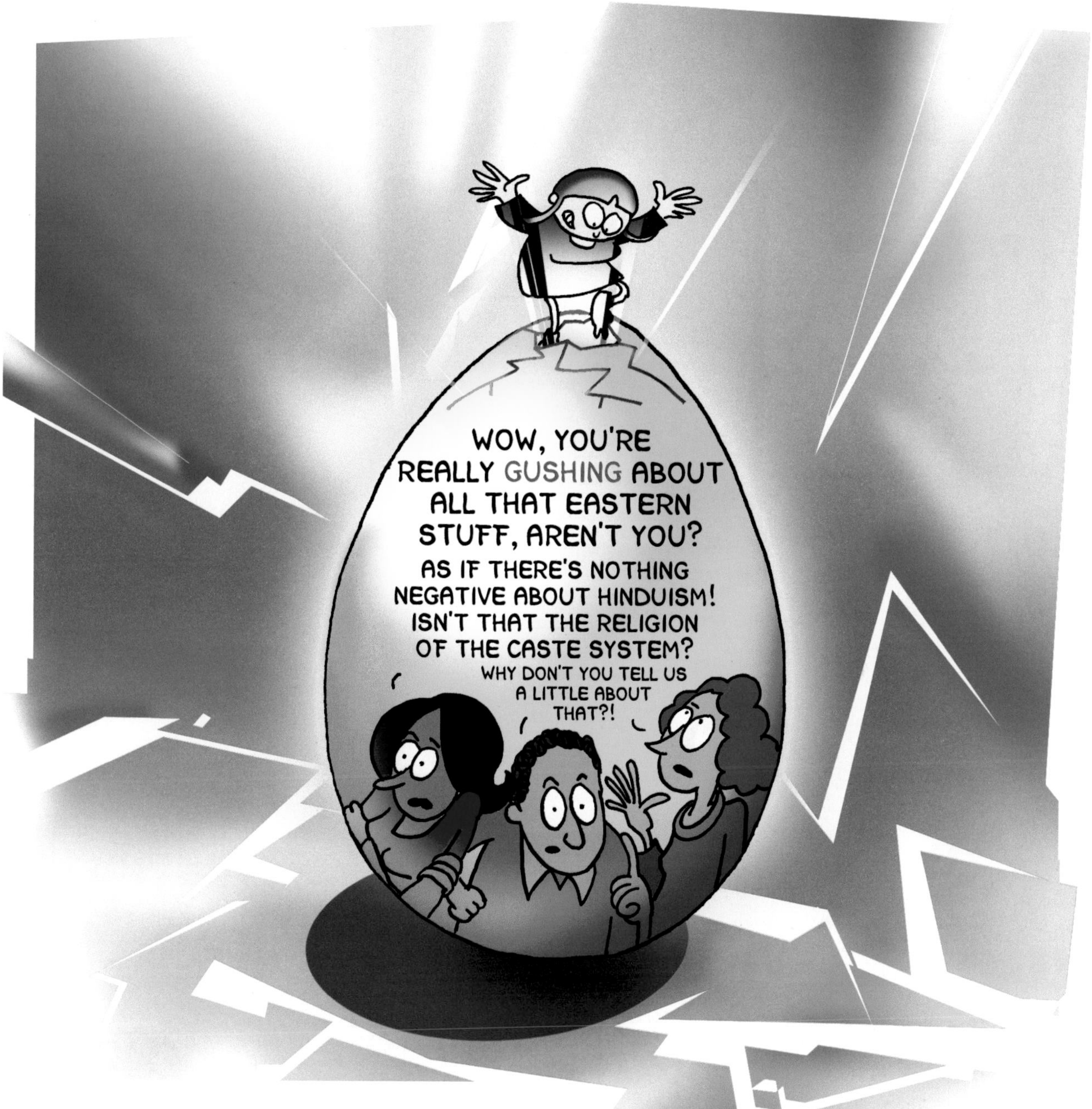
WOW, YOU'RE REALLY GUSHING ABOUT ALL THAT EASTERN STUFF, AREN'T YOU?
AS IF THERE'S NOTHING NEGATIVE ABOUT HINDUISM! ISN'T THAT THE RELIGION OF THE CASTE SYSTEM?
WHY DON'T YOU TELL US A LITTLE ABOUT THAT?!

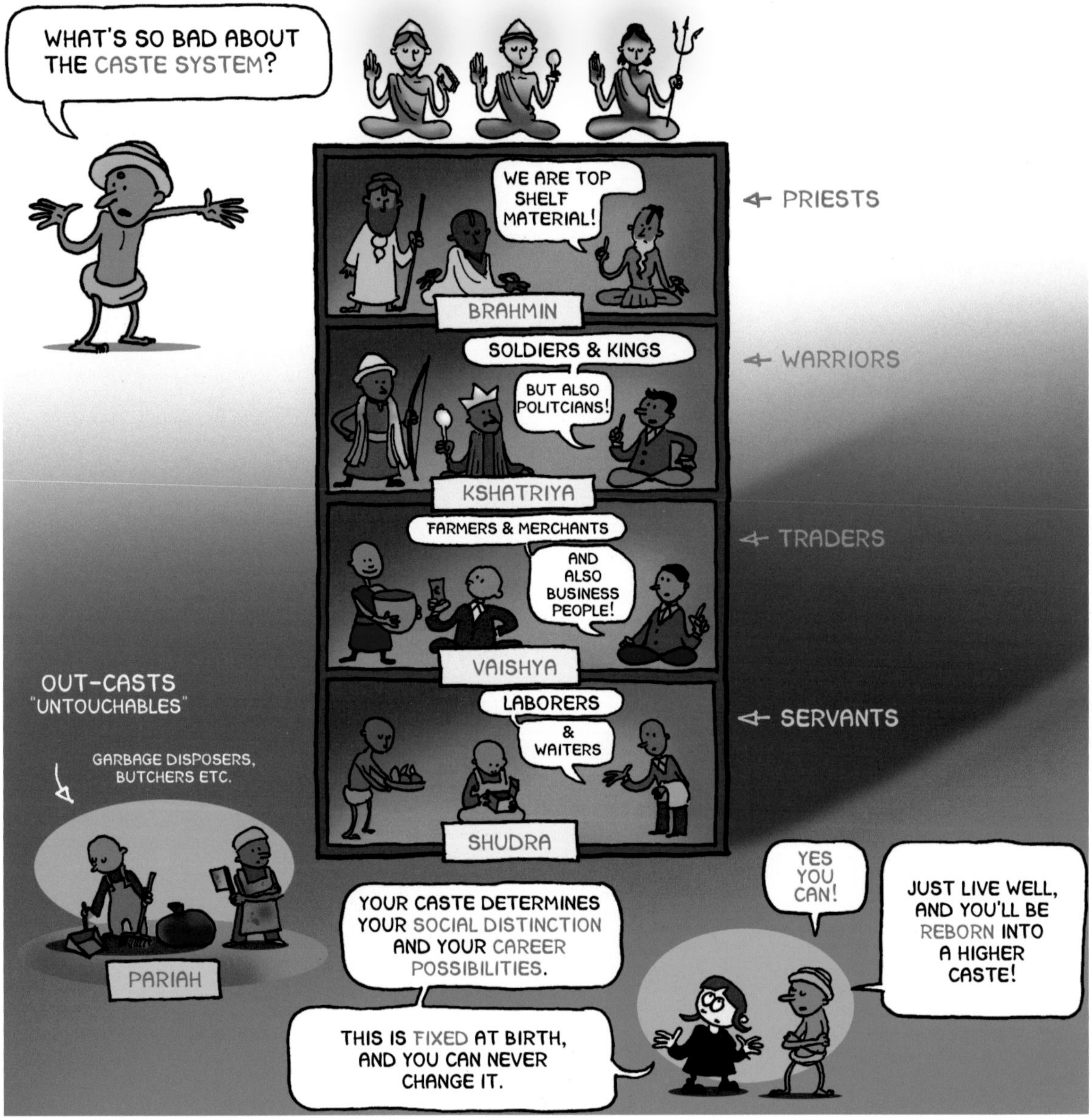
WHAT'S SO BAD ABOUT THE CASTE SYSTEM?
WE ARE TOP SHELF MATERIAL!
BRAHMIN
PRIESTS
SOLDIERS & KINGS
BUT ALSO POLITCIANS!
KSHATRIYA
WARRIORS
FARMERS & MERCHANTS
AND ALSO BUSINESS PEOPLE!
VAISHYA
TRADERS
LABORERS
& WAITERS
SHUDRA
SERVANTS
OUT-CASTS
"UNTOUCHABLES"
GARBAGE DISPOSERS, BUTCHERS ETC.
PARIAH
YOUR CASTE DETERMINES YOUR SOCIAL DISTINCTION AND YOUR CAREER POSSIBILITIES.
THIS IS FIXED AT BIRTH, AND YOU CAN NEVER CHANGE IT.
YES YOU CAN!
JUST LIVE WELL, AND YOU'LL BE REBORN INTO A HIGHER CASTE!

BUDDHISM

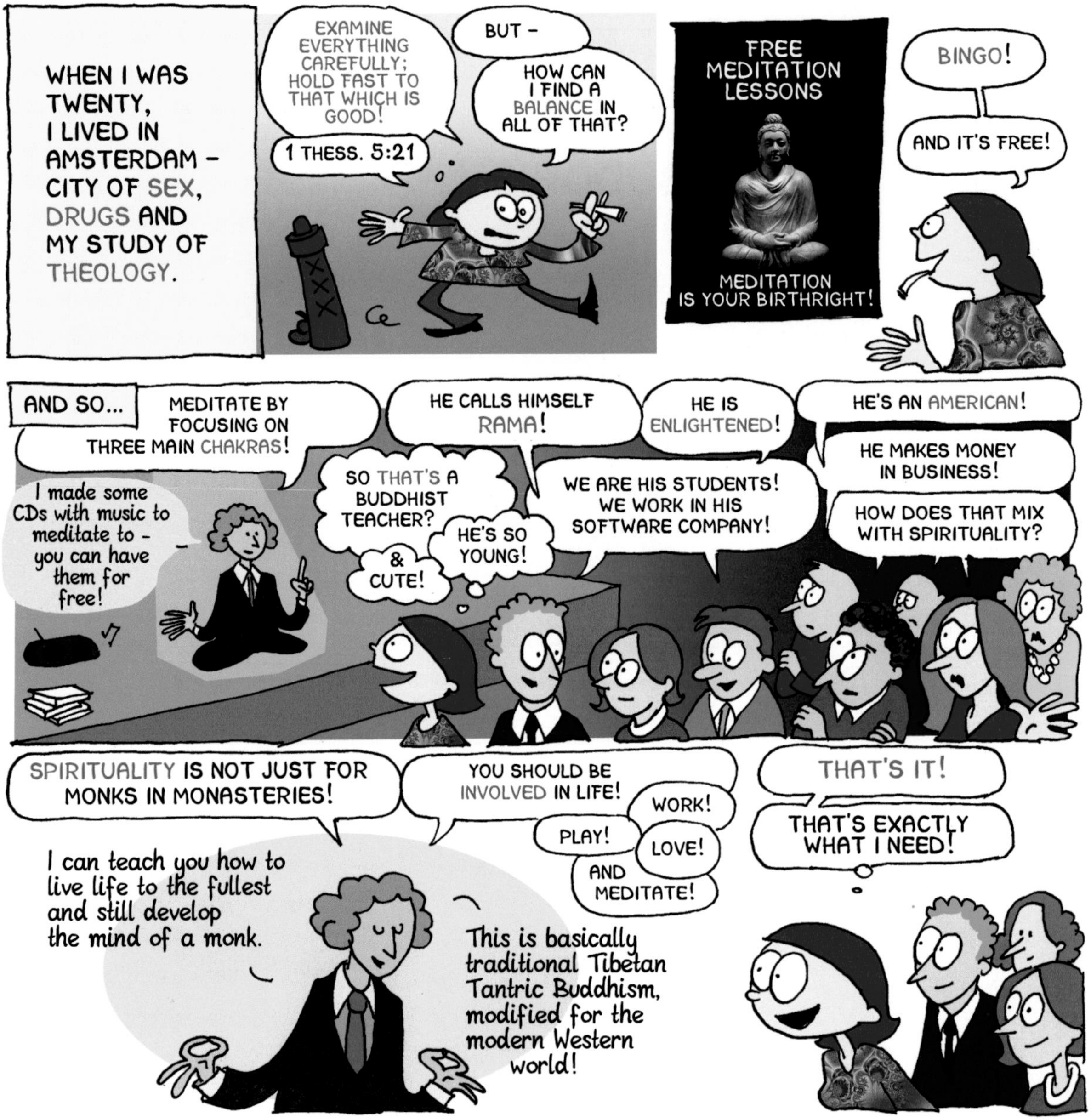
WHEN I WAS TWENTY, I LIVED IN AMSTERDAM – CITY OF SEX, DRUGS AND MY STUDY OF THEOLOGY.
EXAMINE EVERYTHING CAREFULLY; HOLD FAST TO THAT WHICH IS GOOD!
1 THESS. 5:21
BUT –
HOW CAN I FIND A BALANCE IN ALL OF THAT?
FREE MEDITATION LESSONS
MEDITATION IS YOUR BIRTHRIGHT!
BINGO!
AND IT'S FREE!
AND SO...
MEDITATE BY FOCUSING ON THREE MAIN CHAKRAS!
I made some CDs with music to meditate to – you can have them for free!
HE CALLS HIMSELF RAMA!
SO THAT'S A BUDDHIST TEACHER?
HE'S SO YOUNG!
& CUTE!
HE IS ENLIGHTENED!
WE ARE HIS STUDENTS! WE WORK IN HIS SOFTWARE COMPANY!
HE'S AN AMERICAN!
HE MAKES MONEY IN BUSINESS!
HOW DOES THAT MIX WITH SPIRITUALITY?
SPIRITUALITY IS NOT JUST FOR MONKS IN MONASTERIES!
YOU SHOULD BE INVOLVED IN LIFE!
WORK!
PLAY!
LOVE!
AND MEDITATE!
I can teach you how to live life to the fullest and still develop the mind of a monk.
This is basically traditional Tibetan Tantric Buddhism, modified for the modern Western world!
THAT'S IT!
THAT'S EXACTLY WHAT I NEED!

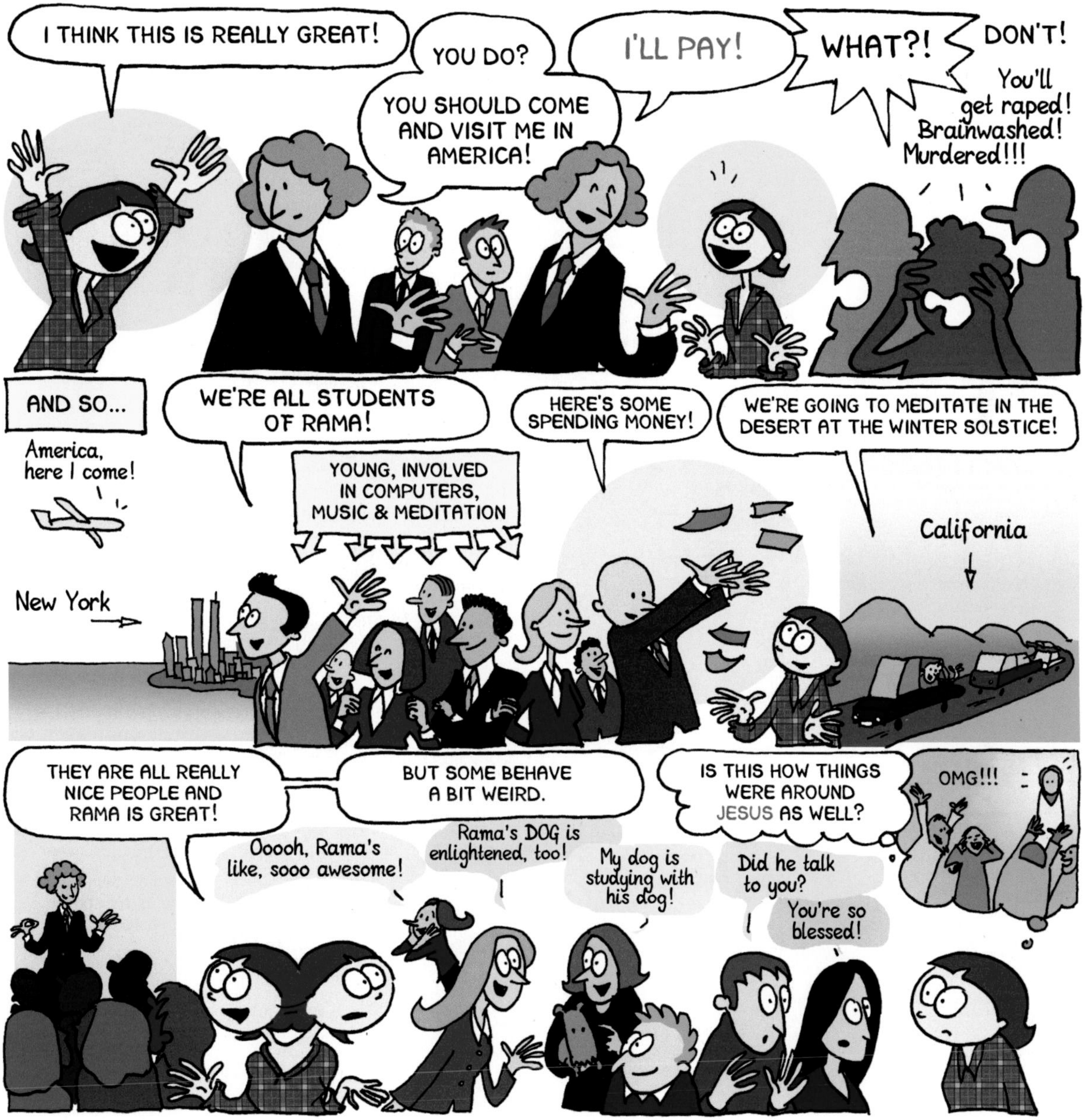
I THINK THIS IS REALLY GREAT!
YOU DO?
YOU SHOULD COME AND VISIT ME IN AMERICA!
I'LL PAY!
WHAT?!
DON'T!
You'll get raped! Brainwashed! Murdered!!!
AND SO...
America, here I come!
WE'RE ALL STUDENTS OF RAMA!
YOUNG, INVOLVED IN COMPUTERS, MUSIC & MEDITATION
HERE'S SOME SPENDING MONEY!
WE'RE GOING TO MEDITATE IN THE DESERT AT THE WINTER SOLSTICE!
New York
California
THEY ARE ALL REALLY NICE PEOPLE AND RAMA IS GREAT!
BUT SOME BEHAVE A BIT WEIRD.
IS THIS HOW THINGS WERE AROUND JESUS AS WELL?
OMG!!!
Ooooh, Rama's like, sooo awesome!
Rama's DOG is enlightened, too!
My dog is studying with his dog!
Did he talk to you?
You're so blessed!

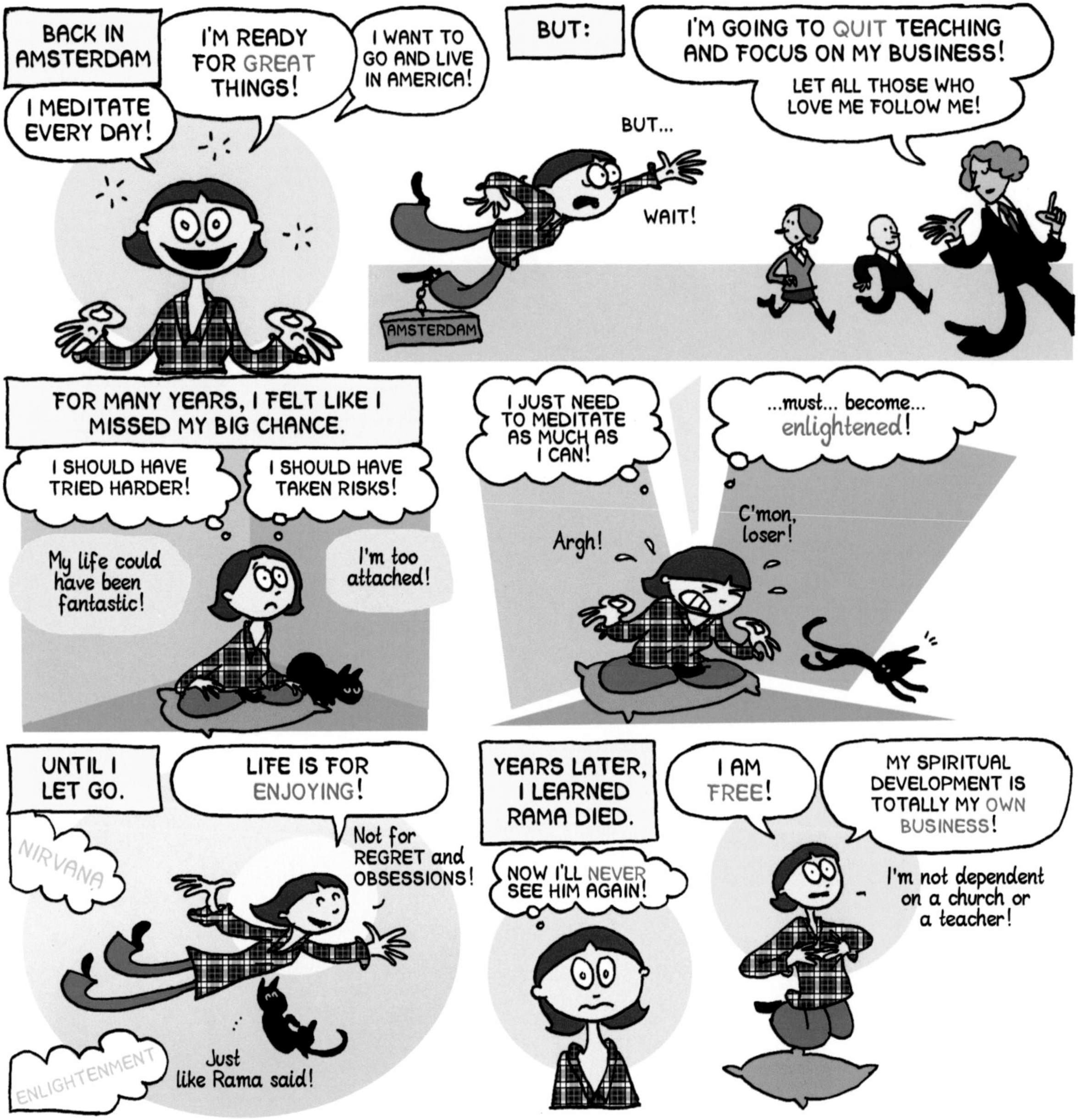
BACK IN AMSTERDAM
I MEDITATE EVERY DAY!
I'M READY FOR GREAT THINGS!
I WANT TO GO AND LIVE IN AMERICA!
BUT:
I'M GOING TO QUIT TEACHING AND FOCUS ON MY BUSINESS!
LET ALL THOSE WHO LOVE ME FOLLOW ME!
BUT...
WAIT!
AMSTERDAM
FOR MANY YEARS, I FELT LIKE I MISSED MY BIG CHANCE.
I SHOULD HAVE TRIED HARDER!
I SHOULD HAVE TAKEN RISKS!
My life could have been fantastic!
I'm too attached!
I JUST NEED TO MEDITATE AS MUCH AS I CAN!
...must... become... enlightened!
Argh!
C'mon, loser!
UNTIL I LET GO.
LIFE IS FOR ENJOYING!
Not for REGRET and OBSESSIONS!
NIRVANA
ENLIGHTENMENT
Just like Rama said!
YEARS LATER, I LEARNED RAMA DIED.
NOW I'LL NEVER SEE HIM AGAIN!
I AM FREE!
MY SPIRITUAL DEVELOPMENT IS TOTALLY MY OWN BUSINESS!
I'm not dependent on a church or a teacher!

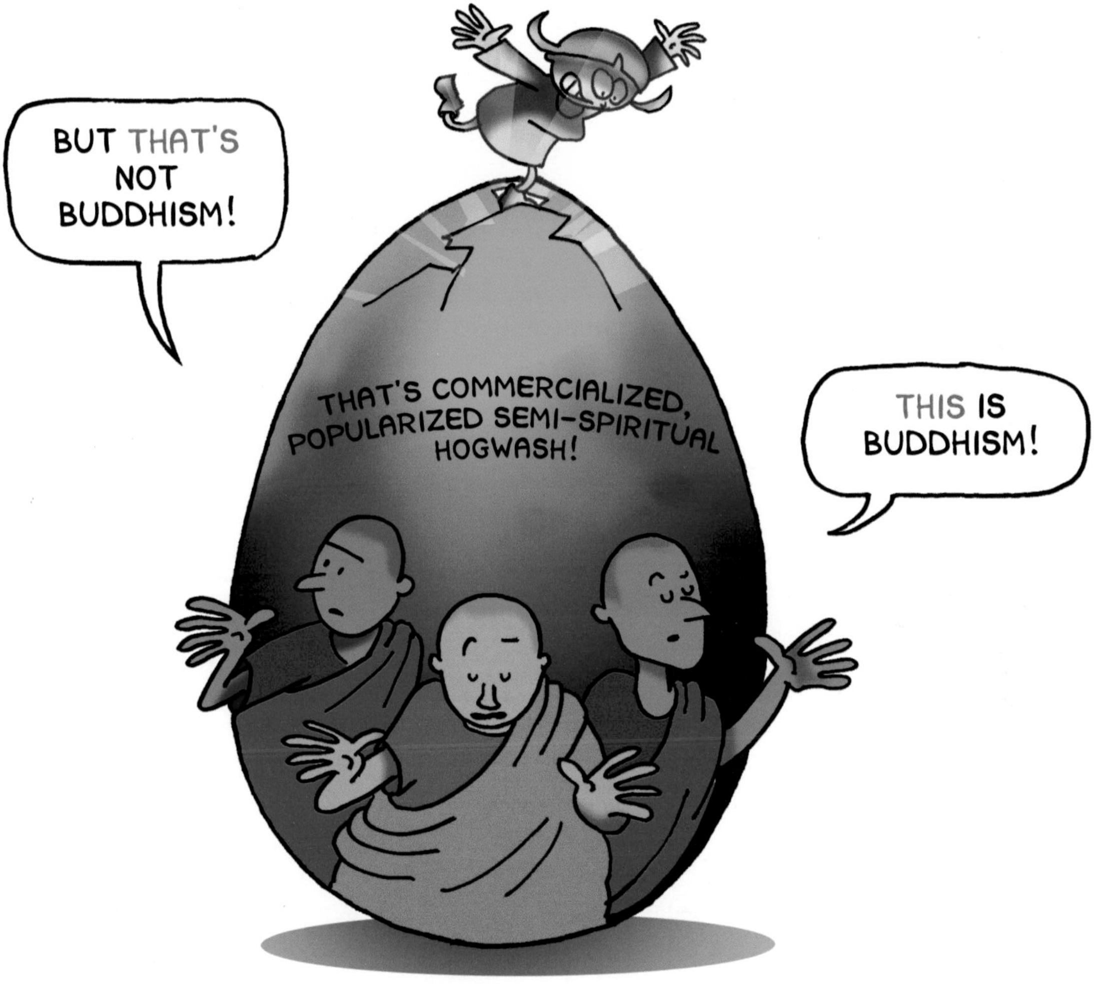
BUT THAT'S NOT BUDDHISM!
THAT'S COMMERCIALIZED, POPULARIZED SEMI-SPIRITUAL HOGWASH!
THIS IS BUDDHISM!

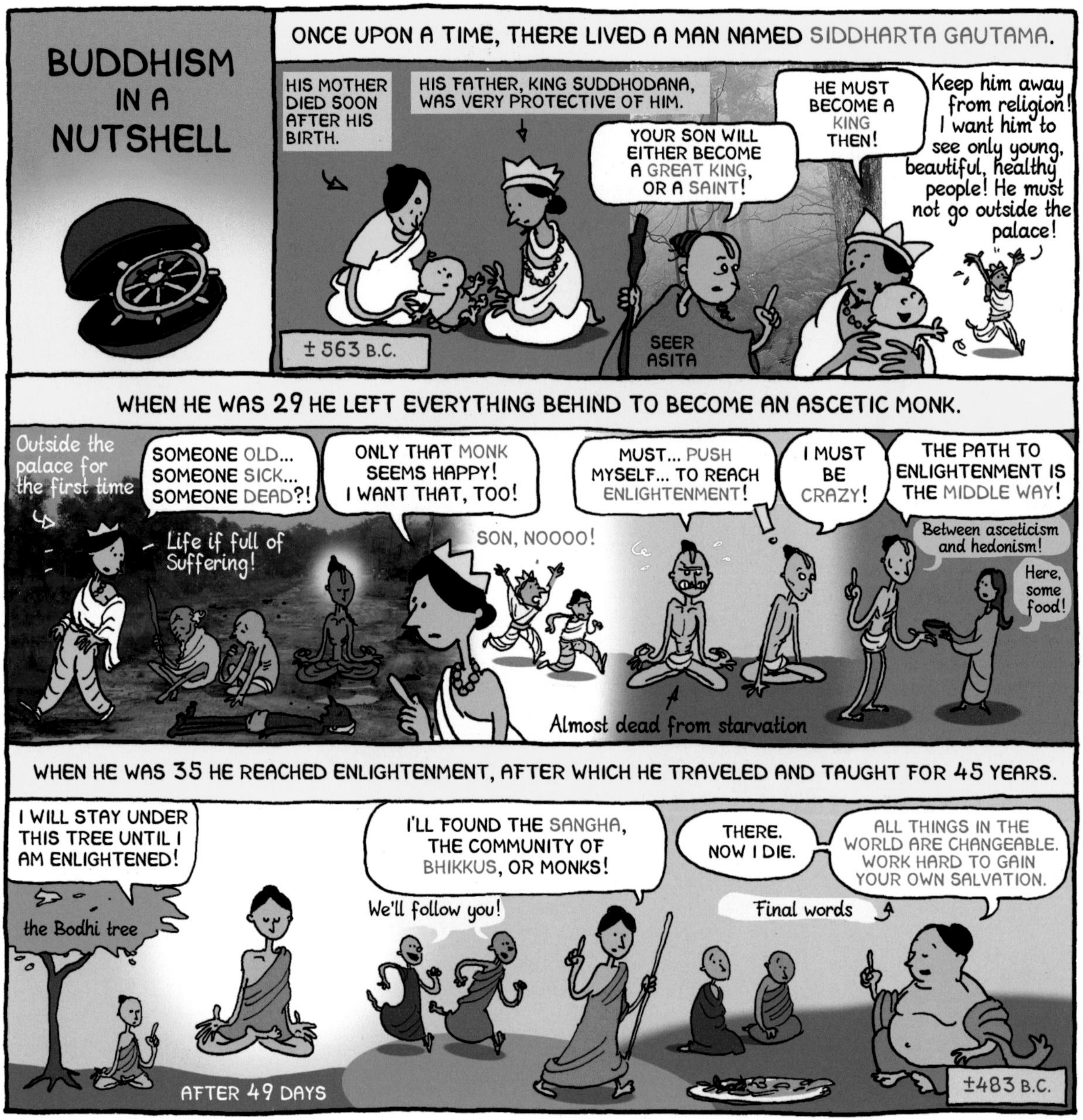
BUDDHISM IN A NUTSHELL
ONCE UPON A TIME, THERE LIVED A MAN NAMED SIDDHARTA GAUTAMA.
HIS MOTHER DIED SOON AFTER HIS BIRTH.
HIS FATHER, KING SUDDHODANA, WAS VERY PROTECTIVE OF HIM.
±563 B.C.
YOUR SON WILL EITHER BECOME A GREAT KING, OR A SAINT!
SEER ASITA
HE MUST BECOME A KING THEN!
Keep him away from religion! I want him to see only young, beautiful, healthy people! He must not go outside the palace!
WHEN HE WAS 29 HE LEFT EVERYTHING BEHIND TO BECOME AN ASCETIC MONK.
Outside the palace for the first time
SOMEONE OLD... SOMEONE SICK... SOMEONE DEAD?!
Life if full of Suffering!
ONLY THAT MONK SEEMS HAPPY! I WANT THAT, TOO!
SON, NOOOO!
MUST... PUSH MYSELF... TO REACH ENLIGHTENMENT!
Almost dead from starvation
I MUST BE CRAZY!
THE PATH TO ENLIGHTENMENT IS THE MIDDLE WAY!
Between asceticism and hedonism!
Here, some food!
WHEN HE WAS 35 HE REACHED ENLIGHTENMENT, AFTER WHICH HE TRAVELED AND TAUGHT FOR 45 YEARS.
I WILL STAY UNDER THIS TREE UNTIL I AM ENLIGHTENED!
the Bodhi tree
AFTER 49 DAYS
I'LL FOUND THE SANGHA, THE COMMUNITY OF BHIKKUS, OR MONKS!
We'll follow you!
THERE. NOW I DIE.
ALL THINGS IN THE WORLD ARE CHANGEABLE. WORK HARD TO GAIN YOUR OWN SALVATION.
Final words
±483 B.C.

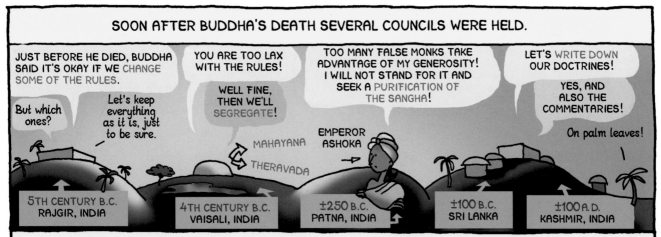

SOON AFTER BUDDHA'S DEATH SEVERAL COUNCILS WERE HELD.

JUST BEFORE HE DIED, BUDDHA SAID IT'S OKAY IF WE CHANGE SOME OF THE RULES.

But which ones?

Let's keep everything as it is, just to be sure.

YOU ARE TOO LAX WITH THE RULES!

WELL FINE, THEN WE'LL SEGREGATE!

TOO MANY FALSE MONKS TAKE ADVANTAGE OF MY GENEROSITY! I WILL NOT STAND FOR IT AND SEEK A PURIFICATION OF THE SANGHA!

LET'S WRITE DOWN OUR DOCTRINES!

YES, AND ALSO THE COMMENTARIES!

On palm leaves!

MAHAYANA
THERAVADA

EMPEROR ASHOKA

5TH CENTURY B.C. RAJGIR, INDIA

4TH CENTURY B.C. VAISALI, INDIA

±250 B.C. PATNA, INDIA

±100 B.C. SRI LANKA

±100 A.D. KASHMIR, INDIA

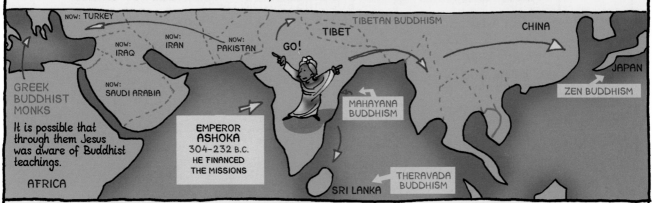

THANKS TO MISSIONARY WORK, BUDDHISM STARTED TO SPREAD RAPIDLY.

NOW: TURKEY

NOW: IRAQ

NOW: IRAN

NOW: PAKISTAN

NOW: SAUDI ARABIA

GREEK BUDDHIST MONKS

It is possible that through them Jesus was aware of Buddhist teachings.

AFRICA

EMPEROR ASHOKA 304-232 B.C. HE FINANCED THE MISSIONS

GO!

TIBET

TIBETAN BUDDHISM

CHINA

JAPAN

ZEN BUDDHISM

MAHAYANA BUDDHISM

THERAVADA BUDDHISM

SRI LANKA

FROM THE 19TH CENTURY ON, BUDDHISM STARTED TO GAIN THE INTEREST OF THE WEST.

MY WORK HAS MANY SIMILARITIES WITH BUDDHISM, ESPECIALLY MY BOOK 'THE WORLD AS WILL AND REPRESENTATION'.

BUDDHISM IS A HUNDRED TIMES MORE REALISTIC THAN CHRISTIANITY!

IN 1927 THE FIRST ENGLISH TRANSLATION APPEARED OF:

I TRAVELED TO SRI LANKA AND INDONESIA AND WROTE A NUMBER OF BOOKS THAT WERE INFLUENCED BY BUDDHISM!

THE TIBETAN BOOK OF THE DEAD

FOREWORD BY C.G. JUNG

1922

SIDDHARTA

H. HESSE

SCHOPENHAUER
German philosopher
1788 - 1860

NIETZSCHE
German philosopher
1844- 1900

HERMANN HESSE
German writer
1877 - 1962

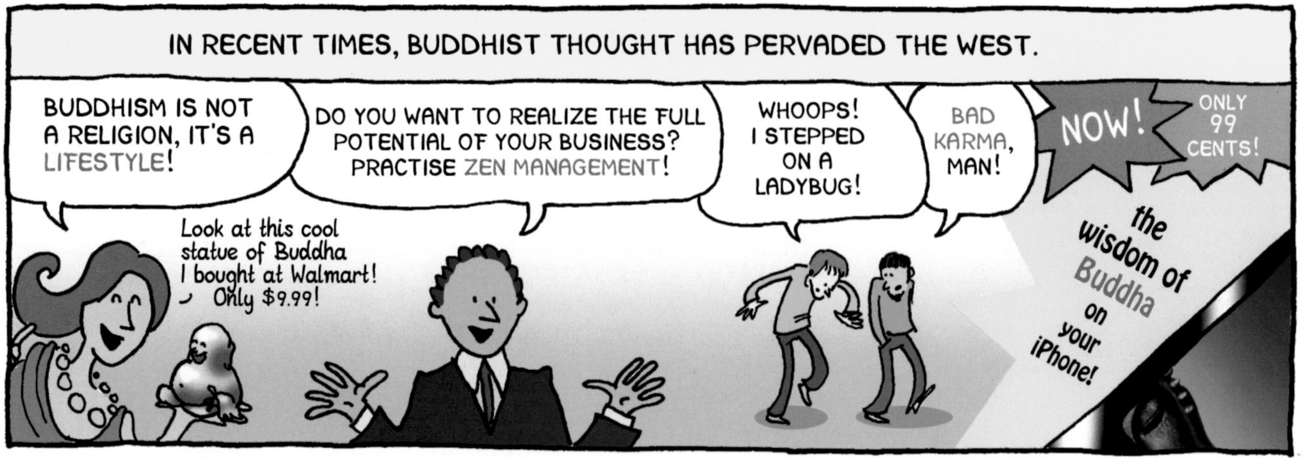
IN RECENT TIMES, BUDDHIST THOUGHT HAS PERVADED THE WEST.
BUDDHISM IS NOT A RELIGION, IT'S A LIFESTYLE!
Look at this cool statue of Buddha I bought at Walmart! Only $9.99!
DO YOU WANT TO REALIZE THE FULL POTENTIAL OF YOUR BUSINESS? PRACTISE ZEN MANAGEMENT!
WHOOPS! I STEPPED ON A LADYBUG!
BAD KARMA, MAN!
NOW!
ONLY 99 CENTS!
the wisdom of Buddha on your iPhone!

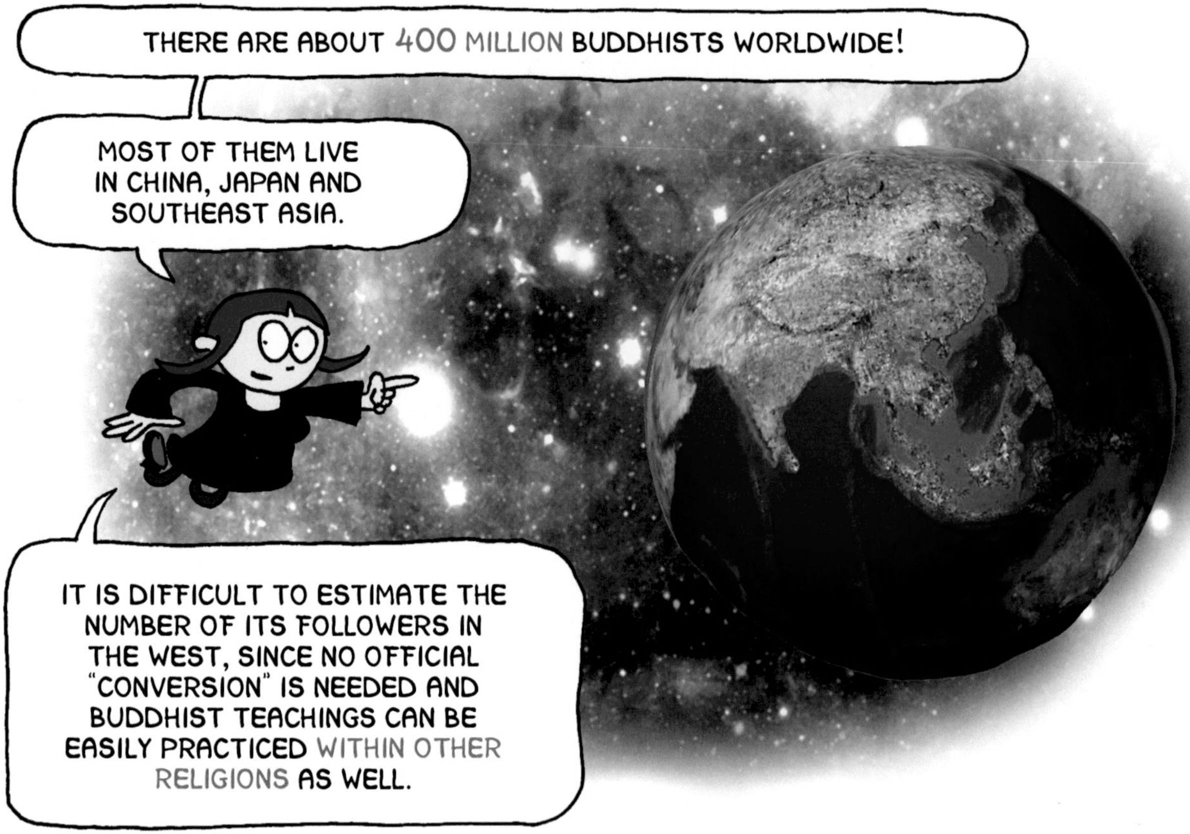
THERE ARE ABOUT 400 MILLION BUDDHISTS WORLDWIDE!
MOST OF THEM LIVE IN CHINA, JAPAN AND SOUTHEAST ASIA.
IT IS DIFFICULT TO ESTIMATE THE NUMBER OF ITS FOLLOWERS IN THE WEST, SINCE NO OFFICIAL "CONVERSION" IS NEEDED AND BUDDHIST TEACHINGS CAN BE EASILY PRACTICED WITHIN OTHER RELIGIONS AS WELL.

THE SYMBOL OF BUDDHISM

THE SYMBOL OF BUDDHISM IS THE DHARMACHAKRA, THE WHEEL OF LAW.

THE CIRCLE SYMBOLIZES THE PERFECTION OF THE DHARMA TEACHINGS.

THE CENTER SYMBOLIZES DISCIPLINE, THE CORE OF MEDITATION!

GANKYIL = "WHEEL OF JOY"

IT STANDS FOR THE INDIVISIBLE, INTERDEPENDENT TRINITY OF BUDDHA, DHARMA (teaching) AND SANGHA (community).

THE EIGHT SPOKES STAND FOR THE EIGHTFOLD PATH!

ENLIGHTENMENT CAN BE ATTAINED BY:

① RIGHT VIEW
of the Four Noble Truths – see page 91

② RIGHT INTENTION
Be non-violent, kind and unselfish

③ RIGHT SPEECH
Abstain from lies, slander & idle chatter

④ RIGHT ACTION
Abstain from killing, stealing & sexual misconduct

⑤ RIGHT LIVELIHOOD
No trading in weapons, slaves, meat, poison or drugs, no prostitution

⑥ RIGHT EFFORT
Avoid bad or unwholesome thoughts; cultivate good and wholesome things

⑦ RIGHT MINDFULNESS
Being conscious of body, mind, emotions and phenomena

⑧ RIGHT CONCENTRATION
Meditate

THE CORE OF BUDDHISM

I THINK THE CORE IS MEDITATION!

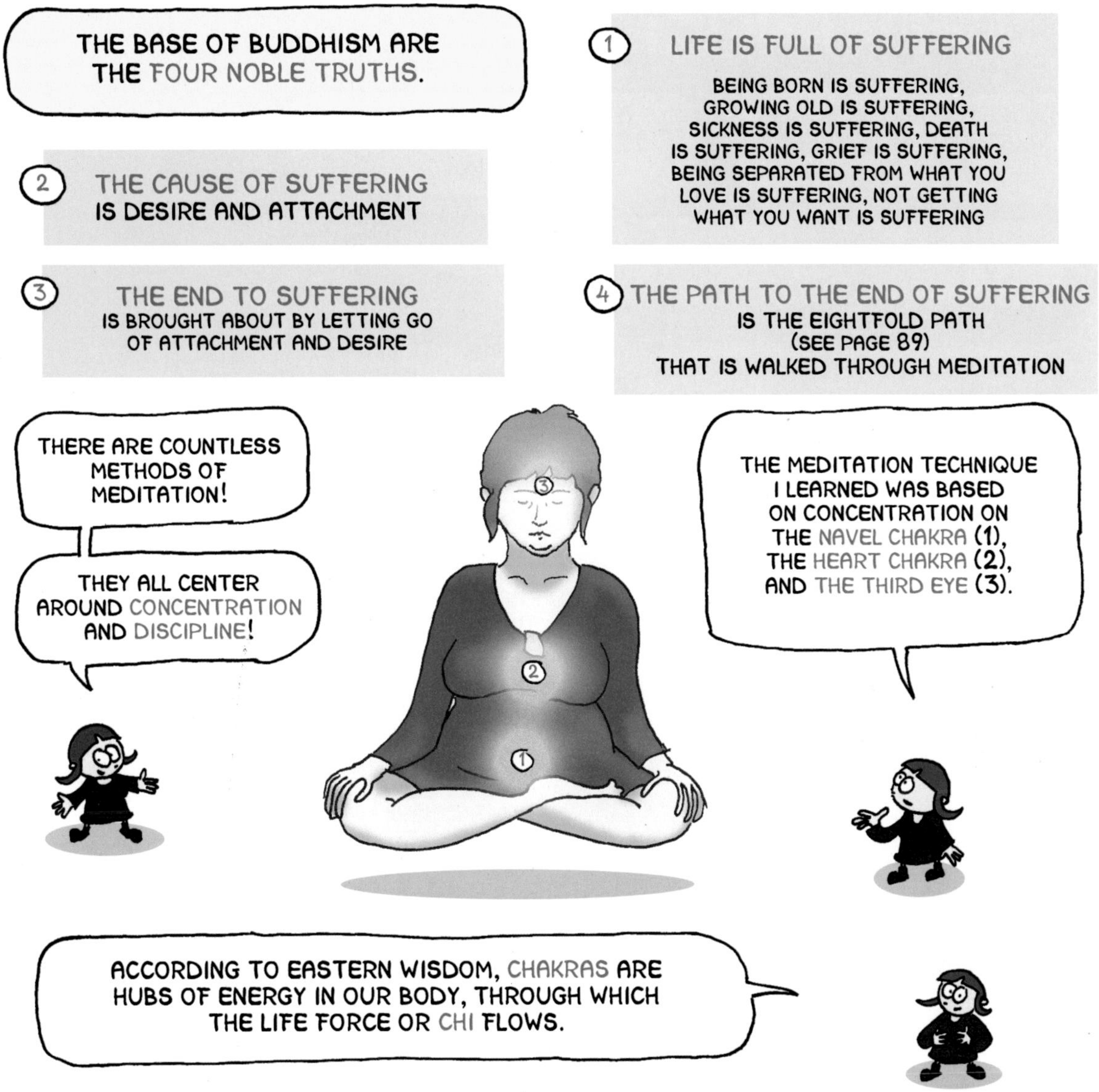
THE BASE OF BUDDHISM ARE THE FOUR NOBLE TRUTHS.
1 LIFE IS FULL OF SUFFERING
BEING BORN IS SUFFERING, GROWING OLD IS SUFFERING, SICKNESS IS SUFFERING, DEATH IS SUFFERING, GRIEF IS SUFFERING, BEING SEPARATED FROM WHAT YOU LOVE IS SUFFERING, NOT GETTING WHAT YOU WANT IS SUFFERING
2 THE CAUSE OF SUFFERING IS DESIRE AND ATTACHMENT
3 THE END TO SUFFERING IS BROUGHT ABOUT BY LETTING GO OF ATTACHMENT AND DESIRE
4 THE PATH TO THE END OF SUFFERING IS THE EIGHTFOLD PATH (SEE PAGE 89) THAT IS WALKED THROUGH MEDITATION
THERE ARE COUNTLESS METHODS OF MEDITATION!
THEY ALL CENTER AROUND CONCENTRATION AND DISCIPLINE!
THE MEDITATION TECHNIQUE I LEARNED WAS BASED ON CONCENTRATION ON THE NAVEL CHAKRA (1), THE HEART CHAKRA (2), AND THE THIRD EYE (3).
3
2
1
ACCORDING TO EASTERN WISDOM, CHAKRAS ARE HUBS OF ENERGY IN OUR BODY, THROUGH WHICH THE LIFE FORCE OR CHI FLOWS.

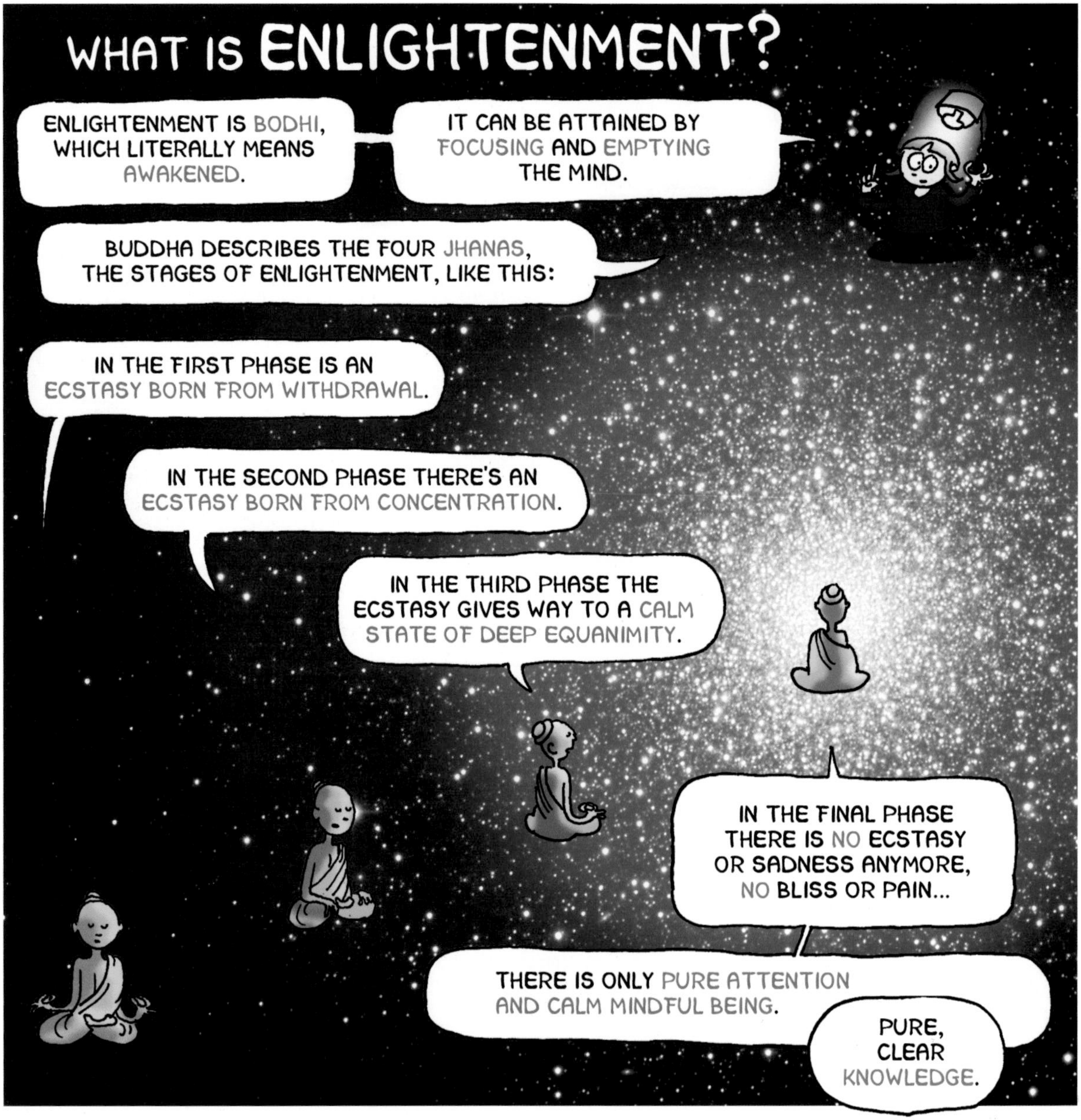
WHAT IS ENLIGHTENMENT?
ENLIGHTENMENT IS BODHI, WHICH LITERALLY MEANS AWAKENED.
IT CAN BE ATTAINED BY FOCUSING AND EMPTYING THE MIND.
BUDDHA DESCRIBES THE FOUR JHANAS, THE STAGES OF ENLIGHTENMENT, LIKE THIS:
IN THE FIRST PHASE IS AN ECSTASY BORN FROM WITHDRAWAL.
IN THE SECOND PHASE THERE'S AN ECSTASY BORN FROM CONCENTRATION.
IN THE THIRD PHASE THE ECSTASY GIVES WAY TO A CALM STATE OF DEEP EQUANIMITY.
IN THE FINAL PHASE THERE IS NO ECSTASY OR SADNESS ANYMORE, NO BLISS OR PAIN...
THERE IS ONLY PURE ATTENTION AND CALM MINDFUL BEING.
PURE, CLEAR KNOWLEDGE.

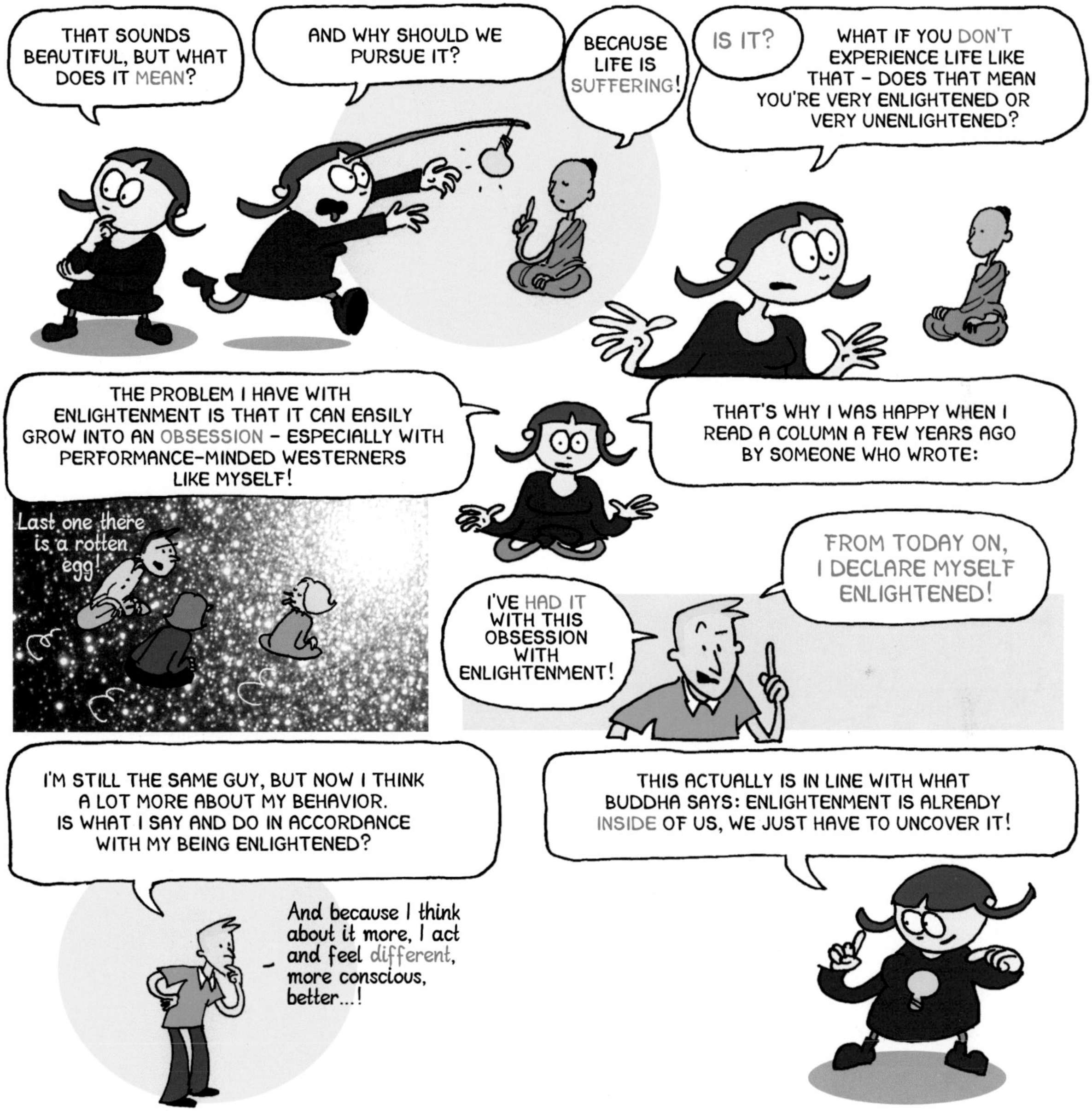
THAT SOUNDS BEAUTIFUL, BUT WHAT DOES IT MEAN?
AND WHY SHOULD WE PURSUE IT?
BECAUSE LIFE IS SUFFERING!
IS IT?
WHAT IF YOU DON'T EXPERIENCE LIFE LIKE THAT – DOES THAT MEAN YOU'RE VERY ENLIGHTENED OR VERY UNENLIGHTENED?
THE PROBLEM I HAVE WITH ENLIGHTENMENT IS THAT IT CAN EASILY GROW INTO AN OBSESSION – ESPECIALLY WITH PERFORMANCE-MINDED WESTERNERS LIKE MYSELF!
Last one there is a rotten egg!
THAT'S WHY I WAS HAPPY WHEN I READ A COLUMN A FEW YEARS AGO BY SOMEONE WHO WROTE:
I'VE HAD IT WITH THIS OBSESSION WITH ENLIGHTENMENT!
FROM TODAY ON, I DECLARE MYSELF ENLIGHTENED!
I'M STILL THE SAME GUY, BUT NOW I THINK A LOT MORE ABOUT MY BEHAVIOR. IS WHAT I SAY AND DO IN ACCORDANCE WITH MY BEING ENLIGHTENED?
And because I think about it more, I act and feel different, more conscious, better...!
THIS ACTUALLY IS IN LINE WITH WHAT BUDDHA SAYS: ENLIGHTENMENT IS ALREADY INSIDE OF US, WE JUST HAVE TO UNCOVER IT!

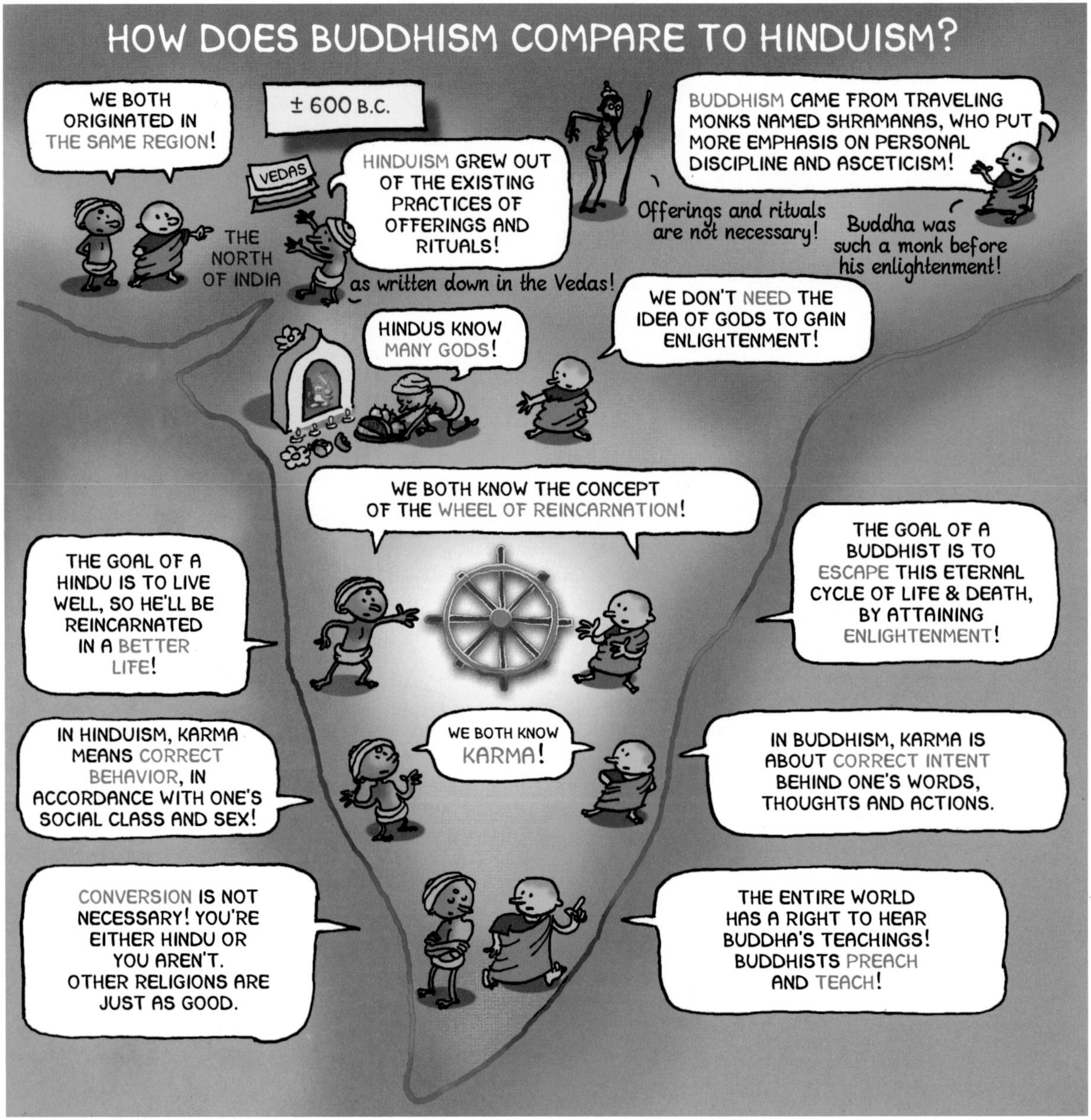
HOW DOES BUDDHISM COMPARE TO HINDUISM?
WE BOTH ORIGINATED IN THE SAME REGION!
± 600 B.C.
VEDAS
THE NORTH OF INDIA
HINDUISM GREW OUT OF THE EXISTING PRACTICES OF OFFERINGS AND RITUALS!
as written down in the Vedas!
Offerings and rituals are not necessary!
BUDDHISM CAME FROM TRAVELING MONKS NAMED SHRAMANAS, WHO PUT MORE EMPHASIS ON PERSONAL DISCIPLINE AND ASCETICISM!
Buddha was such a monk before his enlightenment!
HINDUS KNOW MANY GODS!
WE DON'T NEED THE IDEA OF GODS TO GAIN ENLIGHTENMENT!
WE BOTH KNOW THE CONCEPT OF THE WHEEL OF REINCARNATION!
THE GOAL OF A HINDU IS TO LIVE WELL, SO HE'LL BE REINCARNATED IN A BETTER LIFE!
THE GOAL OF A BUDDHIST IS TO ESCAPE THIS ETERNAL CYCLE OF LIFE & DEATH, BY ATTAINING ENLIGHTENMENT!
WE BOTH KNOW KARMA!
IN HINDUISM, KARMA MEANS CORRECT BEHAVIOR, IN ACCORDANCE WITH ONE'S SOCIAL CLASS AND SEX!
IN BUDDHISM, KARMA IS ABOUT CORRECT INTENT BEHIND ONE'S WORDS, THOUGHTS AND ACTIONS.
CONVERSION IS NOT NECESSARY! YOU'RE EITHER HINDU OR YOU AREN'T. OTHER RELIGIONS ARE JUST AS GOOD.
THE ENTIRE WORLD HAS A RIGHT TO HEAR BUDDHA'S TEACHINGS! BUDDHISTS PREACH AND TEACH!

THE BOOKS OF BUDDHISM

THE PALI CANON

NAMED AFTER THE LANGUAGE IN WHICH THEY WERE ORIGINALLY WRITTEN: PALI

ALSO KNOWN AS TRIPITAKA

"THE THREE BASKETS" – ORIGINALLY THESE TEXTS WERE WRITTEN ON PALM LEAVES WHICH WERE STORED IN BIG WICKER BASKETS

SUTTA
DISCOURSES BY THE BUDDHA

VINAYA
RULES FOR MONKS AND NUNS

ABHIDHAMMA
PHILOSOPHICAL AND PSYCHOLOGICAL WRITINGS THAT WERE ADDED 250 YEARS AFTER BUDDHA'S DEATH

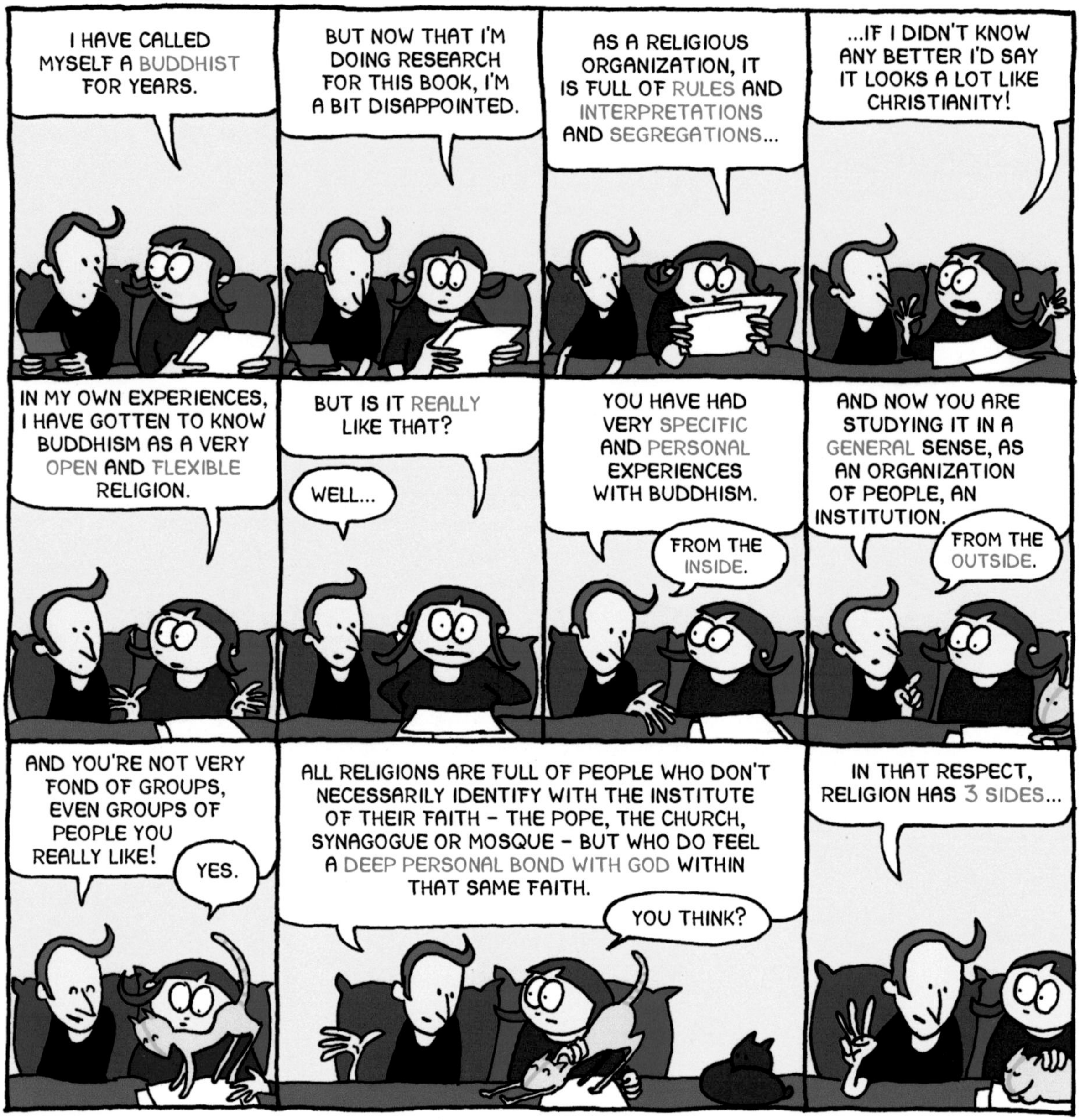
I HAVE CALLED MYSELF A BUDDHIST FOR YEARS.
BUT NOW THAT I'M DOING RESEARCH FOR THIS BOOK, I'M A BIT DISAPPOINTED.
AS A RELIGIOUS ORGANIZATION, IT IS FULL OF RULES AND INTERPRETATIONS AND SEGREGATIONS...
...IF I DIDN'T KNOW ANY BETTER I'D SAY IT LOOKS A LOT LIKE CHRISTIANITY!
IN MY OWN EXPERIENCES, I HAVE GOTTEN TO KNOW BUDDHISM AS A VERY OPEN AND FLEXIBLE RELIGION.
BUT IS IT REALLY LIKE THAT?
WELL...
YOU HAVE HAD VERY SPECIFIC AND PERSONAL EXPERIENCES WITH BUDDHISM.
FROM THE INSIDE.
AND NOW YOU ARE STUDYING IT IN A GENERAL SENSE, AS AN ORGANIZATION OF PEOPLE, AN INSTITUTION.
FROM THE OUTSIDE.
AND YOU'RE NOT VERY FOND OF GROUPS, EVEN GROUPS OF PEOPLE YOU REALLY LIKE!
YES.
ALL RELIGIONS ARE FULL OF PEOPLE WHO DON'T NECESSARILY IDENTIFY WITH THE INSTITUTE OF THEIR FAITH – THE POPE, THE CHURCH, SYNAGOGUE OR MOSQUE – BUT WHO DO FEEL A DEEP PERSONAL BOND WITH GOD WITHIN THAT SAME FAITH.
YOU THINK?
IN THAT RESPECT, RELIGION HAS 3 SIDES...

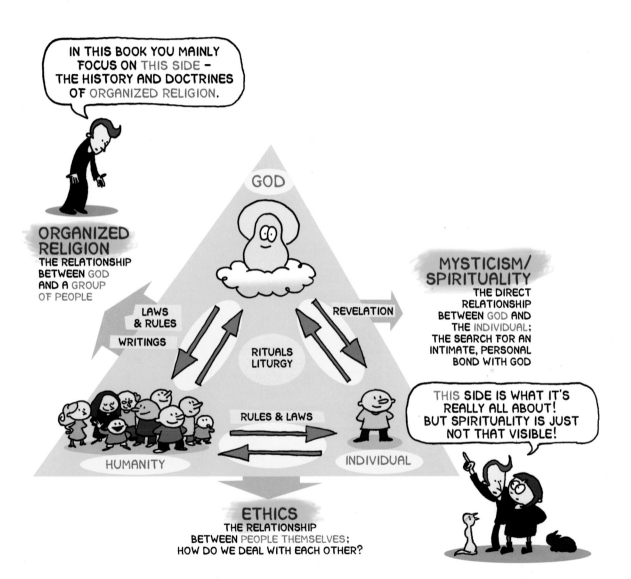

IN THIS BOOK YOU MAINLY FOCUS ON THIS SIDE – THE HISTORY AND DOCTRINES OF ORGANIZED RELIGION.

ORGANIZED RELIGION
THE RELATIONSHIP BETWEEN GOD AND A GROUP OF PEOPLE

GOD

LAWS & RULES

WRITINGS

RITUALS LITURGY

REVELATION

MYSTICISM/ SPIRITUALITY
THE DIRECT RELATIONSHIP BETWEEN GOD AND THE INDIVIDUAL; THE SEARCH FOR AN INTIMATE, PERSONAL BOND WITH GOD

THIS SIDE IS WHAT IT'S REALLY ALL ABOUT! BUT SPIRITUALITY IS JUST NOT THAT VISIBLE!

RULES & LAWS

HUMANITY

INDIVIDUAL

ETHICS
THE RELATIONSHIP BETWEEN PEOPLE THEMSELVES; HOW DO WE DEAL WITH EACH OTHER?

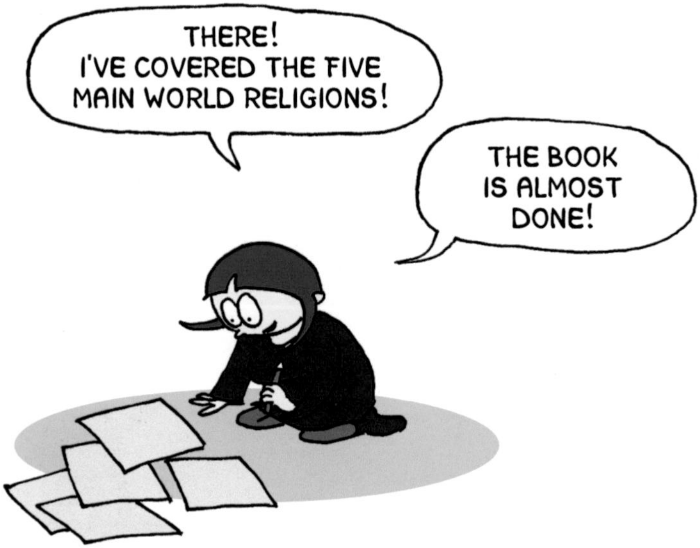
THERE!
I'VE COVERED THE FIVE
MAIN WORLD RELIGIONS!
THE BOOK
IS ALMOST
DONE!

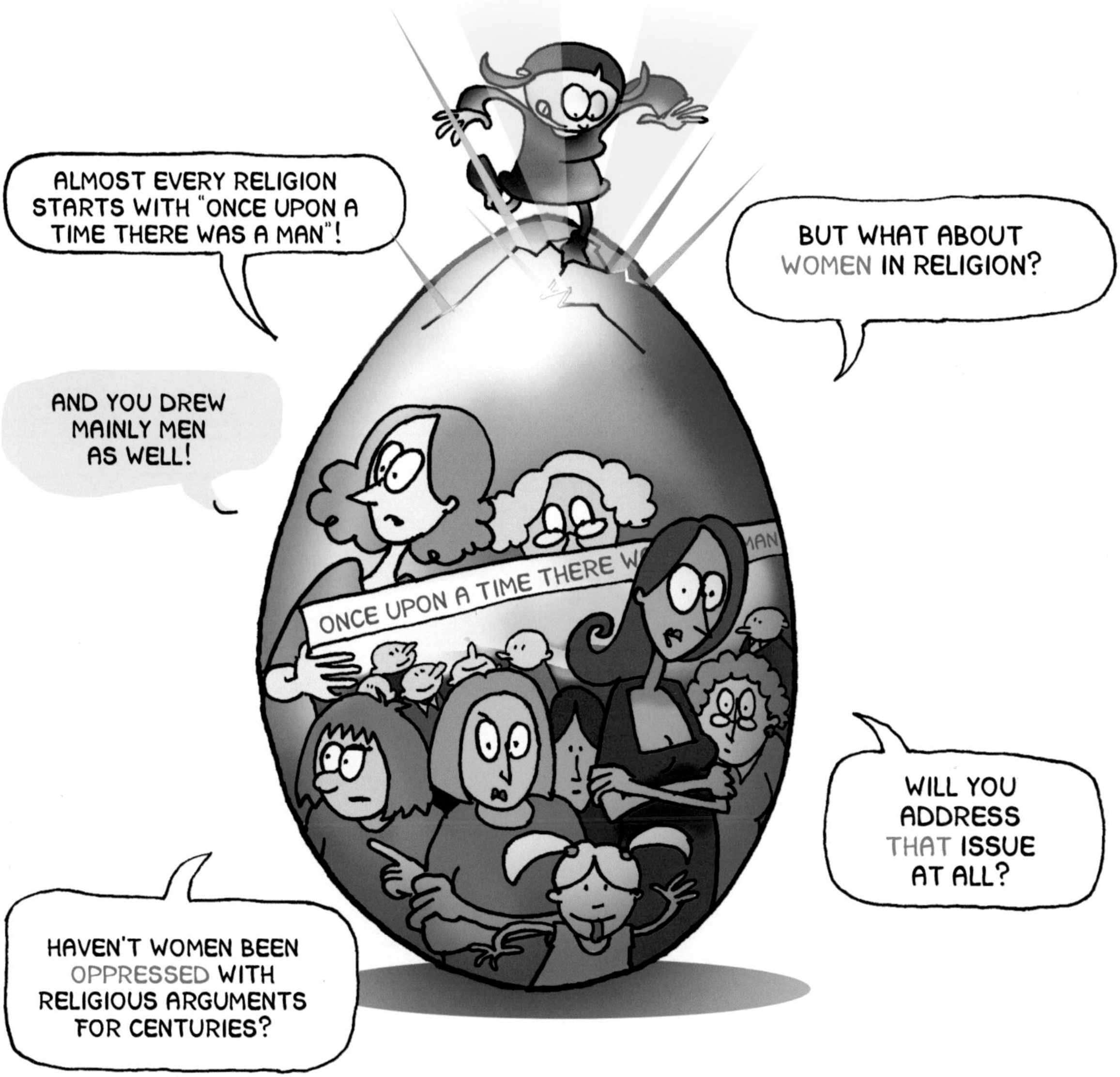
ALMOST EVERY RELIGION STARTS WITH "ONCE UPON A TIME THERE WAS A MAN"!
BUT WHAT ABOUT WOMEN IN RELIGION?
AND YOU DREW MAINLY MEN AS WELL!
ONCE UPON A TIME THERE W
MAN
WILL YOU ADDRESS THAT ISSUE AT ALL?
HAVEN'T WOMEN BEEN OPPRESSED WITH RELIGIOUS ARGUMENTS FOR CENTURIES?

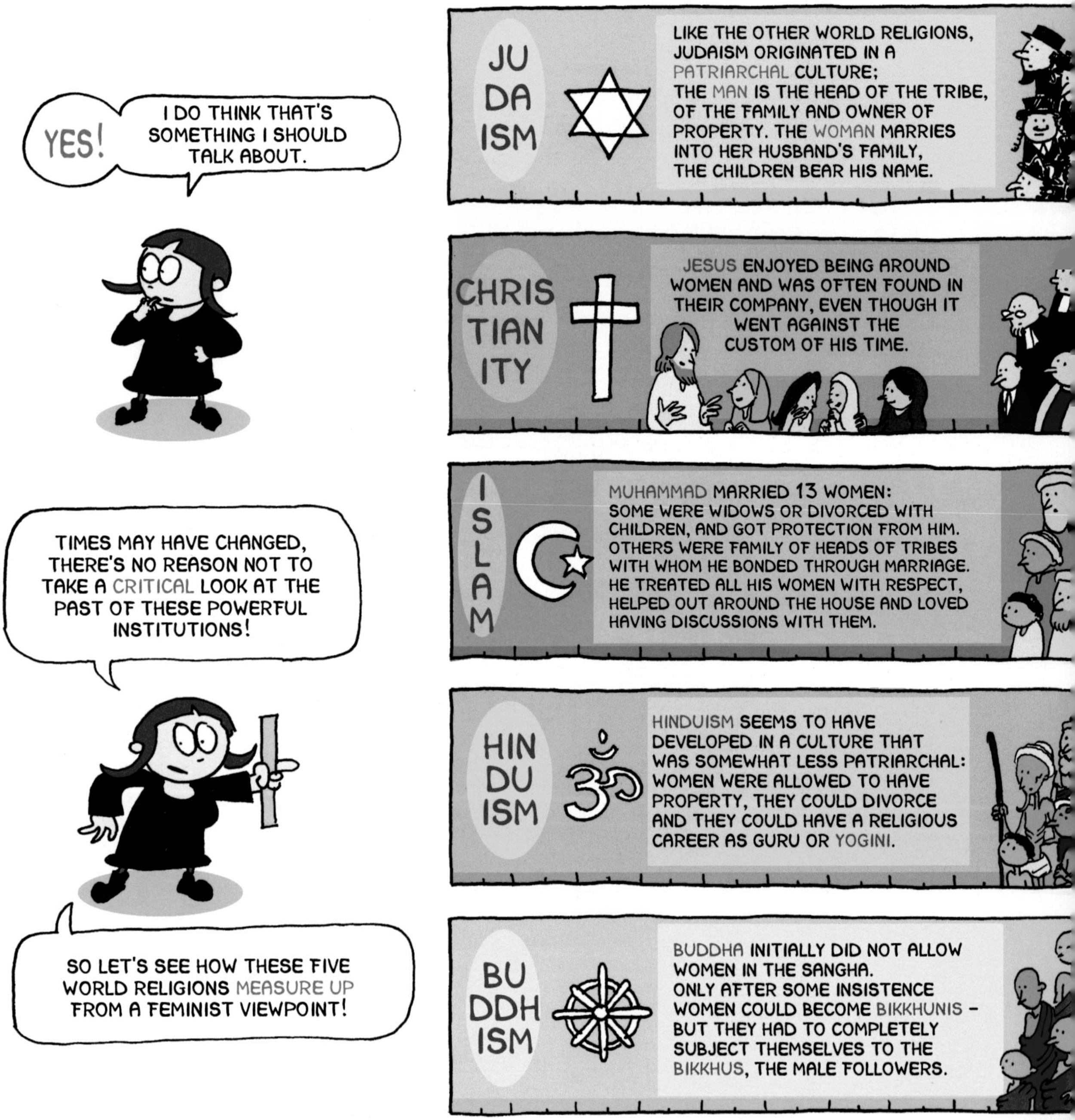

YES!
I DO THINK THAT'S SOMETHING I SHOULD TALK ABOUT.
TIMES MAY HAVE CHANGED, THERE'S NO REASON NOT TO TAKE A CRITICAL LOOK AT THE PAST OF THESE POWERFUL INSTITUTIONS!
SO LET'S SEE HOW THESE FIVE WORLD RELIGIONS MEASURE UP FROM A FEMINIST VIEWPOINT!
JUDAISM
LIKE THE OTHER WORLD RELIGIONS, JUDAISM ORIGINATED IN A PATRIARCHAL CULTURE; THE MAN IS THE HEAD OF THE TRIBE, OF THE FAMILY AND OWNER OF PROPERTY. THE WOMAN MARRIES INTO HER HUSBAND'S FAMILY, THE CHILDREN BEAR HIS NAME.
CHRISTIANITY
JESUS ENJOYED BEING AROUND WOMEN AND WAS OFTEN FOUND IN THEIR COMPANY, EVEN THOUGH IT WENT AGAINST THE CUSTOM OF HIS TIME.
ISLAM
MUHAMMAD MARRIED 13 WOMEN: SOME WERE WIDOWS OR DIVORCED WITH CHILDREN, AND GOT PROTECTION FROM HIM. OTHERS WERE FAMILY OF HEADS OF TRIBES WITH WHOM HE BONDED THROUGH MARRIAGE. HE TREATED ALL HIS WOMEN WITH RESPECT, HELPED OUT AROUND THE HOUSE AND LOVED HAVING DISCUSSIONS WITH THEM.
HINDUISM
HINDUISM SEEMS TO HAVE DEVELOPED IN A CULTURE THAT WAS SOMEWHAT LESS PATRIARCHAL: WOMEN WERE ALLOWED TO HAVE PROPERTY, THEY COULD DIVORCE AND THEY COULD HAVE A RELIGIOUS CAREER AS GURU OR YOGINI.
BUDDHISM
BUDDHA INITIALLY DID NOT ALLOW WOMEN IN THE SANGHA. ONLY AFTER SOME INSISTENCE WOMEN COULD BECOME BIKKHUNIS – BUT THEY HAD TO COMPLETELY SUBJECT THEMSELVES TO THE BIKKHUS, THE MALE FOLLOWERS.

THE TORAH MAINLY TELLS THE HISTORY OF MEN. BUT THERE ARE A FEW REMARKABLE STORIES ABOUT STRONG WOMEN.

I SAVED MY BROTHER MOSES AND HELPED LEAD THE PEOPLE OF ISRAEL THROUGH THE DESERT.

MIRIAM

I LED THE ARMY OF ISRAEL TO VICTORY AGAINST THE CANAANITES!

DEBORAH

I BECAME THE WIFE OF THE PERSIAN KING AHASUERUS AND SAVED MY PEOPLE FROM BEING MASSACRED!

ESTHER

I SEDUCED AND BEHEADED A PERSIAN ARMY LEADER!

Holofernes R.I.P.

JUDITH

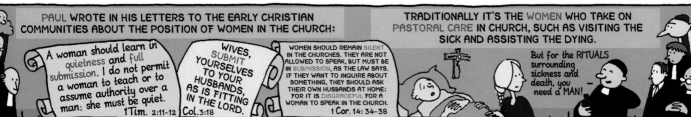

PAUL WROTE IN HIS LETTERS TO THE EARLY CHRISTIAN COMMUNITIES ABOUT THE POSITION OF WOMEN IN THE CHURCH:

A woman should learn in quietness and full submission. I do not permit a woman to teach or to assume authority over a man; she must be quiet. 1Tim. 2:11-12

WIVES, SUBMIT YOURSELVES TO YOUR HUSBANDS, AS IS FITTING IN THE LORD. Col.3:18

WOMEN SHOULD REMAIN SILENT IN THE CHURCHES. THEY ARE NOT ALLOWED TO SPEAK, BUT MUST BE IN SUBMISSION, AS THE LAW SAYS. IF THEY WANT TO INQUIRE ABOUT SOMETHING, THEY SHOULD ASK THEIR OWN HUSBANDS AT HOME; FOR IT IS DISGRACEFUL FOR A WOMAN TO SPEAK IN THE CHURCH. 1 Cor. 14: 34-38

TRADITIONALLY IT'S THE WOMEN WHO TAKE ON PASTORAL CARE IN CHURCH, SUCH AS VISITING THE SICK AND ASSISTING THE DYING.

But for the RITUALS surrounding sickness and death, you need a MAN!

DURING THE GOLDEN AGE OF ISLAMIC CULTURE, MUSLIM WOMEN WERE RATHER EMANCIPATED.

I FOUNDED THE UNIVERSITY OF AL-KARAOUINE IN 859!

WE CAN STUDY AND TEACH!

FATIMA AL-FIHRI

THE ROLE OF WOMEN IN THE MOSQUE HAS ALWAYS BEEN LIMITED, HOWEVER.

MUHAMMAD LET ME LEAD PRAYER FOR WOMEN AS WELL AS MEN!

HMM... WE THINK THAT MIGHT NOT BE SUCH A GOOD IDEA.

UME WARQA

WOMEN DISTRACT MEN! IT'S BETTER IF THEY ARE SEATED IN A DIFFERENT PLACE!

HINDUISM KNOWS MANY POWERFUL GODDESSES.

I WAS THE WIFE OF BRAHMA, BUT I DIVORCED HIM!

I'M THE GODDESS OF MUSICIANS AND OTHER CREATIVE PEOPLE!

SARASWATI

I AM A WARRIOR GODDESS!

DURGA

I AM THE GODDESS OF WEALTH AND HAPPINESS!

AND VISHNU'S WIFE!

LAKSHMI

I AM THE GODDESS OF TIME AND CHANGE!

KALI

THE FEMALE BUDDHIST ORDER OF BHIKKHUNIS SOON BECAME VERY POPULAR.

ACCORDING TO BUDDHA MEN AND WOMEN ARE SPIRITUALLY EQUAL!

AT LAST! A WAY TO ESCAPE THE STRICT RULES OF MARRIED LIFE!

A WOMAN CAN CULTIVATE HER SPIRITUALITY...

A woman who lives well, may reincarnate as a man!

ACCORDING TO BUDDHA ANYONE CAN ATTAIN ENLIGHTENMENT – BUT SOME THOUGHT DIFFERENTLY.

...BUT ONLY A MAN CAN GET ENLIGHTENED!

NONSENSE! THAT KIND OF TALK IS FROM MARA, LORD OF EVIL!

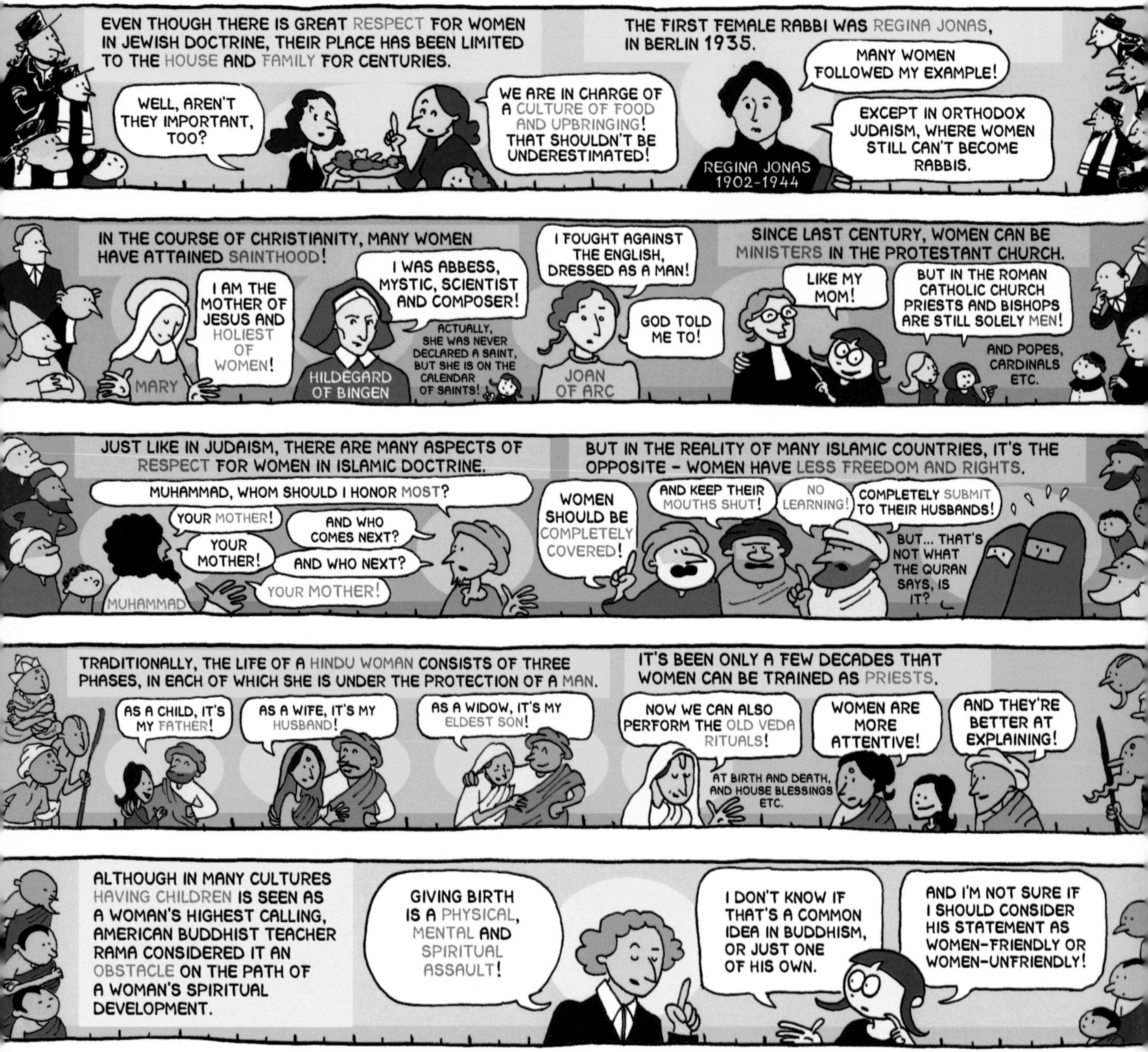
EVEN THOUGH THERE IS GREAT RESPECT FOR WOMEN IN JEWISH DOCTRINE, THEIR PLACE HAS BEEN LIMITED TO THE HOUSE AND FAMILY FOR CENTURIES.
WELL, AREN'T THEY IMPORTANT, TOO?
WE ARE IN CHARGE OF A CULTURE OF FOOD AND UPBRINGING! THAT SHOULDN'T BE UNDERESTIMATED!
THE FIRST FEMALE RABBI WAS REGINA JONAS, IN BERLIN 1935.
MANY WOMEN FOLLOWED MY EXAMPLE!
EXCEPT IN ORTHODOX JUDAISM, WHERE WOMEN STILL CAN'T BECOME RABBIS.
REGINA JONAS 1902–1944
IN THE COURSE OF CHRISTIANITY, MANY WOMEN HAVE ATTAINED SAINTHOOD!
I AM THE MOTHER OF JESUS AND HOLIEST OF WOMEN!
MARY
I WAS ABBESS, MYSTIC, SCIENTIST AND COMPOSER!
HILDEGARD OF BINGEN
ACTUALLY, SHE WAS NEVER DECLARED A SAINT, BUT SHE IS ON THE CALENDAR OF SAINTS!
I FOUGHT AGAINST THE ENGLISH, DRESSED AS A MAN!
GOD TOLD ME TO!
JOAN OF ARC
SINCE LAST CENTURY, WOMEN CAN BE MINISTERS IN THE PROTESTANT CHURCH.
LIKE MY MOM!
BUT IN THE ROMAN CATHOLIC CHURCH PRIESTS AND BISHOPS ARE STILL SOLELY MEN!
AND POPES, CARDINALS ETC.
JUST LIKE IN JUDAISM, THERE ARE MANY ASPECTS OF RESPECT FOR WOMEN IN ISLAMIC DOCTRINE.
MUHAMMAD, WHOM SHOULD I HONOR MOST?
YOUR MOTHER!
AND WHO COMES NEXT?
YOUR MOTHER!
AND WHO NEXT?
YOUR MOTHER!
MUHAMMAD
BUT IN THE REALITY OF MANY ISLAMIC COUNTRIES, IT'S THE OPPOSITE – WOMEN HAVE LESS FREEDOM AND RIGHTS.
WOMEN SHOULD BE COMPLETELY COVERED!
AND KEEP THEIR MOUTHS SHUT!
NO LEARNING!
COMPLETELY SUBMIT TO THEIR HUSBANDS!
BUT... THAT'S NOT WHAT THE QURAN SAYS, IS IT?
TRADITIONALLY, THE LIFE OF A HINDU WOMAN CONSISTS OF THREE PHASES, IN EACH OF WHICH SHE IS UNDER THE PROTECTION OF A MAN.
AS A CHILD, IT'S MY FATHER!
AS A WIFE, IT'S MY HUSBAND!
AS A WIDOW, IT'S MY ELDEST SON!
IT'S BEEN ONLY A FEW DECADES THAT WOMEN CAN BE TRAINED AS PRIESTS.
NOW WE CAN ALSO PERFORM THE OLD VEDA RITUALS!
AT BIRTH AND DEATH, AND HOUSE BLESSINGS ETC.
WOMEN ARE MORE ATTENTIVE!
AND THEY'RE BETTER AT EXPLAINING!
ALTHOUGH IN MANY CULTURES HAVING CHILDREN IS SEEN AS A WOMAN'S HIGHEST CALLING, AMERICAN BUDDHIST TEACHER RAMA CONSIDERED IT AN OBSTACLE ON THE PATH OF A WOMAN'S SPIRITUAL DEVELOPMENT.
GIVING BIRTH IS A PHYSICAL, MENTAL AND SPIRITUAL ASSAULT!
I DON'T KNOW IF THAT'S A COMMON IDEA IN BUDDHISM, OR JUST ONE OF HIS OWN.
AND I'M NOT SURE IF I SHOULD CONSIDER HIS STATEMENT AS WOMEN-FRIENDLY OR WOMEN-UNFRIENDLY!

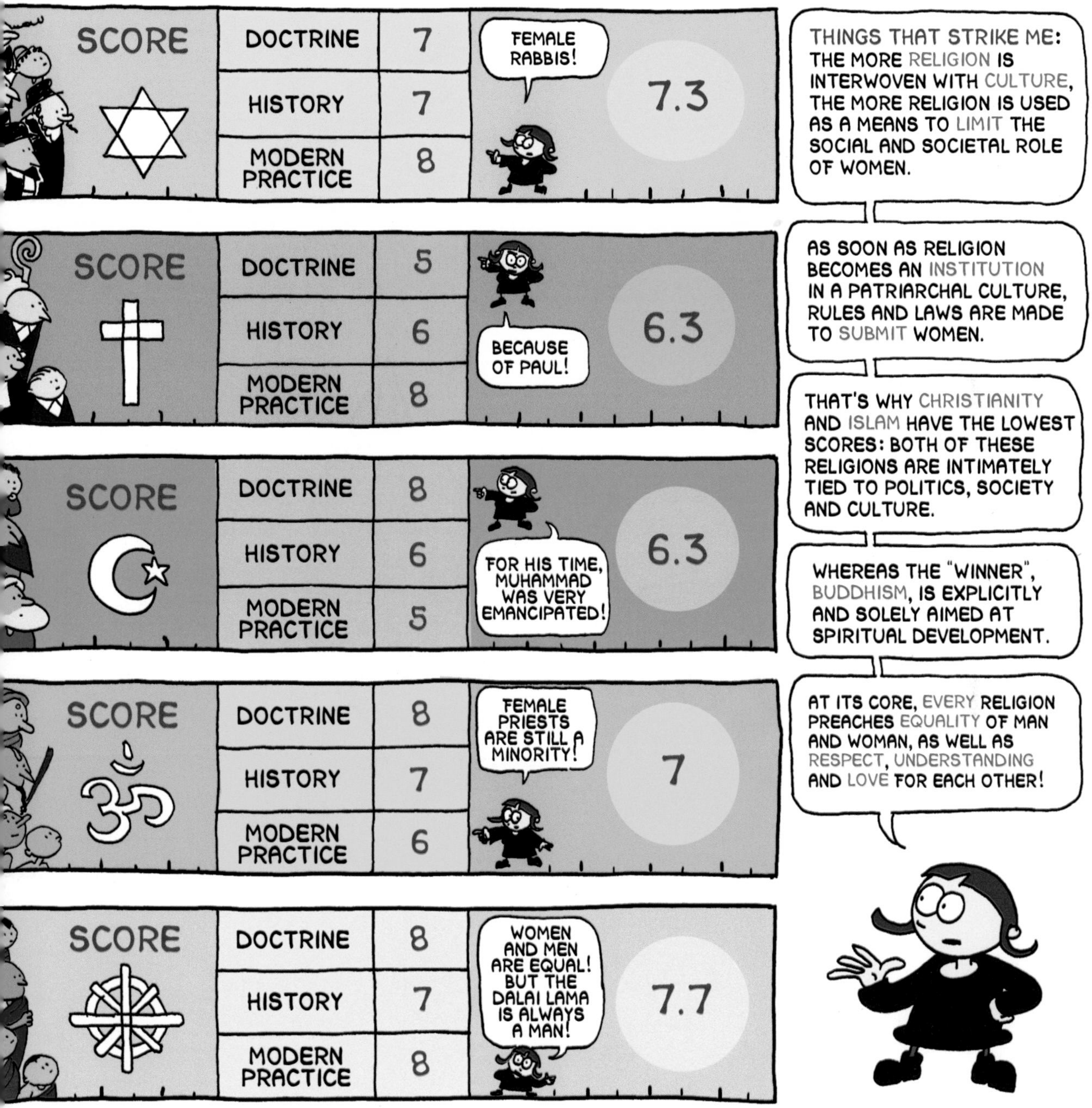
SCORE
DOCTRINE 7
HISTORY 7
MODERN PRACTICE 8
FEMALE RABBIS!
7.3
SCORE
DOCTRINE 5
HISTORY 6
MODERN PRACTICE 8
BECAUSE OF PAUL!
6.3
SCORE
DOCTRINE 8
HISTORY 6
MODERN PRACTICE 5
FOR HIS TIME, MUHAMMAD WAS VERY EMANCIPATED!
6.3
SCORE
DOCTRINE 8
HISTORY 7
MODERN PRACTICE 6
FEMALE PRIESTS ARE STILL A MINORITY!
7
SCORE
DOCTRINE 8
HISTORY 7
MODERN PRACTICE 8
WOMEN AND MEN ARE EQUAL! BUT THE DALAI LAMA IS ALWAYS A MAN!
7.7
THINGS THAT STRIKE ME: THE MORE RELIGION IS INTERWOVEN WITH CULTURE, THE MORE RELIGION IS USED AS A MEANS TO LIMIT THE SOCIAL AND SOCIETAL ROLE OF WOMEN.
AS SOON AS RELIGION BECOMES AN INSTITUTION IN A PATRIARCHAL CULTURE, RULES AND LAWS ARE MADE TO SUBMIT WOMEN.
THAT'S WHY CHRISTIANITY AND ISLAM HAVE THE LOWEST SCORES: BOTH OF THESE RELIGIONS ARE INTIMATELY TIED TO POLITICS, SOCIETY AND CULTURE.
WHEREAS THE "WINNER", BUDDHISM, IS EXPLICITLY AND SOLELY AIMED AT SPIRITUAL DEVELOPMENT.
AT ITS CORE, EVERY RELIGION PREACHES EQUALITY OF MAN AND WOMAN, AS WELL AS RESPECT, UNDERSTANDING AND LOVE FOR EACH OTHER!

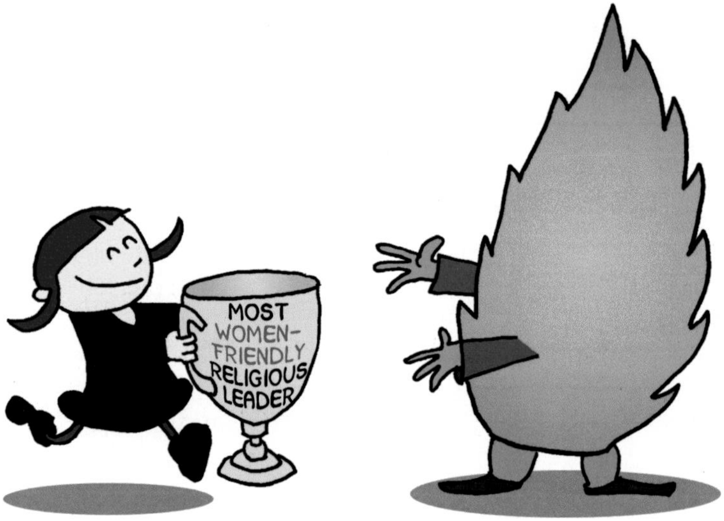
MOST
WOMEN-
FRIENDLY
RELIGIOUS
LEADER

THE RELIGIOUS SMORGASBORD

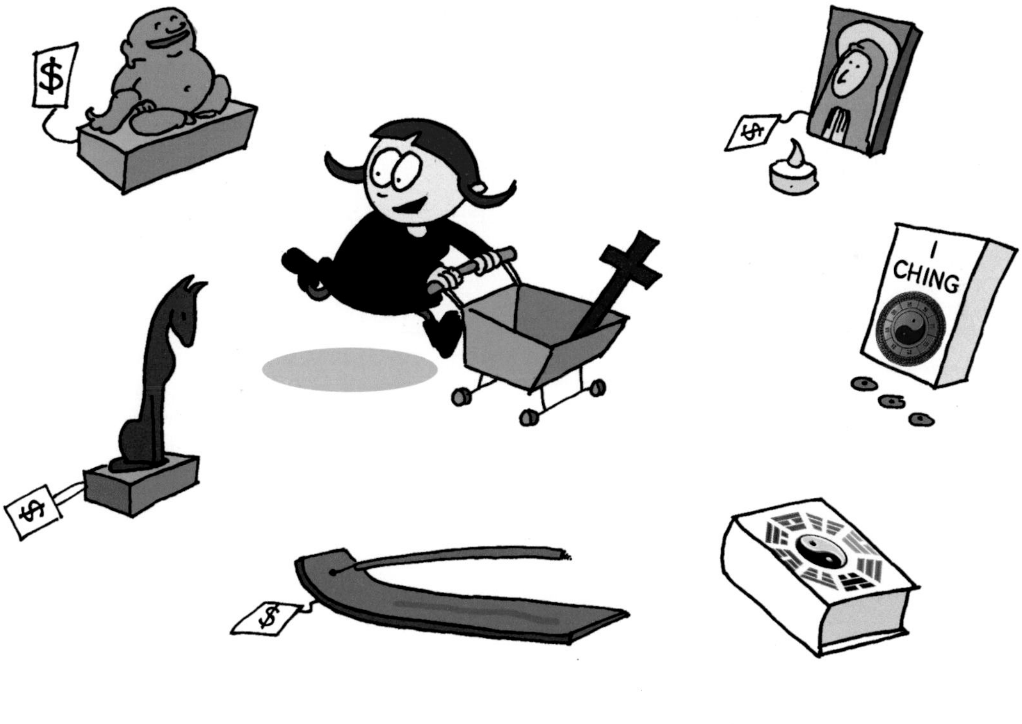
I
CHING

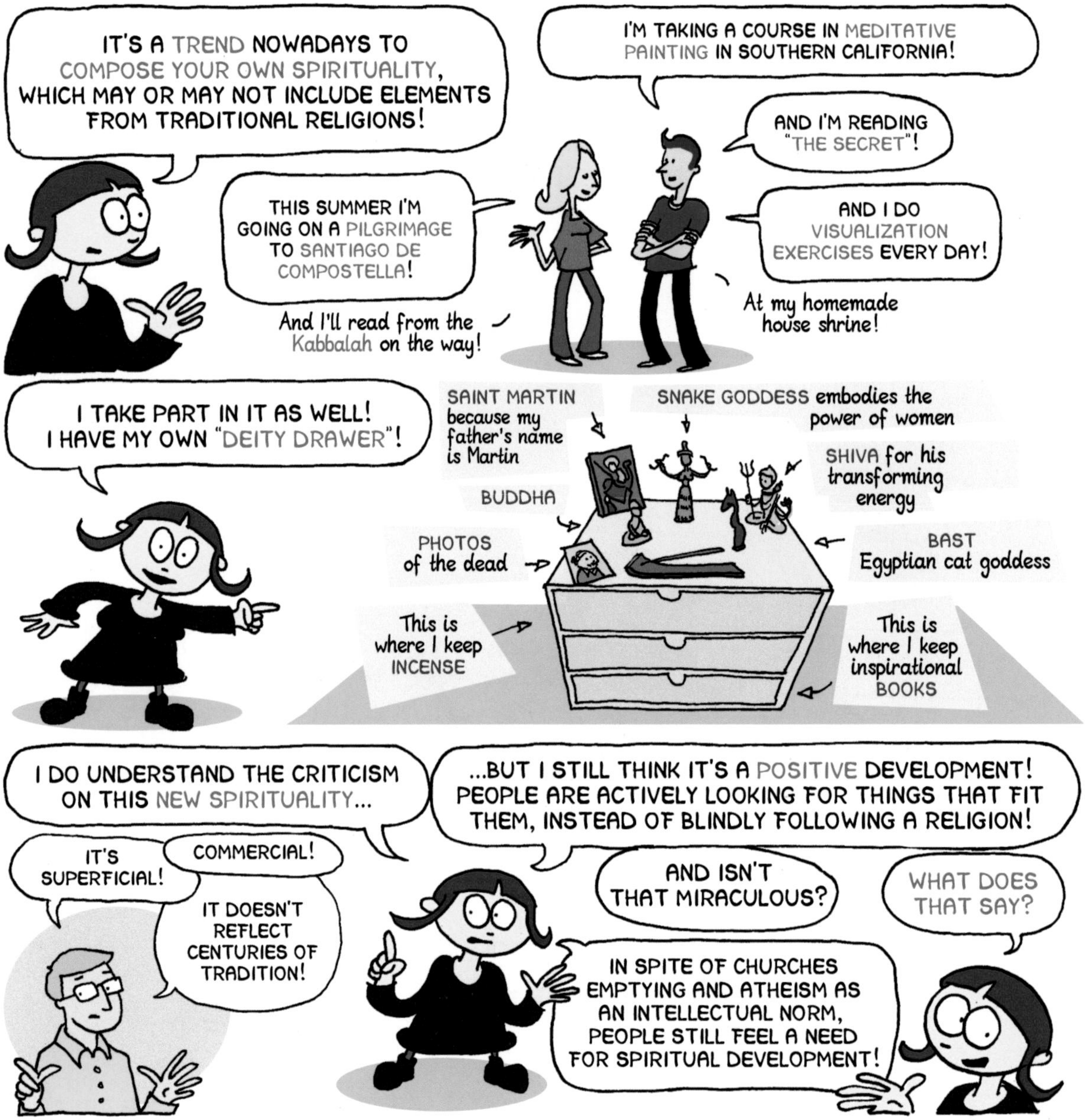
IT'S A TREND NOWADAYS TO COMPOSE YOUR OWN SPIRITUALITY, WHICH MAY OR MAY NOT INCLUDE ELEMENTS FROM TRADITIONAL RELIGIONS!
I'M TAKING A COURSE IN MEDITATIVE PAINTING IN SOUTHERN CALIFORNIA!
AND I'M READING "THE SECRET"!
THIS SUMMER I'M GOING ON A PILGRIMAGE TO SANTIAGO DE COMPOSTELLA!
AND I DO VISUALIZATION EXERCISES EVERY DAY!
And I'll read from the Kabbalah on the way!
At my homemade house shrine!
I TAKE PART IN IT AS WELL! I HAVE MY OWN "DEITY DRAWER"!
SAINT MARTIN because my father's name is Martin
SNAKE GODDESS embodies the power of women
SHIVA for his transforming energy
BUDDHA
PHOTOS of the dead
BAST Egyptian cat goddess
This is where I keep INCENSE
This is where I keep inspirational BOOKS
I DO UNDERSTAND THE CRITICISM ON THIS NEW SPIRITUALITY...
IT'S SUPERFICIAL!
COMMERCIAL!
IT DOESN'T REFLECT CENTURIES OF TRADITION!
...BUT I STILL THINK IT'S A POSITIVE DEVELOPMENT! PEOPLE ARE ACTIVELY LOOKING FOR THINGS THAT FIT THEM, INSTEAD OF BLINDLY FOLLOWING A RELIGION!
AND ISN'T THAT MIRACULOUS?
WHAT DOES THAT SAY?
IN SPITE OF CHURCHES EMPTYING AND ATHEISM AS AN INTELLECTUAL NORM, PEOPLE STILL FEEL A NEED FOR SPIRITUAL DEVELOPMENT!

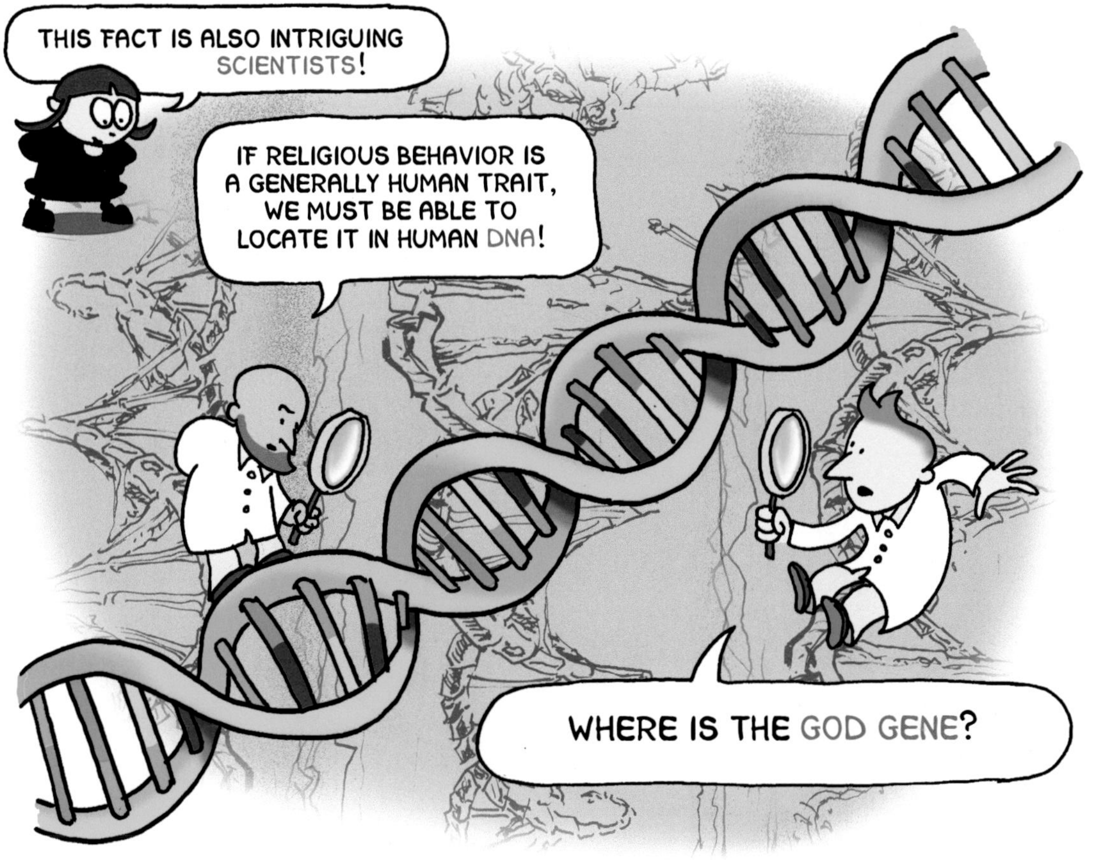
THIS FACT IS ALSO INTRIGUING SCIENTISTS!
IF RELIGIOUS BEHAVIOR IS A GENERALLY HUMAN TRAIT, WE MUST BE ABLE TO LOCATE IT IN HUMAN DNA!
WHERE IS THE GOD GENE?

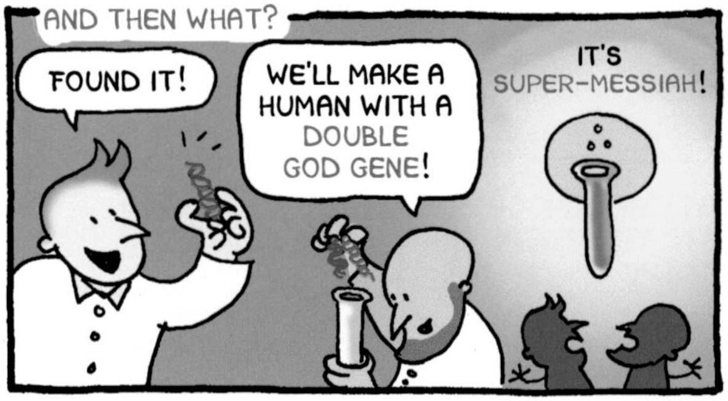
AND THEN WHAT?
FOUND IT!
WE'LL MAKE A HUMAN WITH A DOUBLE GOD GENE!
IT'S SUPER-MESSIAH!

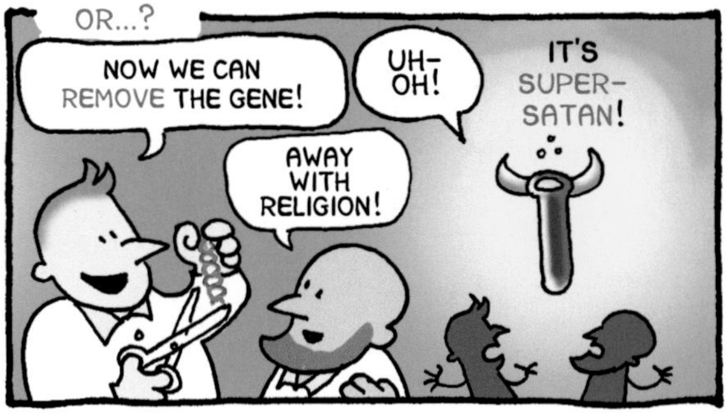
OR...?
NOW WE CAN REMOVE THE GENE!
AWAY WITH RELIGION!
UH-OH!
IT'S SUPER-SATAN!

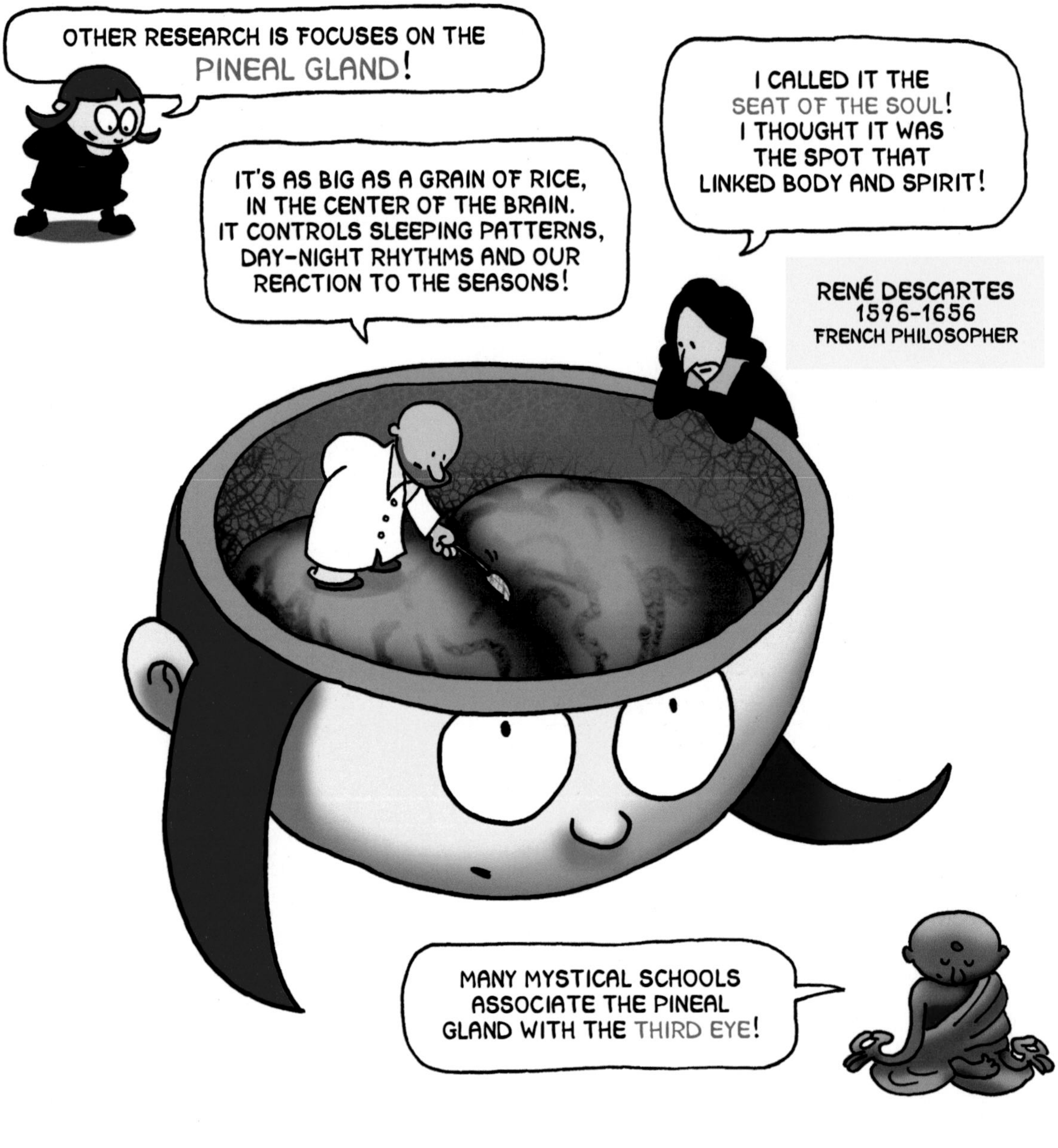
OTHER RESEARCH IS FOCUSES ON THE PINEAL GLAND!
IT'S AS BIG AS A GRAIN OF RICE, IN THE CENTER OF THE BRAIN. IT CONTROLS SLEEPING PATTERNS, DAY-NIGHT RHYTHMS AND OUR REACTION TO THE SEASONS!
I CALLED IT THE SEAT OF THE SOUL! I THOUGHT IT WAS THE SPOT THAT LINKED BODY AND SPIRIT!
RENÉ DESCARTES 1596-1656 FRENCH PHILOSOPHER
MANY MYSTICAL SCHOOLS ASSOCIATE THE PINEAL GLAND WITH THE THIRD EYE!

I MYSELF CAME UP WITH THE FOLLOWING, TOTALLY NON-SCIENTIFIC THEORY:

RELIGIOUS BEHAVIOR IS NOT SHAPED BY SOMETHING THAT'S THERE, BUT BY SOMETHING THAT'S NOT THERE (ANYMORE):
A LINK WITH THE TOTALITY OF ALL LIVING AND NON-LIVING THINGS

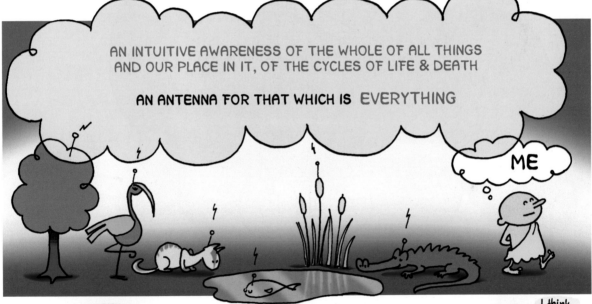

AN INTUITIVE AWARENESS OF THE WHOLE OF ALL THINGS AND OUR PLACE IN IT, OF THE CYCLES OF LIFE & DEATH

AN ANTENNA FOR THAT WHICH IS EVERYTHING

ME

SELF
REASON
LOGIC

IN HUMANS, THIS CONNECTION HAS BECOME DISRUPTED BY OUR OVERDEVELOPED SELF-AWARENESS! WHAT REMAINS IS A LONGING, A FEELING OF LOSS THAT IS EXPRESSED IN RELIGION AND SPIRITUALITY.

I think.

At this moment.

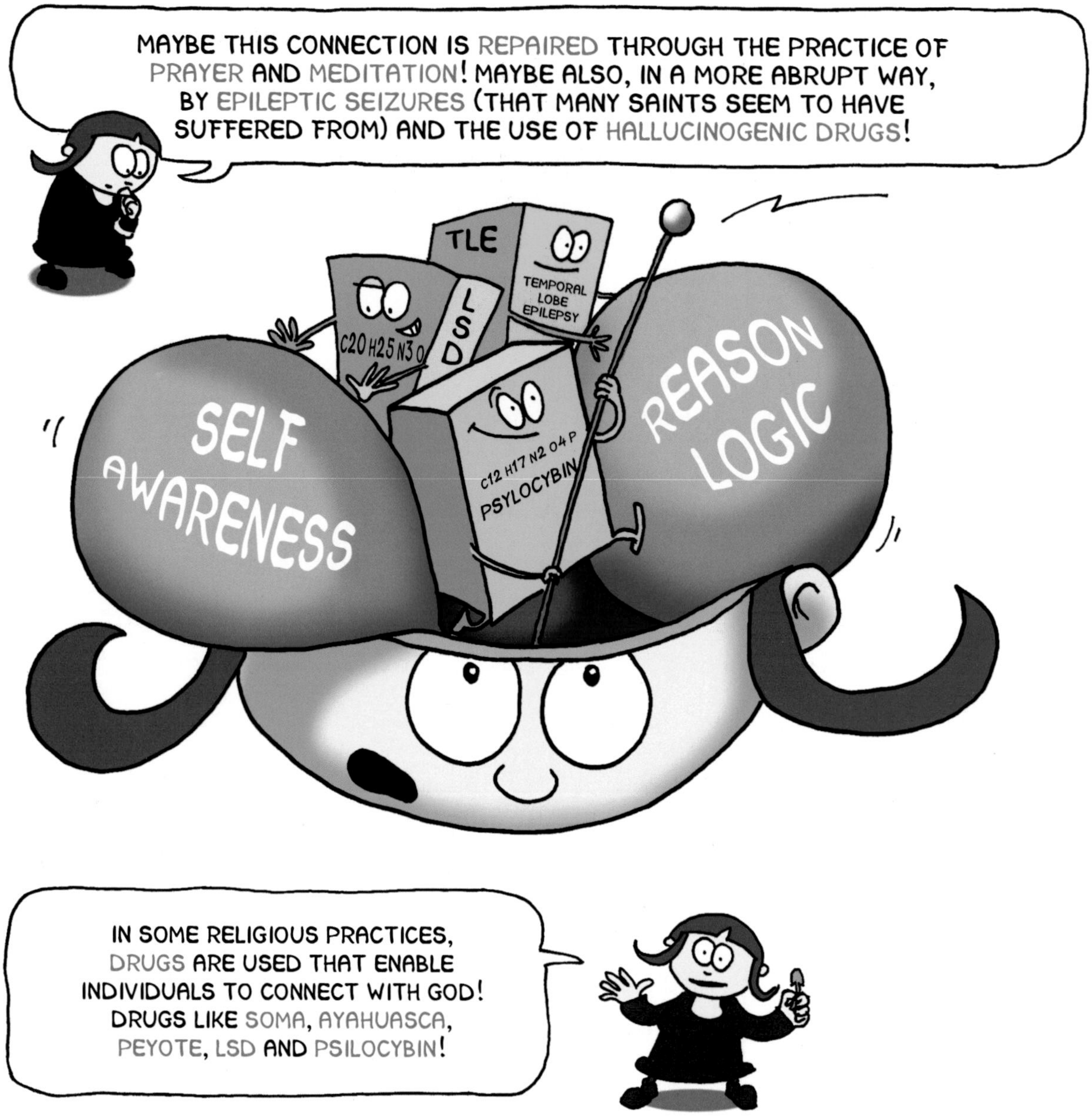
MAYBE THIS CONNECTION IS REPAIRED THROUGH THE PRACTICE OF PRAYER AND MEDITATION! MAYBE ALSO, IN A MORE ABRUPT WAY, BY EPILEPTIC SEIZURES (THAT MANY SAINTS SEEM TO HAVE SUFFERED FROM) AND THE USE OF HALLUCINOGENIC DRUGS!
TLE
TEMPORAL LOBE EPILEPSY
LSD
C20 H25 N3 O
C12 H17 N2 O4 P
PSYLOCYBIN
SELF AWARENESS
REASON LOGIC
IN SOME RELIGIOUS PRACTICES, DRUGS ARE USED THAT ENABLE INDIVIDUALS TO CONNECT WITH GOD! DRUGS LIKE SOMA, AYAHUASCA, PEYOTE, LSD AND PSILOCYBIN!

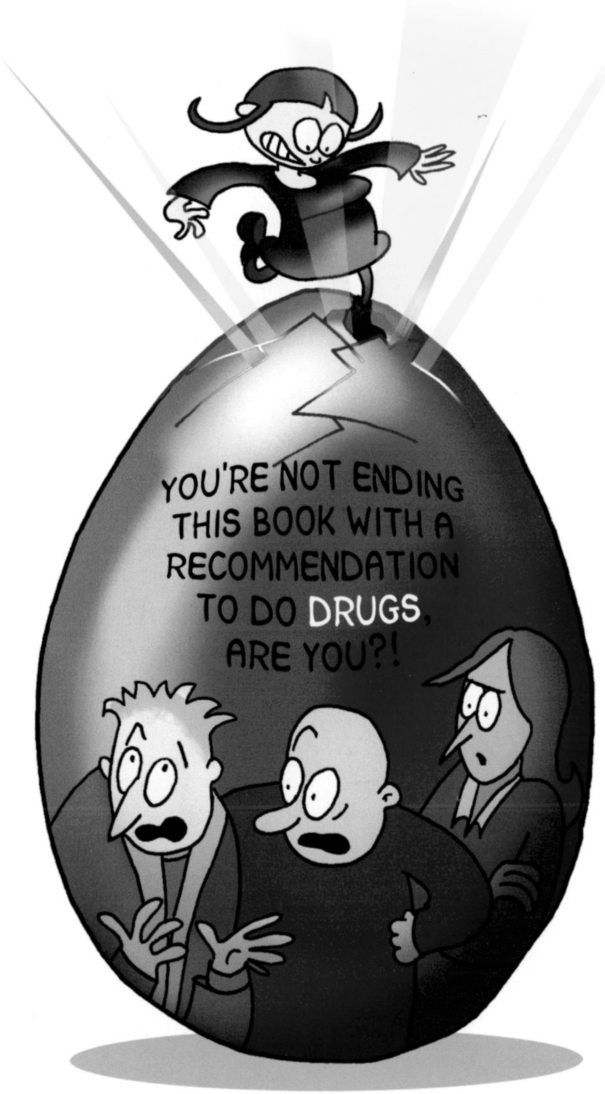
YOU'RE NOT ENDING THIS BOOK WITH A RECOMMENDATION TO DO DRUGS, ARE YOU?!

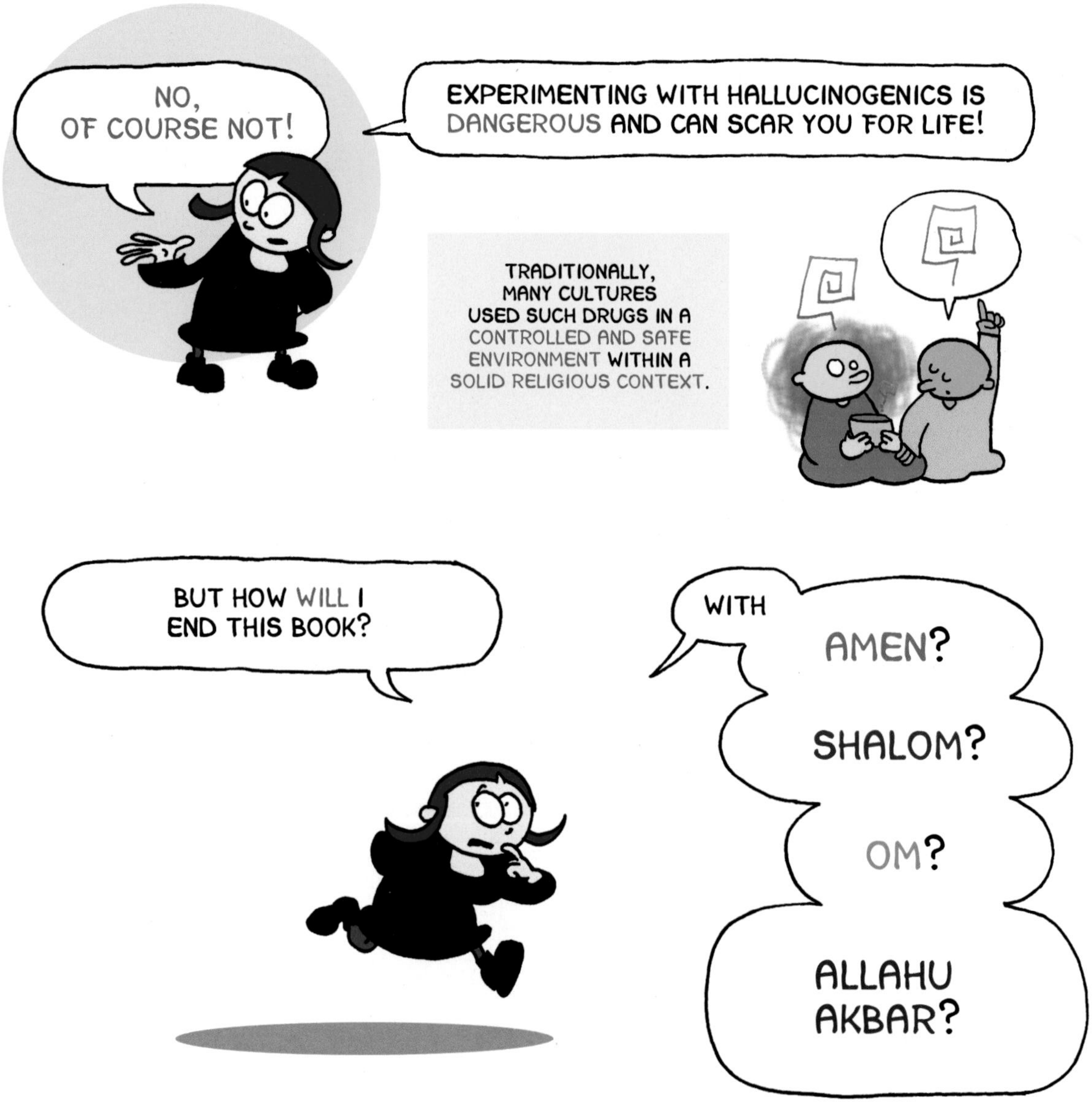
NO, OF COURSE NOT!
EXPERIMENTING WITH HALLUCINOGENICS IS DANGEROUS AND CAN SCAR YOU FOR LIFE!
TRADITIONALLY, MANY CULTURES USED SUCH DRUGS IN A CONTROLLED AND SAFE ENVIRONMENT WITHIN A SOLID RELIGIOUS CONTEXT.
BUT HOW WILL I END THIS BOOK?
WITH
AMEN?
SHALOM?
OM?
ALLAHU AKBAR?

THERE REALLY IS NO END TO THE SEARCH FOR RELIGIOUS TRUTH – IT'S A CONTINUOUS PROCESS OF SEARCHING, FINDING, EMBRACING, QUESTIONING AND REJECTING!

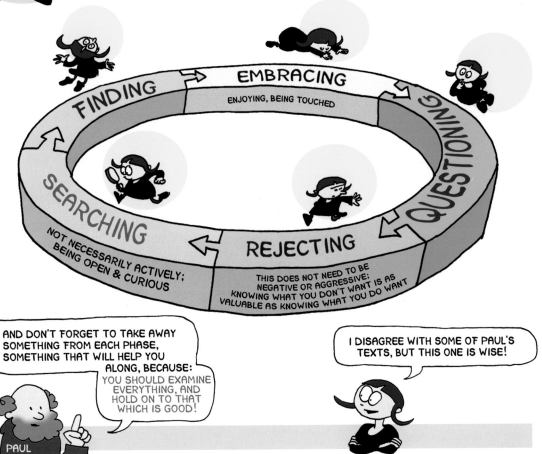

FINDING

EMBRACING

ENJOYING, BEING TOUCHED

QUESTIONING

SEARCHING

NOT NECESSARILY ACTIVELY; BEING OPEN & CURIOUS

REJECTING

THIS DOES NOT NEED TO BE NEGATIVE OR AGGRESSIVE; KNOWING WHAT YOU DON'T WANT IS AS VALUABLE AS KNOWING WHAT YOU DO WANT

AND DON'T FORGET TO TAKE AWAY SOMETHING FROM EACH PHASE, SOMETHING THAT WILL HELP YOU ALONG, BECAUSE: YOU SHOULD EXAMINE EVERYTHING, AND HOLD ON TO THAT WHICH IS GOOD!

PAUL

I DISAGREE WITH SOME OF PAUL'S TEXTS, BUT THIS ONE IS WISE!

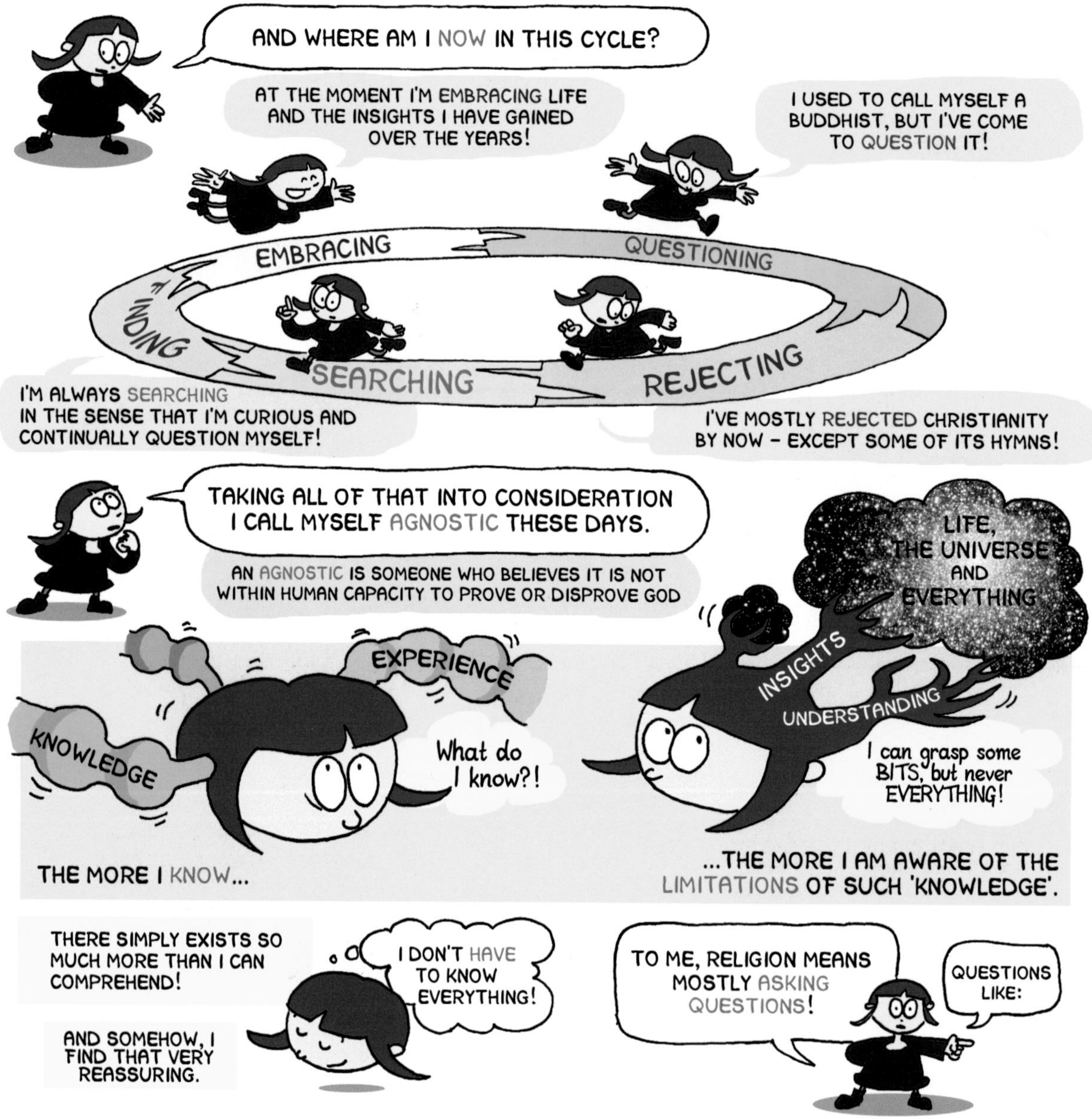
AND WHERE AM I NOW IN THIS CYCLE?
AT THE MOMENT I'M EMBRACING LIFE AND THE INSIGHTS I HAVE GAINED OVER THE YEARS!
I USED TO CALL MYSELF A BUDDHIST, BUT I'VE COME TO QUESTION IT!
EMBRACING
QUESTIONING
FINDING
SEARCHING
REJECTING
I'M ALWAYS SEARCHING IN THE SENSE THAT I'M CURIOUS AND CONTINUALLY QUESTION MYSELF!
I'VE MOSTLY REJECTED CHRISTIANITY BY NOW – EXCEPT SOME OF ITS HYMNS!
TAKING ALL OF THAT INTO CONSIDERATION I CALL MYSELF AGNOSTIC THESE DAYS.
AN AGNOSTIC IS SOMEONE WHO BELIEVES IT IS NOT WITHIN HUMAN CAPACITY TO PROVE OR DISPROVE GOD
LIFE, THE UNIVERSE AND EVERYTHING
EXPERIENCE
KNOWLEDGE
What do I know?!
INSIGHTS
UNDERSTANDING
I can grasp some BITS, but never EVERYTHING!
THE MORE I KNOW...
...THE MORE I AM AWARE OF THE LIMITATIONS OF SUCH 'KNOWLEDGE'.
THERE SIMPLY EXISTS SO MUCH MORE THAN I CAN COMPREHEND!
I DON'T HAVE TO KNOW EVERYTHING!
AND SOMEHOW, I FIND THAT VERY REASSURING.
TO ME, RELIGION MEANS MOSTLY ASKING QUESTIONS!
QUESTIONS LIKE:

WHAT DO YOU BELIEVE IN?

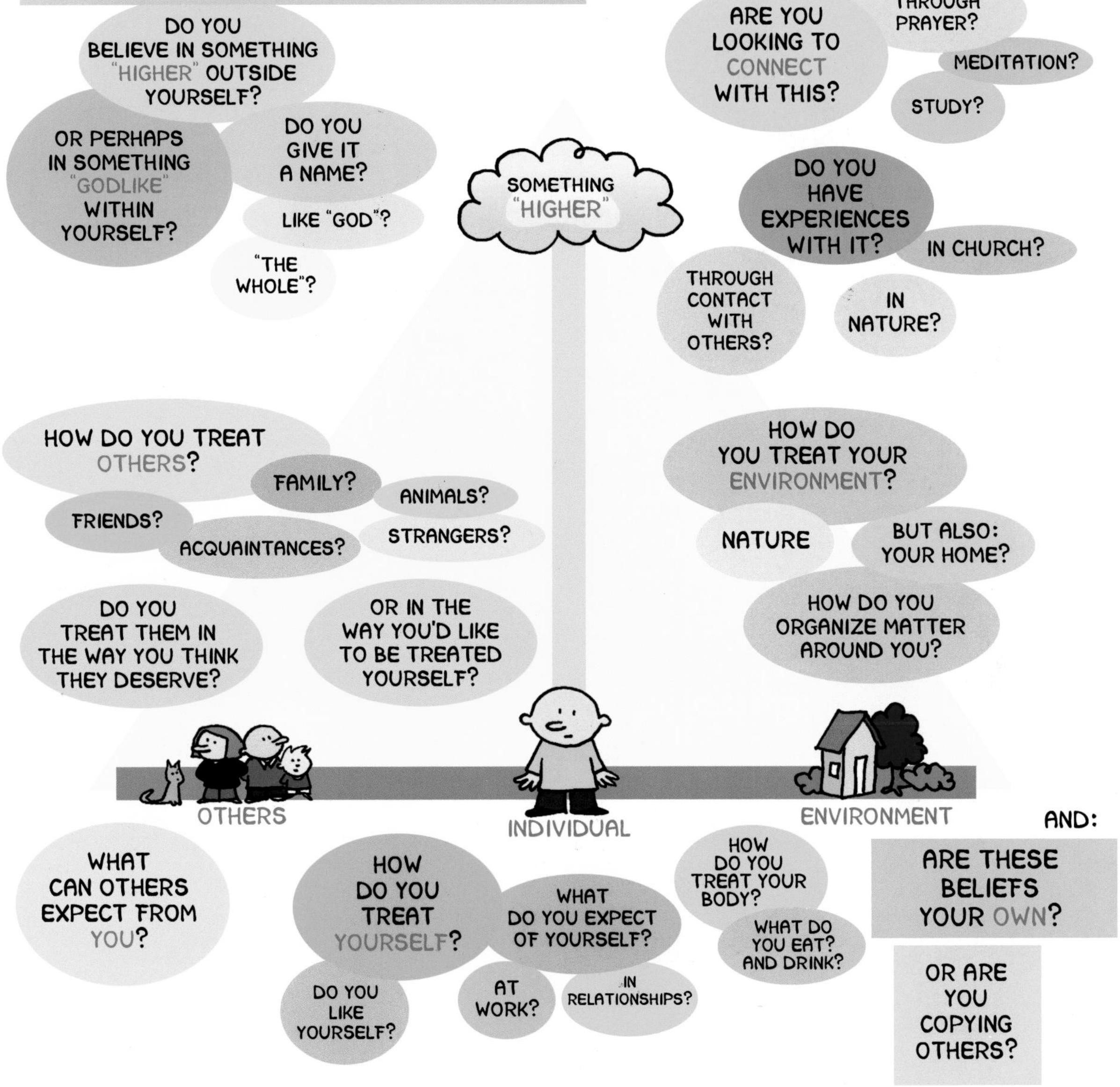

DO YOU BELIEVE IN SOMETHING "HIGHER" OUTSIDE YOURSELF?
OR PERHAPS IN SOMETHING "GODLIKE" WITHIN YOURSELF?
DO YOU GIVE IT A NAME?
LIKE "GOD"?
"THE WHOLE"?
SOMETHING "HIGHER"
ARE YOU LOOKING TO CONNECT WITH THIS?
THROUGH PRAYER?
MEDITATION?
STUDY?
DO YOU HAVE EXPERIENCES WITH IT?
IN CHURCH?
THROUGH CONTACT WITH OTHERS?
IN NATURE?
HOW DO YOU TREAT OTHERS?
FAMILY?
ANIMALS?
FRIENDS?
ACQUAINTANCES?
STRANGERS?
DO YOU TREAT THEM IN THE WAY YOU THINK THEY DESERVE?
OR IN THE WAY YOU'D LIKE TO BE TREATED YOURSELF?
HOW DO YOU TREAT YOUR ENVIRONMENT?
NATURE
BUT ALSO: YOUR HOME?
HOW DO YOU ORGANIZE MATTER AROUND YOU?
OTHERS
INDIVIDUAL
ENVIRONMENT
WHAT CAN OTHERS EXPECT FROM YOU?
HOW DO YOU TREAT YOURSELF?
DO YOU LIKE YOURSELF?
WHAT DO YOU EXPECT OF YOURSELF?
AT WORK?
IN RELATIONSHIPS?
HOW DO YOU TREAT YOUR BODY?
WHAT DO YOU EAT? AND DRINK?
AND:
ARE THESE BELIEFS YOUR OWN?
OR ARE YOU COPYING OTHERS?

INDEX

Also available by the author:

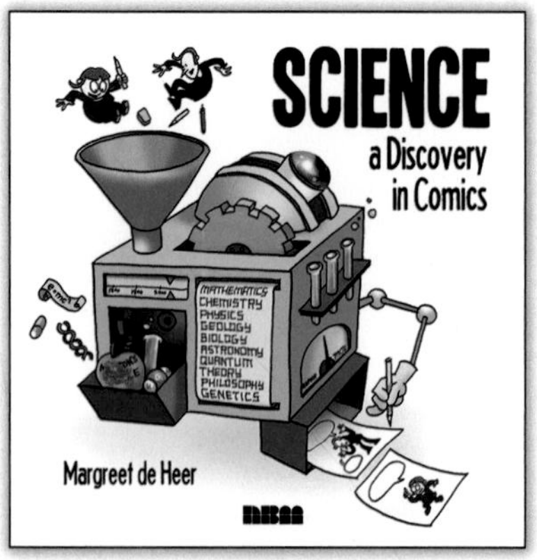
SCIENCE
a Discovery in Comics
MATHEMATICS
CHEMISTRY
PHYSICS
GEOLOGY
BIOLOGY
ASTRONOMY
QUANTUM THEORY
PHILOSOPHY
GENETICS
Margreet de Heer

Science: a Discovery in Comics
$19.99

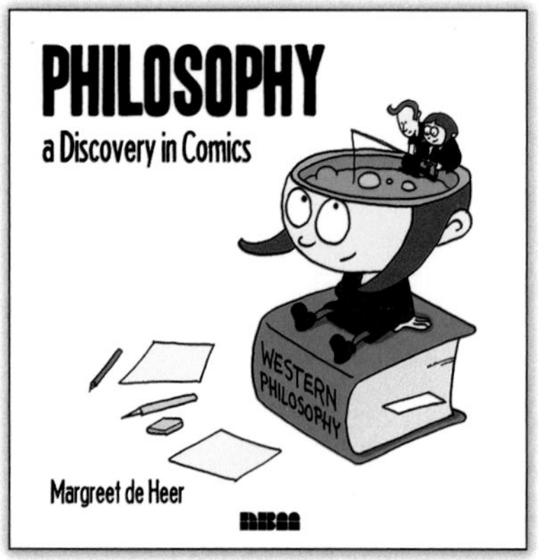
PHILOSOPHY
a Discovery in Comics
WESTERN PHILOSOPHY
Margreet de Heer

Philosophy: a Discovery in Comics
$16.99

See more including reviews, Margreet's blog posts, and order from:
NBMPUB.COM

We have over 200 graphic novels available
write for a complete catalog:
NBM
160 Broadway, Ste. 700, East Wing
New York, NY 10038
If ordering by mail, add $4 p&h for the 1st item, $1 each addt'l.